International Dictionary of Banking and Finance

John Clark

Glenlake Publishing Company, Ltd

Chicago • London • New Delhi

Fitzroy Dearborn Publishers

Chicago and London

ISBN: 1-888998-65-2

Library Edition: Fitzroy·Dearborn Publishers, Chicago and London
Library Edition ISBN: 1-57958-160-9

GPCo
1261 West Glenlake
Chicago, Illinois 60660
Glenlake@ix.netcom.com

Preface

This book is intended to provide access to the specialist terms of banking and general finance for students and professionals in the growing world of banking, and its interaction with building societies and the stock exchange. It should also assist private investors and people who read financial journals and the financial pages of daily newspapers. Like its companion volume the *Dictionary of Insurance and Finance Terms*, it does not limit itself merely to well-established terms. It also includes definitions of the everyday jargon, acronyms and newly adopted words (many from the United States) that are now common in national and international financial dealings.

John O E Clark

John O E Clark is a writer and editor who regularly contributes to dictionaries, encyclopedias and other types of information books for publication in Britain and abroad. He specializes in explaining technical subjects to students and other non-experts, and to people whose first language is not necessarily English.

A

AAA *See* ***triple A.***

ABA Abbreviation of ***American Bankers' Association***

abandonment The express or implied relinquishment of title, possession, or claim of property or an ***asset.***

abatement Reduction.

They expected an abatement in the number of companies making staff redundant in next two months.

The term should not be confused with ***rebate.***

ABA transit number The code number assigned to a bank pursuant to the numerical transit system devised by the American Bankers Association to facilitate collection of transit items (cheques and other items on out-of-town banks).

ABC agreement In a US brokerage company, an agreement with an employee detailing the rights of the company if it buys a membership of the New York Stock Exchange on his or her behalf.

ABC code *See* ***commercial code.***

ability to pay Having sufficient funds to pay one's debts.

ability-to-pay taxation Theory of taxation whereby those who are able to pay more are taxed at a higher rate. Ability-to-pay taxation may be applied to luxury goods, which therefore attract a high rate of tax.

above par Normally used of a share that has a market value above denomination or par value.

The shares of G & B *Electronics were traded above par for the first time today.*

above-the-line Term in accounting for items that are included in the profit and loss account of a business (as distinct from the ***appropriation account***).

above-the-line-advertising Advertising that uses the traditional media of television, radio, cinema, newspapers, magazines and posters.

above-the-line expenditure Alternative name for ***current expenditure***, so called because these items are recorded before the total in a statement of account.

above the market Describing a price that is higher than the usual market price.

absolute advantage Argument in favour of international trade put forward by Adam Smith (1723-90). Absolute advantage applies where, for example, two countries can both produce two commodities they need, but country A is more efficient at producing commodity X and country B is more efficient at producing commodity Y, so they would both profit by concentrating on the particular commodity each produces best and trading them.

absolute bill of sale *Bill of sale* by which goods are transferred to the possession of another.

absolute efficiency Efficiency that depends on discovering and putting into effect the most effective possible combination, distribution, allocation or utilization of limited resources.

absolute monopoly Total monopoly, occurring where there is only one manufacturer of a product or supplier of a service and therefore no competition for the commodity or service in question.

absorbed account Account that has been consolidated with other similar accounts and so ceases to exist.

absorbed business Company that is merged with or taken over by another company and so ceases to exist.

absorbed cost Production cost that is taken into general expenses and not charged to the customer.

absorption costing Allocating manufacturing costs to each product that constitutes the output of a factory.

abstraction of bank funds The wrongful taking of bank funds for personal use from a bank facility.

abusive shelter Investment instrument that gives little in the way of return but allows the investor to reduce income tax liabilities.

a/c Abbreviation of *account*.

acc Abbreviation of *account*.

ACA Abbreviation of Associate of the Institute of Chartered Accountants.

ACCA Abbreviation of Associate of the Chartered Association of Certified Accountants.

accelerated depreciation In accounting, practice of depreciating an ***asset*** at a rate greater than the actual decline in its value in order to gain ***tax concessions***. Accelerated depreciation need not occur throughout the life of an asset; a substantial proportion of its total value is often written off in the first year, and reduced allowances for depreciation are made thereafter.

acceleration Increase in the rate of a price trend, or provision for the early repayment of the amount due in a ***bed-and-breakfast deal***.

acceleration clause Clause in a bank loan agreement which stipulates that the loan becomes immediately repayable if a certain number of repayment instalments are not paid on time.

accelerator principle Theory that growth in production is directly related to the level of investment.

acceptance Broadly, the act of agreeing to do something. In business and finance it can be taken in various ways:

1. Acceptance is one of the two stages in negotiating a ***contract***: ***offer*** and acceptance. A contract is complete only when the offer has been formally accepted by the ***acceptor***.
2. It is the act of writing on a ***bill of exchange***, by which the acceptor accepts the bill and agrees to pay the ***drawer***.
3. It is used to denote a bill that has been endorsed in the above way and has thereby been accepted.

acceptance by intervention *See* ***acceptance for honour***.

acceptance credit Way of financing a sale to a foreign buyer in which a ***commercial bank*** or ***merchant bank*** provides credit to the foreign creditworthy importer, who can draw a ***bill of exchange*** against the credit. The bank charges a ***commission*** to the seller (exporter).

acceptance for honour Situation that occurs when a ***bill of exchange*** is turned down (or protested) and is then accepted by another party, thereby saving the honour of the ***drawer***. It is also termed acceptance supra protest or acceptance by intervention.

acceptance market Part of the ***money market*** that deals in accepted ***bills of exchange***.

accepting (US **acceptance**) **house** Financial institution whose business is concerned mainly with the negotiation of ***bills of exchange,*** by either guaranteeing or accepting them. An accepting house, also called an accepting bank, usually operates in the same way as a ***merchant bank.***

Accepting Houses Committee Committee that represents the London *accepting houses*. Its members get preferential terms on bills sold to the Bank of England.

acceptor Person who accepts either the terms of a ***contract,*** or a ***bill of exchange***. When a bill of exchange is accepted, the ***drawee*** becomes the acceptor.

ACCESS *Credit card* company in the UK owned jointly by Lloyds, Midland and National Westminster banks.

accommodation Money that is lent to someone for a brief period.

accommodation bill *Bill of exchange* signed by one person in order to help another to raise a loan. The signatory (or accommodation party) is acting as guarantor, and normally does not expect to pay the bill when it falls due. Accommodation bills are also known as kites, windbills or windmills.

accommodation payment Euphemism for a bribe. *See* ***kickback***.

accord Frequently used in the USA to mean any form of agreement, especially between companies, the business communities of different countries or the governments of two countries.

The tie-up accord between the country's two leading biotechnology companies will mean some swift and important advances in the field.

accord and satisfaction When one party has discharged its obligations under a **contract,** it may elect to release the other party from its obligations. When this is done in return for a new ***consideration***, the release is known as accord and satisfaction.

account Very generally, a note kept of any financial transaction. It is abbreviated to a/c, acc or acct. The term has three broad meanings:

1. It is used in banking to designate an arrangement made to deposit money with a ***bank***, ***building society*** or a number of other financial institutions. An account may be of many differing types, usually indicated by a qualifying word, depending on the conditions of withdrawal, level of interest, minimum amount of money in the account, or other factors.
2. On the London Stock Exchange it is a period of two weeks (when Bank Holidays occur, this period usually extends to three weeks) in

which trading is carried out. Broadly, transactions are made in the two weeks of the account and the relevant paperwork is carried out during the following week, followed by payments (settlements), made on the sixth business day after the end of the account. This method of working means that transactions may be made with deferred payment, enabling ***speculation*** to take place.

Prices fell sharply at the end of the last account.

3. It is a record of financial transactions, and in this sense, often termed ***accounts***.

He spent three days preparing his accounts for the Inland Revenue.

accountancy Body of knowledge relating to financial matters. Also the work done by an ***accountant***, involving knowledge of the law as it affects financial matters (*e.g.* the ***tax*** laws), ***book-keeping***, and the preparation of ***annual accounts***.

accountant Any person practising accountancy, whether qualified or not. The term may be prefixed with various other terms, denoting the specialism of the accountant (*e.g.* ***cost accountant***, ***management accountant***), that accountant's position within a business (*e.g.* ***chief accountant***), or his or her professional qualifications (*e.g.* ***certified accountant***, ***certified public accountant***, ***chartered accountant***).

account day The Monday ten days or six business days after the end of each stock exchange account, on which all settlements must be made. It is also known as settlement date or day.

account executive In the UK, most commonly used for a person in advertising responsible for service to one client. In the USA, it is an alternative term for ***stockbroker***.

accounting Very broadly, the activity of recording and verifying all monies borrowed, owed, paid or received.

accounting concepts Basic concepts by which sets of accounts are made up. The four generally accepted accounting concepts are the ***accruals concept***, ***consistency concept***, going concern concept and ***prudence concept***.

accounting cost Total expenditure required to undertake an activity. *See also* ***economic cost***.

accounting equation Principle that the capital plus the liabilities equal the total resources of a company.

accounting period Time for which accounts are prepared, such as a year for a company's financial accounts or a month for internal management accounts.

accounting principles Another term for ***accounting concepts***.

accounting ratio One of several ratios that are considered important in assessing the financial viability of a project or company.

accounting standards Standards by which ***annual accounts*** are made up, set by professional bodies such as the ***Accounting Standards Board*** (ASB) in the UK.

Accounting Standards Board (ASB) Organization established in the UK in 1990 to set up and improve standards in the world of accountancy.

account payee Words added to a ***crossed cheque*** to ensure that the cheque is paid only into the account of the person or people named on the cheque, i.e. making the cheque non-transferable. It is sometimes written account payee only.

account payee only *See* ***account payee***.

accounts payable Accounts on which a company owes money (for which it has been invoiced), also termed trade creditors.

accounts receivable Accounts on which money is owed to a company (for which it has issued invoices), also called trade debtors.

account stated Account consisting of items that both parties concerned have agreed as being correct; any balance is thereby also agreed.

accredited Describes someone who is authorized to act on behalf of a company or individual.

accrual Gradual increase by addition over a period of time. *See also* ***accrued charges***.

accruals concept Principle used in ***accounting*** by which ***income*** and ***expenditure*** are taken into the profit and loss account for the period in which they occur. This method of accounting is useful in that it pulls together ***receipts*** and the ***costs*** incurred in generating them, avoiding the time lag between the time ***income*** is received and the time ***liabilities*** become due. *See* ***accounting concepts; consistency concept; profit-and-loss account; prudence concept***.

accrued charges Charges that have not yet been accounted for or paid. E.g. if a demand for ***rent*** is made in arrears, it must appear on the accounts as an accrued charge, because the service has already been used, but not paid for.

accrued dividend Dividend payment due to shareholders but not yet paid.

accrued interest Interest payment that is due, but not yet received.

acct Abbreviation of ***account***.

accumulated depreciation In accounting, the total value of an asset that has been written off so far. *See* ***write off***.

accumulation Something that is allowed to increase in value, such as retained profit that accumulates if a company's dividend payments are always less than the total profit made.

accumulation units In unit trusts or life assurance, an accumulation unit is one for which the dividend is ploughed back into the investment to produce higher earnings.

ACH Abbreviation of ***automated clearing house***.

ACIB Abbreviation of Associate of The Chartered Institute of Bankers.

ACIBS Abbreviation of Associate of The Chartered Institute of Bankers in Scotland.

acid-test ratio Ratio of a company's assets (not including stock) to its current liabilities. It is also called the liquidity ratio or the quick ratio (because it gives a quick assessment of the company's financial state).

acquisition The takeover of control of one company by another or by an individual is known as an acquisition of the target company. The purchase of an ***equity*** stake in the target company is the usual method of acquisition.

acquisition trail Course embarked upon when a company becomes ***acquisitive***.

A & C Electronics reported improving finances after its takeover of BD Small Electronics, indicating a possible return to the acquisition trail.

See also ***takeover***.

acquisitive Describing a company that is always on the lookout to grow by taking over other companies. *See also* ***takeover***.

ACT Abbreviation of ***advance corporation tax***.

active bond crowd New York Stock Exchange members who do most of the trading.

act of bankruptcy There are three specific acts of bankruptcy: attempting to leave the country to avoid creditors; giving away property in order to defraud creditors; failing to comply with a bankruptcy notice filed by a *creditor*. By acting in any of these ways, a person may make himself or herself liable to bankruptcy proceedings.

action Equity stake.

The company seemed to have a great deal of potential and so she bought herself a piece of the action.

actionnaires French term, referring to the holders of shares in a French public company (*société anonyme*). *See* ***public limited company***.

active Busy, in action, constantly changing, as in, *e.g.*, active partner, active stock.

active account Bank account on which deposits and withdrawals regularly occur.

active money Money in circulation.

active partner Partner working for a firm. *See also* ***nominal partner; sleeping partner***.

active stock Shares that are frequently traded on the exchange.

actuals Physical commodities that may be purchased on the commodities market and delivered immediately; also known as spot goods. *See also* ***futures***.

Adam Smith (1723-1790) The father of economics, a Scottish philosopher and the author of *The Nature and Causes of the Wealth of Nations*.

additional personal relief For ***taxation*** purposes, the additional amount allowed against a married woman's earned ***income*** over and above the marriage personal ***allowance*** which the couple receive jointly. *See also* ***tax relief***.

add-on market *See* ***aftermarket***.

add-on sales Further sales made to an existing customer.

address commission In shipping, commission paid to a shipping ***agent*** in return for seeing that the cargo is loaded onto the vessel.

adjudication Act of giving judgement. Adjudication may be the act of resolving a legal problem, industrial dispute or of declaring ***bankruptcy***. *See also* ***adjudication order***.

adjudication of bankruptcy Court order declaring a person or company bankrupt. *See also* ***bankrupt***.

adjudication order Order of court, declaring someone bankrupt. It is also known as adjudication of bankruptcy. *See also* ***bankruptcy***.

adjustable peg System that allows exchange rates to vary between certain narrowly defined limits. *See* ***crawling peg***.

adjustable-rate mortgage (ARM) Mortgage whose rate of ***interest*** rises and falls along with interest rates in general.

administered price Price set and partly controlled by the seller, and based on his or her knowledge of the costs of production and estimates of ***demand*** and ***competition***. An administered price lies between ***monopoly*** and free market prices, and characterizes a state of imperfect competition. *See also* ***free market***.

administration Broadly, the sum of actions involved in the organization or management of a company. *See* ***administration expenses***.

In law, however, administration is either the winding-up of the estate of a deceased person in the absence of an executor or in the event of intestacy, or it is the winding-up of a company. Both cases involve the court appointment of someone to act as ***administrator***.

administration expenses One of the general expenses. In company accounting, this is a blanket term covering expenses incurred in the overall management of a company, but not positively attributable to any particular department or operating arm.

administration order County Court order requiring the administration of the estate of a debtor, who usually has to pay the debts by instalments in order to avoid bankruptcy.

administrative receiver Person appointed by the court to manage a company's assets on behalf of debenture holders or other secured creditors.

administrator Term with two meanings:

1. Person appointed (usually by the court) to manage someone else's property.
2. Person appointed by the court to manage the affairs of someone who has died without making a will (intestate). Proof of his or her authority is a letter of administration issued by the court.

ADR Abbreviation of ***American depositary receipts***.

ad referendum When referring to a contract, ad referendum indicates that while the contract has been agreed and signed, there are still some matters to be discussed.

ad valorem In ***taxation***, ad valorem (literally according to the value) indicates that tax is calculated as a percentage of the value of the transaction, rather than charged at a fixed rate. *E.g.* value-added tax is paid as a percentage of the goods or services sold, whereas car road tax in the UK is paid at a fixed rate. *See* ***value-added tax***.

ad valorem duty Duty charged as a percentage of the total value of the goods or services being taxed. Value-added tax is a form of ad valorem duty. *See* ***value-added tax***.

advance Part-payment for work contracted made ahead of total payment, before the goods or services contracted for have been rendered. Sometimes, if payment depends on sales, the advance is set against those sales.

It is usual to pay rent in advance.

The author received a £1000 advance against royalties.

advance corporation tax (ACT) Corporation tax is levied in two parts. The first part is levied on the distribution of profits and is known as advance corporation tax. The second half of the tax is estimated on the company's earnings. *See* ***corporation tax***.

adventure Commercial or financial risk.

adverse Bad or, at the very least, unhelpful.

adverse balance In general, an account balance that shows a ***loss*** or ***liability***. More especially, it is short for adverse ***balance of trade***.

advertising Range of activities that surround the practice of informing the public of the existence and desirability of a product. The main purpose of advertising is to boost sales, or, in the case of charities and national bodies, to provide information or solicit contributions.

advertising agency Company that specializes in planning and executing ***advertising*** campaigns.

advertising copy Text of an advertisement.

advertorial Form of advertising, usually found in newspapers and magazines. The advertorial is printed in such a way that it looks like an editorial or article, in an effort to add the authority of the publication as a recommendation of the product.

advice note Notice from a supplier giving details of goods ordered or delivered. It either accompanies or precedes the shipment, and precedes the invoice. *See also* ***delivery note***.

advice of acceptance Document from a ***collecting bank*** to the bank from which a ***collection order*** was received that acknowledges receipt of funds and gives details of any charges incurred.

advice of fate *See* ***advise fate***.

advice of non-acceptance Document from a ***collecting bank*** to the bank from a which a ***collection order*** was received that gives notice of non-acceptance or non-payment. It is also termed advice of non-payment.

advice of non-payment *See* ***advice of non-acceptance***.

advise fate Request from a collecting ***banker*** to a paying banker to confirm that the ***cheque*** to which it refers has been honoured. This confirmation cannot be given until the paying banker receives the cheque, because the ***account*** to which the cheque refers may have had other ***debits*** made to it, or the ***payer*** may stop the cheque. It is a speedy method of confirmation, and it circumvents the use of a ***banker's clearing house***. The method is also termed advice of fate.

advising bank Bank in an exporter's country, which deals with ***letters of credit*** from a foreign bank, that tells the exporter when such credit has been opened with the foreign bank.

advisery board Group of specialists who advise others.

advisery funds Funds for investment deposited with a bank but which can be invested only after consultation with the depositor.

AE Abbreviation of ***account executive***.

aerial advertising There are several methods of aerial advertising: banners trailed from aircraft; writing in smoke in the sky; writing on the side of hot air balloons and airships. Aerial advertising using aircraft is now restricted mainly to airshows.

AFBD Abbreviation of ***Association of Futures Brokers and Dealers***.

AFDB Abbreviation of ***African Development Bank***.

affidavit Statement or declaration made in writing and witnessed by a commissioner for oaths (such as a ***solicitor***), often for use in legal proceedings.

affinity card Credit card that requires the issuing bank or credit card company to make specified payments to a named charity. It is also called a charity card.

affirmative action programme Scheme in the USA designed to avoid or discourage discrimination in employment, equivalent to equal opportunities employment in the UK.

affreightment Carriage of goods by sea.

African Development Bank (AFDB) Bank established in 1964 with headquarters in Abidjan, Cote d'Ivoire, to facilitate economic development among African nations.

afghani Standard currency unit of Afghanistan, divided into 100 puls.

after-acquired property Possessions obtained by a bankrupt after bankruptcy has been declared.

after date Written on a ***bill of exchange***, after date indicates that the bill will become due a certain (specified) period after the date on the bill. Hence, the bill might read, "60 days after date, we promise to pay..." See also ***after sight; at sight***.

after hours dealing Alternative term for ***early bargain***.

aftermarket Trading in ***stocks*** and ***shares*** after they have made their initial debut on the ***market***. The aftermarket may also be the market in components and services arising after a product has been sold. This is also known as the add-on market.

The flourishing computer aftermarket is created by enthusiasts who soup up old models in preference to buying new ones.

after sight Written on a ***bill of exchange***, term that indicates that the period for which the bill is drawn is to be calculated from the date on which the ***acceptor*** first saw (or accepted) it. This date is normally written on the bill by the acceptor. *See also* ***after date; at sight***.

after-tax profit Profit calculated after all tax deductions have been made.

AG Abbreviation of the German ***Aktiengesellschaf***.

against the box In a ***short sale***, the individual selling short actually owns the ***stock*** sold short but for some reason does not wish to or cannot deliver the particular stock owned in order to settle the sale transaction with the buyer.

age allowance Tax allowance made to a person over the age of 65 or a married couple where one partner is over that age.

agency Term with two meanings:

1. It is a person or *company* that represents another in a particular field.
2. It is a contractual *agreement*, by which one party agrees to represent another, the agent's word becoming as binding in the affairs of the other as if the latter had acted on his or her own behalf.

agency agreement Agreement between a bank and a customer allowing him or her, for a charge, to deposit cheques at a branch of the bank at which the customer does not have an account.

agency bill *Bill of exchange* that is accepted by the London branch of a foreign bank.

agency fee Fee paid each year to an agent for managing a loan. It is also termed a facility fee.

Agency for International Development Created as an agency within the US Department of State by departmental authority pursuant to Executive Order 10973 (November 3, 1961) and section 621 Foreign Assistance Act of 1961 (22 U.S.C. 2381).

agency of necessity Situation that arises when an *agent* acts to safeguard the principal's interests, without the principal's permission. This situation can only arise when (a) the principal cannot be reached, (b) there is a *contract* of agency already in existence between the two parties and, (c) immediate action is absolutely necessary. If these conditions exist, then the agent's actions are legally binding on the principal.

agenda List of matters to be discussed at a meeting. An agenda can constitute a legal document.

agent Person or company that has entered into a contract of *agency* with another party, and acts as its representative, usually in buying and selling goods or services.

agent bank Bank that oversees the entire issue of securities or the granting of a loan, for which it charges a *commission*.

agent de change Stockbroker on the Bourse in Paris.

aggregate Sum total.

agio *Commission* or *charge* made by a *bank* or *bureau de change* in return for converting cash from one *currency* to another.

AGM Abbreviation of *annual general meeting*.

agreement Verbal or written contract between two or more parties to explain the way they intend to act in respect of each other.

agricultural bank Bank specializing in granting loans for agricultural development. It is aso known as a land bank.

agricultural disarmament Reduction in protectionist practices, such as price subsidizing, in agriculture.

Agricultural Credit Corporation (ACC) Government-sponsored organization established in 1965 to provide guarantees to banks that advance capital funds to farmers.

Agricultural Mortgage Corporation (AMC) Organization established in 1928 by the Bank of England to provide long-term loans to farmers, using their land as security.

aids to trade Activities (often services) that assist other businesses, such as advertising, banking, insurance and transport.

AIM Abbreviation of ***Alternative Investment Market***.

air-pocket stock Stock whose price suddenly falls, usually after rumours of the company's poor performance.

air waybill Document that accompanies goods being shipped by air, itemizing the goods and constituting evidence of the existence of a ***contract*** to make the shipment.

Aktiengesellschaft Equivalent of a ***public limited company*** (plc) in Austria, Germany or Switzerland. It is abbreviated to AG.

alligator spread Profit made on an ***option*** that is instantly snapped up by the broker as commission, leaving nothing for the investor.

all-in Including everything, most often used to describe a price or service. *She bought the lot at auction for £25 all-in.*

allocatur ***Certificate*** of approval of ***costs*** incurred in an action (e.g. ***liquidation***) for ***taxation*** purposes.

allonge Slip attached to a ***bill of exchange*** that provides extra space for the noting of ***endorsements***. Allonges were most useful when bills of exchange moved freely from one holder to another, but now are less common.

A

allotment Broadly, the sharing out of something, usually funds, among a group of people.

allotment of shares When a company issues ***shares*** by publishing a ***prospectus*** and inviting applications, allotment is the assignment of shares to each applicant. In cases where the issue is oversubscribed, shares are allotted in proportion to the quantity requested and so applicants do not always receive the number of shares they originally requested. *See also* ***application and allotment; oversubscribed.***

allowable expenses Expenses that are tax-deductible.

allowance Term with two meanings:

1. It is money that is allotted (allowed) to individuals for a specific reason, or a provision made for unusual or uncertain events.
2. It is the amount deducted for one of various reasons before **income** is calculated for **tax** purposes.

alpha Stock Exchange categorization of the top100 most actively traded shares with a large capitalization value. *See also* ***beta; delta; gamma.***

alternate director Person who shares a directorship with another. Each member of a pair of alternate directors has a vote on the board.

Alternative Investment Market (AIM) Replacement for the Unlisted Securities Market, which closed at the end of 1996, aimed at helping smaller companies to raise capital.

alternative payee Cheque or bill of exchange can be made payable to either of two people, each of whom is an alternative payee.

amalgamation The coming together or unification of two or more companies. *See also* ***merger; takeover.***

ambulance stock Securities recommended to a client whose investment portfolio has done badly. The practice is especially common in Japan.

American depositary receipts (ADR) Receipts that are issued by American banks declaring that a certain number of a company's shares have been deposited with them. ADRs are denominated in dollars and although they usually refer to non-American companies, they are traded on the American markets as US securities.

American Express (AMEX) International ***credit*** company based in the United States.

American Express card ***Plastic card*** issued by American Express, used as a no-limit debit card by its holders. It is not a true ***credit card*** because long-term credit is unavailable, and debts must be paid by a given due date.

American Plan Also known as the white plan or the Bretton Woods Agreement, a proposal to encourage international ***trade*** by fixing international currency ***conversion*** rates and enabling those currencies to be freely converted. *See also* ***Bretton Woods Conference.***

American Stock Exchange (AMEX) New York stock exchange that deals in stocks and bonds of smaller companies.

AMEX Abbreviation of ***American Express*** and ***American Stock Exchange.***

amortize To pay off a ***debt*** by means of payments over a period of time. More specifically, in ***accounting***, the cost of a fixed ***asset*** is written in to the profit and loss account over a period of years, rather than being taken into account when it is first bought. The cost of the asset has been amortized when this period is over.

The capital cost of the packaging equipment will be amortized over 5 years.

See ***depreciation; profit-and-loss account.***

amortizing mortgage ***Mortgage*** in which all the principal and interest has been repaid, usually by equal payments, by the end of the mortgage term. Although the payments are equal, early payments are made up mostly of interest, whereas later payments are mostly repayments of the principle.

analysis Determination of the composition or the significance of something. In business and finance, an analysis can be a detailed study or investigation of a particular subject, often culminating in a report, upon which executives may base their decisions.

analysis-paralysis What happens when managers spend their time having endless meetings and writing interminable reports, but never making any decisions. It is characterized by a desire for more and more statistics and information.

analyst Person who undertakes ***analysis.***

ancillary credit business Business that does not directly provide credit but is engaged in credit brokerage, debt adjusting, debt counselling, debt collection or the operation of a credit reference agency. *See* ***credit broker; debt collection agency.***

& Co Abbreviation of "and company", words sometimes added to a crossed cheque.

annual accounts Report submitted annually, showing the current financial state of a company and the results of its operations for that year. *See also* ***annual report***.

annual charges For ***taxation*** purposes, that part of a person's or company's income that has been paid after tax has been deducted. *E.g.* a ***covenant*** to a person is deemed by the Inland Revenue to have been paid net of tax.

annual general meeting (AGM) ***Shareholders'*** meeting, required by law to be held yearly by every public company. An AGM is normally used to discuss the ***annual report*** and ***accounts***, to announce ***dividends*** and to elect ***auditors*** and ***directors***. This is often the only opportunity the shareholders have to air their views. *See* ***public limited company***. *See also* **EGM;** ***gadfly***.

annual increment Amount by which money (often a salary) or goods increase in the course of one year.

annualized percentage rate (APR) Also known as annual percentage rate, the rate of ***interest*** charged on a monthly basis (*e.g.* on a ***hire purchase*** transaction) shown as a yearly ***compound*** rate.

annual report Document required by law to be released annually by public companies, describing the company's activities during the previous year. It usually includes the company's balance sheet for the year.

annual return Document that in the UK must be submitted to Companies House each year by every company with share capital, detailing such items as the address of the registered office, a list of current members, charges on the company, etc.

annual value Income that accrues annually from the possession of, say, property or a portfolio of shares. A distinction is normally made between net annual value and gross annual value, the former being the annual income from a possession after expenses of ownership have been deducted, and the latter being the income before expenses have been taken into account. *See also* ***rateable value***.

annul To make void in law, to cancel.

The contract was annulled by the courts.

Annunzio-Wylie Anti Money Laundering Act (Title XV of H.R. 5334) Legislation giving the power to certain governmental agencies to revoke the US federal charter of any institution convicted of money ***laundering***.

answer on cheque Reason for non-payment of a cheque, stamped or written on the face of the cheque by the paying banker. *E.g.*, "refer to drawer" on a cheque usually indicates that the cheque has not been paid because of lack of funds in the drawer's account.

antedate To put on a document, *e.g.* a ***cheque*** or ***invoice***, a date which is already past.

The invoice was antedated to 1 December last year.

See also ***postdate.***

antedated cheque Cheque whose date is long past. A cheque more than six months old is invalid (it is said to be stale) and will not be paid by the receiving bank.

anti-trust laws Legislation in the USA enacted to prevent the formation of ***monopolies***. It is similar to the Monopolies and Mergers Act in the UK.

AOB Abbreviation of any other business. AOB normally appears at the end of an ***agenda*** and provides an opportunity for discussion of any matters not already dealt with or arising too late for inclusion on the formal agenda.

APACS Abbreviation of ***Association for Payment Clearing Services.***

APCIMS Abbreviation of ***Association of Private Client Investment Managers and Stockbrokers.***

application and allotment System whereby a company may issue ***shares***. This is done by publishing a ***prospectus***, inviting applications from institutions and individuals to buy shares, and then allotting shares to those who take up the offer. *See also* ***allotment; stag***.

apportion To share out. The term is normally applied to ***costs***.

They decided to apportion start-up costs equally between the members of the co-venture.

appreciation Increase in value. In ***accounting***, appreciation is an increase in value of (fixed) ***assets***.

Over the years the company directors were pleased to see their office block appreciate.

See also ***depreciation.***

A

appro Informal abbreviation of approval.

appropriate financial services vehicle Subsidiary of a ***building society***

that functions as a tied agent or an independent financial adviser.

appropriation Act of putting aside (funds) for a special reason.

They decided to appropriate funds from the production budget to set up a marketing department.

There are three specialist meanings of the term:

1. In company accounting, it is the division of pre-tax ***profits*** between corporation ***tax***, company ***reserves*** and ***dividends*** to shareholders. The term works in the same sense in a ***partnership*** situation.
2. In the shipping of produce, the appropriation is the document by which the seller identifies to the buyer the relevant unit in the shipment.
3. If a ***debtor*** makes a payment to a ***creditor*** and does not specify which debt the payment is in settlement of, the creditor may appropriate it to any of the debts outstanding on the debtor's account. This is often known as appropriation of payments.

*See also **appropriation account**.*

appropriation account Account that shows net profits (current and carried forward) and how they are split between dividends and reserves.

APR Abbreviation of ***annualized percentage rate***.

arb Shortened form of ***arbitrage***.

arbitrage Practice of dealing on two markets almost simultaneously in order to profit from differing exchange ***rates***. Arbitrage may take place when dealing in ***commodities***, ***bills of exchange*** or ***currencies***. It also occurs in situations where prices and returns are fixed and in this sense arbitrage may be contrasted with ***speculation*** in that there is little risk involved. In the USA, often shortened to arb. *See also **reverse arbitrage; soft arbitrage**.*

arbitrager (or **arbitrageur)** Person who practises ***arbitrage***.

arbitration In disputes arising out of a ***contract***, the parties involved may either go to court or appoint someone (an arbitrator) to settle the dispute. The agreement to go to arbitration does not preclude either of the parties taking legal proceedings if it desires. *See also **umpirage**.*

ARBs Abbreviation of ***arbitragers***.

Ariel Name of a computerized system that makes possible share dealing between subscribers (all of whom are institutions) without having to deal through the London Stock Exchange.

ARM Abbreviation of ***adjustable-rate mortgage***.

arrangement Generally, the settlement of any financial matter. More specifically, a deed of arrangement is an agreement between a ***debtor*** and some or all of his or her ***creditors***, reached in order to avoid the debtor's ***bankruptcy***. Arrangement may be encountered in various forms: as a letter of licence, deed of inspectorship, ***assignment*** of property or a deed of composition. It may take place either before or after a bankruptcy petition has been presented to the courts.

arrangement fee Fee charged by a bank for certain services, such as setting up a ***bridging loan***.

arrears Money owed but not yet paid.

Having been out of work for several months, she found that her rent payments were in arrears.

See also ***advance***.

arrestment Scottish term for ***attachment***.

articled clerk Kind of apprentice, generally working in one of the professions, such as law or accounting.

articles of association *See* ***memorandum of association***.

ASAP Informal abbreviation of as soon as possible.

ASB Abbreviation of ***Accounting Standards Board***.

AsDB Abbreviation of ***Asian Development Bank***.

A-shares Shares with rights different from those legally attached to ***ordinary shares***. There are also B-shares, C-shares, etc. The term is frequently used to describe ***non-voting shares***.

Asian Development Bank (AsDB) International bank established in 1966 to facilitate economic development among developing Asian countries.

as per advice Term normally found as a note on a ***bill of exchange***, indicating that the ***drawee*** has already been notified that the bill has been drawn on him or her.

assay Testing of a metal or ore to determine the proportion of precious metal it contains. Assay most often applies to metals used in coinage, and to gold and silver. Metals assayed are stamped with a hallmark or an assay mark.

assay master Official who is responsible for the testing and grading of metals in the above way.

ASSC Abbreviation of Accounting Standards Steering Committee. *See* ***accounting standards.***

assented In a situation where a company is threatened with a ***takeover***, assented stocks or shares are those whose owner is in agreement with the takeover. In these circumstances, there may arise separate markets in assented and non-assented stock. Assented stock may also be stock whose owner is in agreement with a proposed change in the conditions of issue.

assessment Act of calculating ***value.***

I am waiting for my Income Tax assessment.

asset Something that belongs to an individual or company and which has a ***value***, *e.g.* buildings, plant, stock, but also ***accounts receivable.*** There are several types of assets for business purposes, and they are usually classified in terms of their availability for ***exchange.***

asset-backed Term that refers to investments that are related to tangible assets, *e.g.* property, so that the investment participates in ***growth*** which can easily be determined. *See* ***tangible assets.***

asset-based financing Loans secured on a company's assets, especially its accounts receivable or its stock.

asset card US term for a ***debit card.***

asset management Broadly, the efficient control and exploitation of a firm's assets, most commonly used to describe the management of any ***fund*** by a fund manager.

asset play Activities of a company, the major part of whose value is based on its assets rather than its operations.

assets-to-equity ratio Value of assets owned by a company compared to the total of issued capital and reserves.

asset stripping Practice, normally frowned upon, whereby a company is bought so that the buyer may sell off its assets for immediate gain.

asset value Value of the assets of a company.

asset value per share Value of the assets of a company, minus its liabilities, divided by the number of shares.

assignment Legal transfer of a property, right or obligation from one party to another. Assignment takes place most commonly where a ***contract*** is involved.

associate Term prefixed adjectivally to indicate a company or individual linked in some way to another, as in, *e.g.*, associate company.

associate company Company that is partly owned by another, which has a stake of less than 50%.

associate director Director who is a member of the ***board*** but lacks full voting powers. The position is normally held by able but comparatively junior managers; it rewards their enthusiasm and reinforces their commitment without giving them real power.

associated operation Operation that is somehow linked to another within a company. Associated operations within a company may, *e.g.*, manufacture similar products or use similar production methods.

association Group of people or companies with a common interest. *E.g.* a trade association is a group of companies operating in the business, who come together to provide information and services to each other. Association is also what happens when a company is formed.

Association for Payment Clearing Services (APACS) Organization established in 1985 for managing and controlling the main payment clearing systems and methods of money transmission in the UK.

Association of British Factors (ABF) Organization established in 1977 of representatives of companies whose main business is providing full ***factoring*** services.

Association of Futures Brokers and Dealers (AFBD) Former ***self-regulating organization*** (SRO) , established in 1986, which regulated the activities of brokers and dealers on the London futures market. In 1991 it became part of the ***Securities and Futures Authority*** (SFA).

Association of Private Client Investment Managers and Stockborkers (APCIMS) Organization established in 1990 that represents the interests of private-client investment managers and stockbrokers in the UK.

AST Abbreviation of ***automated screen trading***.

at best Instruction to a ***broker*** to buy or sell ***shares*** or ***commodities*** at the best price available. *See* ***at limit***.

at call Money at call has been borrowed but must be repaid on demand. *See also* ***at short notice***.

at limit Instruction to a ***broker*** to buy or sell ***shares*** or ***commodities*** with a limit on the upper and lower prices.

A

ATM Abbreviation of ***automatic telling*** (US ***teller***) ***machine***.

at par Equal, indicating a share price equal to the paid-up or nominal value. *See also* ***parity***.

at short notice Describing money that is borrowed for a very short period of time, say twenty-four or forty-eight hours, usually at a low ***interest*** rate. *See also* ***at call***.

at sight Note on a ***bill of exchange*** indicating that the payment is due on presentation of the bill. *See also* ***after sight***.

attachment Act of court whereby the court is able to recover money owed by a debtor by ordering a person owing money to the debtor to pay that money direct to the court. ***Arrestment*** is the equivalent of attachment in Scottish law.

at-the-money-option Call or put option where the price of the security on the market is the same as the ***exercise price***.

attorney In the UK, someone who is legally authorized to act for another, or a person practising at the bar. In the USA, however, the term is more often used to denote a ***lawyer***.

attractive stock Ordinary shares that promise a good return.

at warehouse ***Goods*** or ***commodities*** that are waiting at a warehouse either to be bought or delivered to a customer. A price at warehouse (or ex-warehouse) does not normally include freight charges. *See also* ***futures; spot goods***.

auction Method of selling goods in public. The auctioneer acts as an agent for the seller, offers the goods and normally sells to the highest bidder (for which service the auctioneer charges a ***commission***).

audit Examination of the ***accounts*** of a company. It is a legal requirement in the UK that the accounts of all companies over a certain size (in terms of annual turnover) be scrutinized annually by a qualified ***auditor***.

auditor Person appointed by a company or other organization to perform an ***audit***.

audit trail System whereby each stage of a transaction is formally recorded.

authenticate To state that something is true. *E.g.* an ***auditor*** signs a company's ***accounts***, thereby authenticating them.

authority Broadly, authority is the given power to act in a certain way.

Hence, a ***banker*** receives an authority from a client to operate the account in a certain way, or an ***agent*** receives authority to act in such a way on behalf of his or her principal.

authorized capital Amount of capital a company is authorized to raise through the issue of shares, as set down in the company's articles of association (*see* ***memorandum of association***).

authorized clerk Employee of a ***stockbroker***, who is authorized to make transactions on his or her behalf.

automated clearing house (ACH) Computer system used by the US Customs Service for making electronic transfer of funds (instead of using cheques or cash) for paying duty and taxes on imported goods.

automated screen trading (AST) System that uses computers to display prices and deal in securities.

automatic debit transfer Service provided in the UK by ***Girobank*** that, for a small charge, allows a business to collect regular sums of money from a large number of customers.

automatic (or **automated) telling machine** (ATM) Computer-linked machine, usually mounted on the wall of a bank or other financial institution, which dispenses cash, statements and balances on production of a card and the provision of the correct ***personal identification number***.

aval Guarantee given by a bank at a customer's request that a ***bill of exchange*** will be paid on presentation.

AVC Abbreviation of additional voluntary ***contribution*** paid into an approved pension scheme by an employee.

average Single number or value that indicates the general tendency of a collection of numbers or value. The average of *n* values is the sum of the values divided by *n*. It is also called the mean.

average available earnings ***Profit*** available for distribution to shareholders.

average balance Sum of the daily balances of a bank account over a period of time divided by the number of days in the period.

average cleared credit balance ***Average balance*** on a credit account, used to estimate the allowance that can be made against the cost of maintaining the account (before the actual commission charge is known).

average cost pricing Determination of a price in accordance with the average cost of producing a good. The manufacturer makes neither a profit nor a loss.

average due date If the due date falls within a range of days, the average due date is the mid-point of that range. *See* ***due date***.

average price Alternative term for ***target price***.

average revenue Total amount of money received divided by the number of units of a product sold.

avoirdupois System of weights used in the UK and USA (using, *e.g.*, ounces and pounds), now gradually being replaced by the metric system.

axe Used as a verb, the term means to stop abruptly or to cut back (normally for financial reasons).

The R & D department was the first to be axed when the company found it was in financial trouble.

B

baby bonds Friendly society bonds that yield growing funds for a child usually over a ten-year term.

back Term with two meanings:

1. It is used adjectivally to refer to the past.
2. To back is to lend money to a project to enable it to start or continue operating.

He finally found a bank to back his idea. It is lending him £50,000.

back date To date a document with a date previous to that on which it was actually signed. Back dating indicates that the provisions of the document became effective on the back date rather than the date on which the document was signed.

back dating Assigning value to an entry (credit or debit) on a date that is earlier than that on which the entry is actually made.

back door System by which the Bank of England purchases Treasury bills at the market rate, rather than assist ***discount houses*** by lending cash to them directly, in order to inject funds into the ***money market***. *See also **front door**.*

back duty Also known as back tax, retrospective tax levied on profits or goods on which no tax was paid at the time.

backer Person or institution that financially backs projects or operations.

She found it relatively easy to find a backer for such an interesting business proposition.

backfreight Freight for the return of cargo paid by the consignor when goods are not delivered through the consignor's own fault, or are refused by the consignee.

backhander Informal term for a bribe or unofficial payment in cash for work done.

You won't get any orders from that company's purchasing manager unless you give him a backhander.

back-in ***Poison pill*** tactic sometimes used by the shareholders of a company threatened by ***takeover***, whereby the shareholders sell their holdings back to the company at a price agreed by the board.

backing away Failure of a securities dealer to carry through a deal at the price he or she has quoted. Backing away is usually frowned upon in all markets.

backing support Gold or other security that supports an issue of banknotes.

back interest Alternative term for ***accrued interest***.

back month On financial ***futures*** markets, those contracts that are being traded for the month that is furthest in the future.

back office Alternative term for ***backroom***.

backroom Informal name given to the department in a stockbroking firm that deals in matters other than the buying or selling of shares, *e.g.* share ***dividends***, shareholder registrations, and payment.

backroom backlog Delay in processing stockbroking transactions, caused by a large volume of business.

A huge backroom backlog followed the deregulation of the London market.

back tax Also known as back duty, payment of tax on income that was not paid at the time it was earned or first claimed. *See also* ***tax evasion***.

back-to-back Form of ***credit*** by which a finance house acts as an intermediary between a foreign seller and a foreign buyer, concealing the identity of the seller. The seller passes to the finance house the documents relevant to the sale and the house reissues them to the buyer in its own name.

back-to-back loan Type of ***loan*** between companies in different countries (and perhaps in different currencies) employing a bank or finance house which uses funding from a third party to provide the loan.

backwardation Two meanings are possible:

1. In a commodity market, it is the situation in which the future price is lower than the spot price, because of excessive present demand, which is expected to fall as time passes. Opposite, in commodity terms, to contango.
2. In stock markets, the situation in which the highest bid price is higher than the lowest offer price, making it theoretically possible to buy from one market maker and sell to another immediately, at a profit. *See also* ***choice price***.

backward integration Amalgamation of a company that operates at one stage of production with another that is located farther back in the chain. *E.g.* a manufacturing company amalgamates with a company that provides raw materials.

BACS Company established in 1986 whose name is based on its previous title, Bankers Automated Clearing House. It processes automated credits, direct debits and standing orders, as well as other types of payments.

bad cheque Cheque that bounces because it is drawn on an account that has insufficient funds to cover payment. *See* ***bounce***; ***refer to drawer***.

bad debt Debt that has not been, and is not expected to be, paid. Such losses are practically unavoidable in business (and allowances are almost always made for such instances), although some bad debts may be sold to a ***factoring*** company, which attempts to recover the debt on its own account.

bagging the Street Concealment of information about the sale of ***stock*** from dealers and specialists by institutional investors or ***brokers***. Such information may include reasons why the stock is being sold off, and the number and price of the shares in question.

baht Standard currency unit of Thailand, divided into 100 satang.

bailee Person, such as a banker, to whom goods are entrusted for safe keeping. *See* ***bailment***.

bailment Act of placing goods into the care of someone else. The person who places the goods is the bailor and must be the rightful owner. The bailee is the person who receives the goods.

bailor Person who leaves goods with somebody (the bailee) for safe keeping. *See* ***bailment***.

bailout Government intervention in the affairs of a public company to prevent it going bankrupt, providing loans at low interest, or tax concessions. Bailout also means the withdrawal of capital from a public company by its founders before the public has a chance to do so.

bail out To go to the rescue of a company that is experiencing financial difficulties by providing it with ***capital***.

bad paper ***Bill of exchange*** that is never likely to be honoured.

bailee Person who holds goods on behalf of another.

balance Quite apart from its general applications, the term is used, primarily in double-entry book-keeping, to refer to the sum owed or owing when an ***account*** has been reckoned. Hence, the phrase to balance the books means to add in this sum to the relevant side of the account so that both columns show the same total.

balance of payments Account of all recorded financial exchanges made between the residents of a country and those of other countries. The balance of payments is divided into current and capital accounts. The current account takes stock of all ***invisible*** and ***visible trade*** (the ***balance of trade*** is part of the balance of payments current account), and the capital account includes all movements of ***capital*** in or out of the country.

balance of trade Also known as the visible balance, the difference between the value of a country's ***visible imports*** and ***visible exports***. When the value of visible imports total more than the value of visible exports, it is known as an adverse balance of trade. *See* ***balance of payments***.

balance sheet Statement that shows the financial position of a company in respect of its assets and liabilities at a certain time.

balance the books *See* ***balance***.

balance ticket Alternative term for certification of transfer. *See* ***certification of transfer***.

balboa Standard currency unit of Panama, divided into 100 centisimos.

balloon Large irregular part-payment of a loan, made when funds are available. Such an arrangement is termed a balloon loan.

balloon mortgage Mortgage in which a lump sum has to be paid at the end of the mortgage period to pay off outstanding principal and interest. It is also called a non-amortizing mortgage.

ballot While in general terms a ballot is a method of voting by marking a paper, in finance it more specifically refers to a method of allotting ***shares*** to applicants in the event a share issue is ***oversubscribed***. All applications are entered for the ballot and those drawn at random receive some or all of the shares applied for. *See* ***application and allotment***.

banco Funds held on account by a bank, as opposed to cash.

bank An institution that carries on the business of banking and is so authorized by the ***central bank*** (in Britain the Bank of England). *See also* ***central bank;merchant bank***.

bank (US **banking) account** Arrangement to deposit money with a bank. *See* ***current account; deposit account; savings account.***

bank advance *See* ***bank loan.***

bank advisery committee Informal organization consisiting of the leading banks in a foreign debtor country. It proposes debt restructuring plans to its government, which may in turn pass them on foreign lending governments.

bank balance Statement relating to an account with a bank, showing only the level of funds in the account and not details of recent transactions. *See also* ***bank statement.***

bank bill Instruction to a bank to pay someone a certain sum of money. The term is usually employed in transactions involving foreign currencies. In the USA the term refers to a banknote.

bank book Book showing debits and credits made to a bank account.

bank certificate Document signed by a bank manager, often requested by an auditor, stating the balance of a company's account on a specified date.

bank charges Charges made by a bank on many types of account. Typically, charges are made each time a cheque is drawn or a facility used, although many banks are now advertising no charges on current accounts that remain in credit.

bank cheque Cheque drawn by a bank and not one of its account holders. It is also called a cashier's cheque.

bank deposit Money paid into a bank account, usually into either a ***current account*** or an interest-earning ***deposit account.***

bank draft Also called a banker's draft, a ***cheque*** drawn on a bank by itself. A bank draft must be honoured, because it is drawn on the bank itself rather than on the debtor's account. The debtor must pay the bank the sum drawn in advance.

banker Person involved in the business of banks and banking, or an institution that performs the same task for other institutions.

banker's acceptance Draft ***bill of exchange*** drawn on a bank and accepted by it.

Bankers Automated Clearing Services *See* BACS.

banker's bank Bank comprising several independent banks that acts as a *clearing house* for various financial transactions. The term is also used for the Bank of England.

banker's card Plastic card issued by a bank to its creditworthy customers, which guarantees the payment of a cheque up to a certain sum (usually £50-£100).

banker's cheque Cheque that is drawn on one bank by another bank, usually in order to transfer a customer's funds.

Banker's Clearing House The best known of the clearing houses in the UK, which facilitates the passing of cheques that are presented at the many branches of each member bank, by making an account of each bank's indebtedness to the others at the end of each banking day.

banker's draft Another name for a ***bank draft***.

banker's lien Banker's right to hold and, after giving notice, sell bills of exchange, cheques, promissory notes and other property obtained through banking belonging to a customer who is also a debtor. The right does not apply to property left at the bank for safe keeping.

banker's opinion Statement about the financial status of a customer supplied by a bank to another bank or authorized enquiry agent. The statement should not breach confidence and is carefully worded in non-actionable terms. It is also called a banker's reference.

banker's order Alternative term for ***standing order***.

banker's payment Draft or order drawn on a bank by one of its own branches in favour of another bank.

banker's reference *See* ***banker's opinion***.

bank examination An inspection of the financial condition of a bank, initiated by the bank itself or conducted by legally constituted authorities, to assure the depositors, stockholders and the public that the affairs of the bank are being conservatively and efficiently managed.

bank examiners Persons appointed pursuant to US banking laws, the Federal Reserve Act, Federal Deposit Insurance Act and state banking laws to examine the affairs of banks and banking institutions within each jurisdiction.

Bank for International Settlements (BIS) An international bank that acts as agent and trustee for various international organizations. It is also a clearing house for interbank transactions using European currency. The Bank of England is the agent of BIS in London. BIS was originally established in Basle, Switzerland, for dealing with German war reparations after World War I.

bank giro System for tranferring funds between accounts held at different banks, usually by means of ***credit transfers***.

bank giro credit (BCG) *See **bank transfer**.*

bank guarantee Guarantee made by a bank that it will pay an exporter for goods shipped if a foreign purchaser defaults; the guarantee is obtained by the foreign purchaser.

bank holding company Company that holds or controls more than 5% of the voting shares of a bank.

Bank Holding Company Act (US) The Bank Holding Company Act of 1956 (May 9, 1956, 70 Stat. 133) for the first time allowed actual ***holding companies*** in the banking field and put them under comprehensive banking regulations.

bank holiday *See **non-business days**.*

Banking Act of 1933 (US) Approved June 16, 1933 (48 Stat.164), the first of the major banking laws enacted by the Roosevelt Administration, effecting important changes in the banking laws. The Act was created in order to control abuses in the banking system and prevent future, large-scale bank failures as had occurred in the United States during the early 1930s.

Banking Act of 1935 (US) Approved August 23, 1935 (49 Stat. 717), the second of the major banking laws of the Roosevelt Administration, amendatory of the Banking Act of 1933, The Federal Reserve Act, and other banking statutes.

Banking Acts Acts of Parliament in the UK, of 1979 and 1987, which define banks (as a takers of deposits), authorize their supervision (by the Bank of England) and specify their minimum paid-up capital reserves (£1 million).

banking education service Service available to schools and colleges, financed by the major banks. It makes available information in the form of printed matter and computer disks about banks and careers in banking.

Banking Federation of the European Union Organization of national professional banking associations devoted to complying with the terms of the Treaty of Rome and putting forward the opinions of banks in an attempt to shape the decisions of the European Parliament and other EU bodies.

banking information service Former public information service organized by the major banks.

Banking Ombudsman A person charged with investigating complaints against any of the member banks of the scheme made by individuals, group depositors or small businesses.

banking practice *See* ***Code of Banking Practice***.

bankings Money (cash or cheques) deposited with a bank, typically by a retail business.

bank interest Any interest involved in banking, such as interest paid on a deposit account or interest charged on a loan or overdraft.

bank interest certificate Document issued by a bank, usually for tax purposes, stating the amount of interest paid to a customer on a deposit account or paid by a customer on a bank loan.

bank loan Loan made by a bank for a specified term and at a specified rate of interest, usually against some form of security. It is also called a bank advance.

bank mandate Written request given to a bank by someone wanting to open an account; it includes specimen signatures of those authorized to use the account.

banknote Paper currency produced by a bank of issue that carries a promise to pay the bearer on demand the sum specified on the note. Often called simple a note, it is also known as a bill in the USA.

Bank of England The ***central bank*** of the UK. Founded in 1694, it now has various functions including the supervision of other banks, acting as a ***banker's bank*** and a ***lender of the last resort***, and issues banknotes in the UK.

Bank of Scotland Commercial bank in Scotland which, while not a ***central bank***, issues its own banknotes.

bank rate Official rate of interest charged by the central banks as ***lender of the last resort***. The term has fallen out of use in the UK, to be replaced by ***minimum lending rate***.

bank reconciliation At any time a bank statement is unlikely to agree with the balance in a firm's cash book, because cheques received or paid may not have been banked. A reconciliation is thus prepared to prove that a true record is being kept by the company. This is done by taking the balance in the cash book, and taking into account transactions not detailed on the statement. At the end of the exercise the two balances should be the same.

bank reconciliation statement Document issued by a bank to explain any difference between the balance shown on a ***bank statement*** and the actual balance as shown in a ***bank book*** at a particular time, usually due to delay in transmission of credits or presentation of cheques by drawees.

bank reference *See* ***banker's opinion.***

bank return Weekly statement from the Bank of England giving financial information about its banking and issuing departments.

bankrupt Person who is unable to pay his or her debts, as determined by the court.

bankruptcy State of being unable to pay debts, as determined by the court.

bankruptcy debt Debt owed by a bankrupt at the beginning of bankruptcy or for which he or she becomes liable after the beginning of bankruptcy because of an obligation that pre-dates it.

bankruptcy level Amount of money owed for which a person can be made bankrupt, currently £750, or any other amount specified in a statutory instrument by the Secretary of State.

bankruptcy order Order of the court adjudging someone bankrupt.

bankruptcy petition Application to the court to be declared bankrupt or to have someone else declared bankrupt.

Bank Service Corporation Act (US) An act that provides that an insured bank may invest not more than 10 per cent of paid-in and unimpaired capital and unimpaired surplus in a bank service corporation.

bank statement Document from a bank giving details of all financial transactions and the balance on a particular account over a given period, usually a month.

bank sweep arrangement Standing instruction to a bank to move funds between accounts (such as from a ***deposit account*** to a ***current account***) as necessary without the need for specific instructions from the customer.

bank transfer Way of making payments at any branch of any bank into an account held in the same or any other bank. It is also called bank giro credit (BCG).

bar Term with three meanings:

1. It is the profession of a ***barrister***.

In 1976 she was called to the bar.

2. It is an obstacle that prevents something happening.

His inadequate knowledge of accounting acted as a bar to his career progress.

3. It is an informal term meaning one million.

Barclaycard Plastic card issued by Barclays Bank that functions as a ***cash card***, ***cheque card*** and ***credit card*** with a pre-set spending limit. As well as Barclays Banks, any bank in the VISA organization will accept the card for over-the-counter cash withdrawals.

bard card *See* ***cheque card***.

bargain In Stock Exchange jargon, any deal struck involving the buying and selling of ***shares***.

bargaining Act of negotiating a price or other terms.

barrier to entry Set of economic and other conditions that make it difficult to set up a business, *i.e.* to enter the market.

base Lowest or starting point from which calculations are made, especially calculations of relative stock price movements.

base currency Currency that forms the basis of an ***exchange rate***. For example, a foreign currency may be quoted in terms of the pound sterling or the American dollar, which are base currencies.

base date Alternative term for ***base year***.

base drift Situation that occurs when a country's central bank tries to limit the money supply but it drifts above the target base.

base money In the USA, the minimum percentage of its deposits that a bank must have in its reserves.

base period Time period selected as the base for an ***index*** number series. The index for a base period is usually 100, and changes in prior or subsequent periods are expressed relative to it.

base rate Minimum amount of interest a bank charges on a loan. The base rate is normally augmented in actual circumstances, according to current market pressures and the risk involved in the loan.

base stock (method) Method of stock valuation whereby stock levels are assumed to be constant and the goods are valued at their original cost.

base year Sometimes also known as the ***base date***, the time from which an index (*e.g.* the Financial Times All Share Index) is calculated. *See also* ***index***.

basis Value of an ***asset*** for ***tax*** purposes.

basis point Unit used to measure the rate of change of investment payments for bonds or notes. Each basis point is equal to 0.01 per cent.

basket of currencies Group of currencies against which the value of some other currency is measured.

basket pegger Country that uses the average of a group of foreign currencies (rather than a single currency) to fix its exchange rate.

Basle Statement Also known as the Basle Concordat, an agreement made in 1975 (revised 1983) that acts as a basis of co-operation between the central banks of the European Union.

bear Stock Exchange dealer or analyst who believes that prices or investment values will go down.

bear closing Situation that occurs when a dealer has sold shares or commodities he or she does not yet own and then buys them back, at a lower price, thus making a profit.

bearer Someone who holds a ***bill***, ***cheque*** or certificate.

bearer bill Also called a bearer note, a bill of exchange, cheque or other negotiable instrument that is payable to the bearer (or is endorsed in blank).

bearer bond Bond payable to the bearer rather than to a specific, named individual. *See also* ***registered bond***.

bearer note *See* ***bearer bill***.

bearer securities Securities that are payable to the bearer and thus easily transferable.

bearer scrip Temporary document achnowledging acceptance of an offer form and cheque for a new issue, exchanged for a bearer bond when the bond is available (or when all instalments have been paid).

bearer stocks Like bearer bonds, securities that are payable to the bearer, not to a named holder.

bear hug In ***corporate finance***, an informal term for notice given to the board of a ***target*** company that a ***takeover*** bid is imminent.

bearish Someone or something (e.g. a market) with the qualities of a ***bear***.

Some market analysts believe that reaction to this week's money-supply figures will not be so bearish after all.

bear market Condition in which share prices are falling. ***Bears*** are speculators who sell shares in anticipation of falling prices.

bear position Position of an investor whose sales exceed his or her purchases, and who therefore stands to gain in a falling or bear market. *See* ***bear***.

bear raid Vigorous selling in concert in order to force down the price of a particular commodity or share. *See also* ***concert party***.

After the 1929 crash, massive bear raids on stocks were recognized as an activity that must be stopped.

bear slide What happens when stock and share prices move towards a bear market situation.

bear squeeze Situation in which bears who have been ***selling short*** are faced with a price rise rather than a fall.

bed-and-breakfast deal Transaction used to minimize the impact of ***capital gains tax***. A ***shareholder*** sells his or her holding after trading closes for the day, for tax purposes. Next morning, the shareholder buys his or her holding back. The US term for a bed and breakfast deal is swap.

bed and PEP Transaction used to comply with the rules about PEPs. A shareholder sells his or her holding after trading closes for the day and buys it back next morning for a ***personal equity plan*** (PEP).

bells and whistles Extras added to a financial product to make it more attractive. ***Options*** are a typical incentive.

below par Share price that has fallen below the nominal value at which the share was issued.

below-the-line accounts Those items included in company accounts that refer to the distribution of profits. Details of *e.g.* ***dividends*** would thus be included in below-the-line accounts. *See also* ***above-the-line***.

below-the-line advertising Advertising by direct mail and merchandising etc. *See* ***above-the-line advertising.***

below-the-line expenditure Alternative term for ***capital expenditure***, because such expenditure is listed below the line recording the total in a statement of account and is regarded as an additional cost. *See also* ***above-the-line expenditure.***

below the market Describing a price that is lower than the usual market price. *See also* ***above the market.***

benchmark Point on an ***index*** that has a significance and is used as a reference point.

beneficial interest Possession or involvement that gives a person the right to take some form of benefit (*e.g.* profit or use) from a property.

beneficial owner When a shareholding is held by a ***nominee*** such as a stockbroker, the nominee's name appears on the register of shareholders. The real owner is known as the beneficial owner. *See* ***nominee shareholder.***

beneficiary Person who gains money or property from something; *e.g.* from a financial transaction such as a life assurance policy or a will.

She was surprised to find herself the principal beneficiary of the will.

benefits in kind Benefits that an employee receives instead of or in addition to salary or wages. Examples include company cars, mobile telephones and medical insurance. Most of such benefits can be assigned a value and assessed for income tax.

benefit taxation Theory of taxation by which taxes to cover public services are paid by those who use them, rather than by the general public at large.

Besloten Vennootschap (BV) Dutch equivalent of private ***limited company*** (Ltd).

best advice Term reflecting the fact that legally an independent financial adviser must offer a potential client the best package to suit him or her out of all the financial products available in the marketplace.

best execution rule Requirement that a stockbroker must obtain the lowest available price when buying securities for a client and the highest possible price when selling.

best price Order to buy or sell something at the best price available at the time.

beta factor (or **coefficient**) Measurement of the volatility of a company's shares, *i.e.* how sensitive the stock is to market fluctuations. The beta is denoted in figures, *e.g.* 1.5, which means that this share will rise 15% in a market that has risen 10%. Shares that under-perform the market are rated below 1.

beta shares (US **stocks**) Second-line shares, as opposed to the less numerous highly-capitalized alpha (first-line) or more numerous gamma (third-line).

bet the ranch To take a substantial risk in stock exchange dealing or other financial transaction.

BCG Abbreviation of ***bank giro credit***. *See* ***bank transfer***.

bid Offer to buy something (*e.g.* shares) at a certain price. A seller may make a certain offer and a prospective buyer may make a bid. The bid cancels out the offer. More especially, a bid is an offer by one company to buy the shares of another, a ***takeover bid***.

bidding ring Group of stock market or antique dealers acting in concert in order to drive prices up or down. This practice is illegal. *See also* ***concert party***.

bid-offer spread Difference between the ***bid price*** and the ***offer price*** offered by a ***market maker***.

bid price Price a market maker is prepared to pay to buy securities. *See also* ***bid-offer spread; offer price***.

bid rate Rate of interest offered for deposits. It is also short for London Offer Bid Rate.

Big Bang Popular term for the deregulation of the London Stock Exchange on 27 October 1986. Among the changes implemented were the admission of foreign institutions as members of the Exchange, the abandonment of rigid distinctions between ***stockbrokers***, ***jobbers*** and ***bankers***, and the abolition of fixed ***commissions***. *See also* ***Little Bang; single capacity***.

Big Blue Nickname for IBM (International Business Machines).

Big Board Nickname for the New York Stock Exchange.

Big Eight Nickname for the eight largest firms of accountants: Arthur Anderson, Arthur Young, Cooppers and Lybrand, Deloitte Haskins and Sells, Ernst and Whinney, Peat Marwick Mitchell, Price Waterhouse and Touche Ross.

Big Four Nickname for the four main commercial banks in the UK: Barclays, Lloyds TSB, Midland and NatWest. They are also known as the High Street banks (*see also* ***commercial bank***). Big Four is also the name given to Japan's largest stock marketing companies: Daiwa, Nikko, Nomura and Yamaichi.

bigger fool theory Justification for buying shares that are over-priced, which runs that there is always a bigger fool somewhere on the market who will buy them from you at an even higher price.

bilateral bank facility Credit facility arranged between a bank and a particular company.

bilateral netting System in which two companies offset their payments and receipts with each other each month and then make a single payment and receipt, thus reducing paperwork and bank charges.

bill Term with four possible meanings:

1. It is a list of charges to be paid on goods or services. In this sense the usual US term is check.

   The supplier presented an exorbitant bill which we refused to pay.

2. It is a document, issued by a bank, promising to pay someone a certain amount of money. It is in this sense that the US meaning of the term is a banknote.
3. It is a document describing goods, most often used in dealings with customs.
4. It is short for ***bill of exchange***.

bill broker Person or company that buys or sells ***bills of exchange***, either on their own account, or as an intermediary.

billion One thousand million, 1,000,000,000. Formerly in the UK a billion was a million million.

bill leak Method used by banks to get round the Bank of England restrictions on lending and the growth of bank deposits by using the acceptance of bills to lend to non-banking organizations. *See also* ***corset***.

bill of exchange Document indicating that one party (the drawee) agrees to pay a certain sum of money on demand or on a specified date, to the drawer. Two very familiar bills of exchange are cheques and banknotes.

bill of imprest Order that entitles its bearer to have money paid in advance.

bill of lading Document detailing the transfer of goods from a (foreign) supplier to a buyer. It may be used as a document of ***title***.

bill of sale Document certificating the transfer of goods (but not real estate) to another person. Goods transferred in this way may not become the property of the receiving party but may be redeemed when the bill is paid.

bill of sight Document passed to a customs inspector by an importer who is unable to describe in detail the imported goods. When the goods are landed a full description must be given, known as perfecting the sight.

bill rate Rate at which a ***bill of exchange*** is discounted. *See* ***discounting***.

bills in a set Foreign ***bills of exchange*** are normally made out in triplicate and sent to the drawee separately to prevent loss. These copies are known as bills in a set.

bills payable In accounting, ***bills of exchange*** that are held and must be paid at some future date. These are effectively liabilities. *See also* ***bills receivable***.

bills receivable In accounting, ***bills of exchange*** that are held and are due to be paid at some future date. These are effectively assets. *See also* ***bills payable***.

BIMBO Abbreviation of buy-in management buy-out, a type of ***management buy-out*** that involves also venture capital from outside.

bimetallism Historic monetary system, once used in the USA (but never in Britain) in which stability of the money supply was attempted by backing it with two precious metals, such as gold and silver.

birr Standard currency unit of Ethiopia, divided in to 100 cents.

BIS Abbreviation of ***Bank for International Settlements***.

black To forbid or boycott trade in certain goods or with certain trading partners. An account that is said to be in the black is in credit. *See also* ***red***.

black book Company's pre-planned strategy to be put into action in the event of a hostile ***takeover*** bid.

black economy Illegal economic activity conducted largely for cash by companies and individuals who pay no taxes on the proceeds. *See also* ***moonlighting; tax evasion***.

blacklist List of companies, products or people that are undesirable and to be avoided.

In the USA the term means more specifically the denial of work to certain people on the grounds of their past beliefs or actions.

John Smith believes he has been blacklisted by management because of his prominence during the 1991 strike.

black market Wholly illegal market; one that is illicit and uncontrolled. Black markets deal in scarce or stolen goods, and frequently come into existence in wartime, because the goods concerned are rationed, or because the market is exceptionally high – in which case counterfeit or imitation goods often appear. Trading is often in kind, one valued commodity being exchanged for another.

Black Monday Monday 19 October 1987. The phrase was coined shortly after the huge losses sustained on the equities markets on that day.

black money Money usually obtained illegally through the international drug trade.

Black Tuesday 18 October 1983, the day IBM announced the launch of two new microcomputers, causing extreme concern on the part of US market analysts over competition in the computer industry and fears that there would be a market ***shakeout***. During the day share prices of competing companies fell considerably.

Black Wednesday 16 September 1992, the day sterling left the ***Exchange Rate Mechanism*** (ERM). The result was a fall of 15% in sterling against the Deutschmark.

blank In general, any form that has not been filled in or not filled in completely, such as a ***blank cheque***.

blank bill ***Bill of exchange*** on which the payee is not specified.

blank cheque Cheque that has been signed (and possibly dated) by the drawee, but that does not specify the amount to be drawn.

blank credit Credit facilities with no upper limit.

blank endorsement A blank cheque endorsed on the reverse. *See* ***blank cheque***.

blanket agreement Agreement that covers many, if not all, items concerning one party's relationship with another.

blanket rate Fixed charge that covers a series of transactions or services.

blank transfer In the transfer of shares, a transfer form that is left blank as regards the name of the transferee. *E.g* if the shares are to be put up as security to a mortgage, the transfer form will be left blank, as the mortgagor has the right to complete the transfer form and sell the shares if the mortgagee defaults.

bliss point In marketing theory, the point at which the consumer is most satisfied with the goods or a combination of goods, so that any change in combination or quantity brings about less consumer satisfaction.

block Group of something (*e.g.* shares); or an obstruction of prevention of entry or exit, as in a ***blocked account***.

blocked account Bank account that becomes subject to restrictions, especially those imposed by governments.

After the coup. the new military government blocked the accounts of all foreign nationals.

See also ***frozen account***.

blocked currency Currency that may not be removed from a country, sometimes for political reasons.

blowout Informal term referring to unexpectedly strong sales of something, *e.g.* goods sold at retail.

Traders regard the Eurobond issue as a blowout because it sold quickly and sparked much excitement on launch.

Blue Book Popular term for a UK government publication entitled *National Income and Expenditure*, best described as the national annual ***report*** and ***accounts***.

blue chip Describing an investment that is regarded as extremely safe, without being ***gilt-edged***. It also describes a company whose shares are regarded as an extremely safe investment.

Analysts believe that blue-chip stocks will continue strong, but that other shares will continue to drift.

blue-chip investment Investment in the ***stock*** of one of the blue-chip companies; hence, a safe but conservative investment. *See* ***blue-chip***.

blue month Month with the greatest trading activity in products such as ***futures*** and ***options***.

blue-sky ***Security*** that is worthless or highly speculative, or something with no specific aim.

Along with its research and development programme, the company invested in a certain amount of blue-sky research.

blue-sky laws Laws in some US states intended to protect investors from potentially worthless share issues.

board Group of people who run a company, society or trust; *see* ***board of directors***. A second meaning refers to goods loaded onto a ship or aircraft.

board of directors Decision-making group comprising all the directors of a company, who are legally responsible for their actions. The board of directors is specifically charged with the management of the company and in the case of a ***public limited company*** is elected by the shareholders at the company's ***annual general meeting*** (AGM). In the USA, the board of directors draws up company policy and appoints executives to run the company. It is sometimes also known simply as "the board".

board meeting Meeting of a ***board of directors***.

bogus Fake or counterfeit.

The police are investigating reports of a con man posing as a salesman, carrying a bogus identity card.

boilerplate language Overly detailed or obscure language found mainly in standard contracts.

A special contract takes time to draft, whereas a boilerplate contract can be used almost immediately.

boiler room Little-known firm of brokers or dealers that sells securities over the telephone.

bolivar Standard currency unit of Venezuela, divided into 100 centimos.

bolivano Standary currency unit of Bolivia, divided into 100 centavos.

bomb Something that happens suddenly with disastrous results.

bona fide Latin for in good faith. It usually appears in reference to contracts, especially contracts of insurance. All parties to a contract are expected to reveal all information relevant to the contract in hand, that is, they are expected to contract in good faith. It is also used simply to mean honest or trustworthy. *See also* ***mala fide***.

After completing an in-depth investigation, the authorities decided that the company was bona fide after all.

bona vacantia Property such as real estate or shares that has no owner and no obvious claimant, *e.g.* property that remains in the hands of a liquidator after the creditors have been paid.

bond Term with three meanings:

1. It is a security issued at a fixed rate by central government, local authorities or occasionally by private companies. It is essentially a contract to repay money borrowed, and as such represents a debt. Normally, bonds are issued in series with the same conditions of repayment and denominations. It is also known as a fixed-interest security.
2. It refers to the importing of goods from abroad. If goods are imported and import duty is not paid immediately, the goods are placed in a bonded warehouse (*i.e.* they are held in bond) until all customs formalities are completed.
3. It is a firm tie or agreement between individuals. "My word is my bond" is the motto of the London Stock Exchange.

bonded Held in ***bond***.

bonded warehouse Warehouse for goods on which excise duty need not be paid until the goods are removed.

bond note Document indicating that imported goods held in bond may be released, because all import formalities have been completed.

bond-washing Practice of buying bonds ***cum dividend*** and selling them ***ex dividend***, to reduce the rate of tax payable on the transaction. The dividend on the bond becomes a capital gain, on which a lower rate of tax is payable than if tax were paid on the proceeds as dividend income. Because of changes in the tax laws in the UK, there is no longer scope for this kind of manoeuvring, although it still happens in the USA.

bonus Additional payment.

bonus dividend Unexpected extra ***dividend*** paid to a shareholder.

bonus issue Issue of ***shares*** made by a company wishing to reduce the average price of its shares. Shareholders receive a number of extra shares in proportion to the number already held. It is also known as a capitalization issue.

A & T Publications has announced a three-for-one bonus issue.

boodle Informal term for money obtained through illegal dealings, often in the form of a ***bribe***.

book In business, the books most frequently referred to are the books of ***account*** in which business transactions are recorded. Books of account are normally held to be legal documents.

book debt Debt recorded in an account book.

book-keeping Business of keeping records of financial transactions.

book of original entry Alternative term for ***book of prime entry***.

book of prime entry Account book in which transactions are recorded from day to day before being transferred to the main ***ledger***.

book value Alternative term for written down value. *See* ***write down***.

boom Popular term for a period when employment, prices and general business activity are at a high level and resources are being used to the full. *See also* ***recession***.

bootstrap Mostly used in the USA where ***takeover*** activity is most prevalent, to describe a cash offer for a controlling interest in a company which, if accepted, is followed by another offer (usually at a lower price) for the remainder of the shares.

The tycoon found bootstrapping a very cost-effective method of taking over other companies.

borrowing Most widely used in the sense of accepting money that is not one's own on the understanding that it will be repaid, usually with interest, at a later date.

On the London Metal Exchange, borrowing is the process of buying a metals contract due to be completed on a near date, and at the same time selling forward a contract for a date further in the future. *See also* ***carry; lending***.

Borse Stock exchange in Europe.

bottom Generally refers to the lowest point of something. In shipping, however, the term refers to a ship, and bottomry is anything to do with shipping.

bottom line Last line of an ***account***, showing either ***profit*** or ***loss***. In this sense the phrase has come to mean the "brutal truth" in general usage.

bottoming out Informal term for a very sudden and serious fall in market prices.

bought deal Practice common in the USA, and becoming more common in the UK, of a major financial institution purchasing a large ***portfolio***

of ***securities*** which it then passes on to its clients piecemeal.

bought ledger Account book in which a business records purchases and, by extension, the credit-control department of an organization.

bounce Term with two meanings:

1. When a ***cheque*** is not honoured by the paying banker, it is said to bounce, because it is passed back to the collecting banker. This may happen for several reasons, but the most common is that there are not enough funds in the account to cover the cheque. A cheque that bounces may be popularly called a rubber cheque. *See* ***refer to drawer***.
2. On the stock market, sudden sharp rise in the value of a share that has been performing badly.

bounced cheque *See* ***bounce***.

bouncing Act of dishonouring a cheque, usually because of lack of funds. *See* ***bounce***.

bounty In a modern business context, a government ***subsidy*** given to aid particular industries. It may be in the form of ***tax*** concessions or a cash handout.

bourse Stock exchange in France; "the Bourse" is the Paris stock exchange.

boutique Relatively new form of financial services company, operating in much the same way as a high street shop, into which customers may walk to seek investment advice and services. It is also known as a financial supermarket.

boycott Refusal to trade with a certain company or nation or in certain goods.

bracket Broadly, a group of people or things that are in some way similar to each other. *E.g.*, the term is applied to a group of banks involved in an issue of new shares.

bracket creep What happens when ***inflation*** forces groups of people into the next tax or income bracket. Normally brackets are fixed annually to account for inflation, but bracket creep can occur if inflation runs at a higher level than anticipated. *See also* ***income bracket; tax backet***.

brain-drain Popular term describing the migration of specialists (usually scientists or technologists) from their home country to another country, often lured by higher salaries and more sympathetic research grants.

branch Part of a business, such as a bank or shop, that functions apart from but under the overall control of the central organization.

branch banking Banking system whereby a small number of commercial banks have many branches and serve a large number of customers. The UK's ***Big Four*** banks are examples of this type of banking. *See also* ***unit banking***.

branch clearing System in which cheque collection from branch banks is organized by a department in the bank's head office.

branch credit Funds deposited for a customer of another branch of the same bank.

brand To put a name (the brand name) on something or to design and package a product so that it is easily recognizable by a consumer. A brand name can be protected by law against misuse by competitors hoping to benefit from the reputation associated with a particular branded product.

branded goods Goods that are packaged by the manufacturer with the brand name clearly visible. Branded goods may often be sold at a higher price than others because of the selling power of the name.

brand leader Brand of a certain type of goods that has the largest share of the market. A brand leader may often be seen as a company's most valuable ***asset***.

brand loyalty Marketing concept by which consumers continually purchase certain gods which they identify by brand name (and associate with quality and value for money).

brand manager Person, usually employed by a large supplier of consumer goods, who co-ordinates the activities of developing and marketing a group of branded products.

brassage Government charge for minting coins, or the actual cost of doing so.

break When prices have been rising steadily over a period, the break is a sudden and substantial drop in prices.

break even To cover one's costs, making neither a ***profit*** or ***loss***.

break-even chart Graph showing the relationship between total fixed costs, variable costs and revenues for various volumes of output.

B

break-even point Point at which fixed and variable costs are exactly covered by sales revenue. At greater volumes of output an operation would normally expect to make a ***profit***.

break-forward On the money market, a combination of a ***currency option contract*** and a ***forward-exchange contract***, which can be broken at a pre-set fixed rate of exchange if exchange rates move in favour of the consumer

breaking an account Closing an account and transferring the balance to another one.

breakout What happens when a share or commodity price breaks a previously fixed, or at least stable, pattern.

break-up Term with two meanings:

1. In real estate, a tenanted property is worth less on the property market than a vacant one. A property with some tenanted and some vacant apartments may be bought and then broken up, so that the tenanted flats may be sold to the tenants and the vacant flats may be sold to outsiders at a much higher rate.
2. In corporate terms, break-up occurs when several or all of the operating arms of a company are sold off, usually after a ***takeover***.

See also ***asset stripping; break-up value.***

break-up value Value of a share or company on the assumption that the company is being disbanded or broken up. The break-up value of a share is calculated by dividing the probable net proceeds from the sale of the company's assets by the number of shares. Sometimes, the term is used as a loose synonym for asset value per share.

Bretton Woods Conference Held in 1944 in Bretton Woods, New Hampshire, this conference between the USA, Canada and the UK formed a new system of international monetary control and resulted in the setting up of the ***International Monetary Fund*** (IMF) and the International Bank for Reconstruction and Development. *See also* ***American Plan.***

bribe Illicit payment made by one person to another in order to gain rights or privileges that the recipient would not normally be entitled to. Offering or accepting a bribe is often a criminal offence.

brick Bundle of brand new banknotes.

bricks and mortar Informal term for the ***fixed assets*** of a company.

bridge financing Any form of short-term funding in anticipated arrival of funds, whether for a venture company on the verge of raising new capital, or a bridging loan for a home buyer who needs to pay for a house before receiving the proceeds on the sale of the former property.

bridging loan Also called bridging advance, *see* ***bridge financing***.

Britannia coins Gold coins minted in the UK in 1987 in competition with the ***Krugerrand***. They were available in denominations of £10, £25, £50 and £100.

British Bankers' Association Organization established in 1919 by British banks with businesses in the UK and by members of the British Overseas Banks Association. In 1972 membership was extended to include foreign banks trading in the UK.

British Overseas and Commonwealth Banks' Association Organization established in 1917 (originally as the Overseas Bankers Association), currently with representatives at the British Bankers' Association.

British Venture Capital Association (BVCA) Trade association of companies that deal in ***venture capital***.

broad money Alternative term for **M3**. *See* ***money supply***.

broadside Informal term for a publicity leaflet or handout.

broker Broadly, an intermediary between a buyer and a seller. There are several forms of broker, the job title referring to what it is that a particular broker deals in; *e.g.* a ***stockbroker*** deals in stocks and shares.

brokerage Payment made to a ***broker*** for services rendered. Also known as a broker's ***commission***.

brokerage account Record kept by a stockbroker of sales and purchases of securities.

broker-dealer Firm that acts in the dual capacity of share broker for its clients and as dealer for its own account.

broker-trader On the London International Financial Futures Exchange, a firm that acts as both broker and trader for its own account. It is similar to a ***broker-dealer***.

bronze coins Lowest-value coins in the UK made of an alloy containing 95% copper, 4% tin and 1% zinc. Currently available only in denominations of 1 penny and 2 pence, they are legal tender up to a total value of 20 pence (20p).

bubble Industry or trend with no substance in it. A bubble usually bursts with more-or-less disastrous consequences for those involved. Probably the most famous bubble was the South Sea Bubble which burst in 1720.

bubble company Company formed with no real business to undertake.

bucket shop Popular phrase describing brokers of stocks, shares and commodities who are not recognized as members of any ***exchange***.

budget Plan that details expected future income and outgoings, normally over a time span of a year. It is also the sum of money set aside for a given activity or project.

The Budget is a government's financial plan for the forthcoming financial year, announced as a statement by the Chancellor of the Exchequer, and concerned principally with the raising of revenue by ***taxation***.

budget account Form of current account on which an agreement is made that the holder pays into the account a fixed amount each month and is then guaranteed ***overdraft*** facilities to cover periods of high ***expenditure*** within a twelve month period. The total of the 12-monthly payments equals the total of the cheques to be issued on the account over the 12-month term. It is also called a continuous credit account.

budget-day value (BDV) Value of an asset on Budget Day (6 April) 1995, used to calculate ***capital gains tax***, which was introduced on that day.

budget deficit Budgetary imbalance, caused by excess of ***expenditure*** over ***income***. In the case of the British government budgets, the deficit is generally funded by the authorization of an increase in the ***National Debt***.

buffer stock In manufacturing industries, a stock of raw materials held as an insurance against shortages or sudden price rises.

On the commodity markets, buffer stocks are held for release at certain strategic times in order to stabilize prices and markets.

building and loan association US organization roughly equivalent to a ***building society*** in the UK and also known as a savings and loan association.

Building Societies Act Act of Parliament passed in the UK in 1986 defining and considerably widening the permitted activities of ***building societies***.

Building Societies Ombudsman A person charged with investigating complaints against any of the member building societies of the scheme made by individual customers.

building society Institution in the UK that accepts ***deposits*** upon which it pays varying rates of ***interest*** and lends money, originally only in the form of a ***mortgage***, to enable people to purchase property. Some building societies issue cheque books and cash cards, and so operate in much the same way as a ***bank***. *See also* ***building and loan association***.

building society cheque *See* ***personal cheque***.

built-in Something that is planned or accounted for at the outset.

bull Stock exchange dealer or analyst who believes that prices or investment values will increase. On this conviction, the dealer buys now and profits by selling later at a higher price.

bulldog bond Sterling denominated bond issued by foreign governments for sale on the UK market.

bullet Term with two meanings:

1. It is the final payment of a loan consisting of the whole principal (previous payments being of interest only).
2. It is a security that pays a guaranteed (fixed) interest at a specific date.

bullet loan Loan in which all early payments are of interest only; the final payment (bullet) includes the principal.

bullion Bars or ingots of a precious metal (such as gold or silver), as opposed to coins.

bullish Describes a market or person with the qualities of a ***bull***.

bull market Condition in which share prices are rising. ***Bulls*** are speculators who buy shares in anticipation of rising prices.

bull position Position of an investor whose purchases exceed his or her sales, and therefore stands to gain in a rising or bull market. *See* ***bull***.

Bundesbank Central bank of Germany, with headquarters in Frankfurt.

bunny bond ***Bond*** with the option of yielding either interest or additional bonds instead of interest.

burden of debt When a ***debt*** is passed on to successive generations, the burden of debt is the ***interest*** payments on the accumulated debt.

bureau Office that specializes in a certain form of business, *e.g.* an employment bureau specializes in supplying temporary or permanent staff to employers for a ***commission***.

bureau de change Office at which currencies may be exchanged on payment of a ***commission***. Some bureaux offer additional services, such as the encashment of personal cheques.

Bureau of the Mint US equivalent to the ***Royal Mint*** in the UK.

burn-out turnaround Strategy to prevent a badly-performing company going into ***liquidation***, involving a total restructuring of the company and a large injection of capital which dilutes the percentage shareholding of existing holders.

burn rate When a new company begins trading on venture capital, the burn rate is the rate at which the company consumes capital in financing fixed overheads. *See* ***venture capital***.

business account Bank account opened in the name of a business. *See also* ***personal account***.

business adviser A professional person who provides business cutomers with advice and information about the bank's services.

business credit card *Credit card* whose payments are charged to the account of a company, not a private individual.

business development loan Loan made for buying fixed assets such as plant and premises, usually over a five-year term.

bust Informal term meaning bankrupt.

After as bad a year as this one has been, I would not be surprised if a large number of small companies went bust.

busted bond Bond whose issuer has defaulted on the loan raised to finance the issue. Valueless except as collectors items, busted bonds are also called old bonds.

buy back A company that is originally financed by venture capital may pay back the capital invested either by seeking a ***quotation*** or by being taken over. In either case, it will be buying itself back from the venture capitalist. *See* ***venture capital***.

buy earnings To buy earnings is to invest in shares that have a low yield but a good earnings growth record.

buyer credit System in which a seller makes a cash contract with an overseas buyer, who pays up to 20% of the price and funds the rest through a long-term loan with a UK bank. The repayment of the loan to the bank is guaranteed by the Export Credits Guarantee Department (ECGD).

buyer's market Market in which there are too many sellers and not enough buyers, so that buyers are in a position to influence prices or conditions of purchase.

buyers over On the Stock Exchange, a situation in which there are more buyers than sellers. The opposite is ***sellers over***.

buy forward To buy shares, commodities, etc. for delivery at a later date. In essence, buying forward is a gamble on the current price, *i.e.* that it will rise in the future and the buyer will then be able to sell at a profit. *See also* ***selling short***.

buy in Refers to a situation in which a seller of shares, etc. fails to deliver on the agreed date, which sometimes happens if the seller is ***selling short***. In this case the buyer is entitled to buy shares from another source and to charge the seller with any expenses incurred. This process is known as buying in.

buy on close Buying contracts on a financial ***futures*** market at a price within the ***closing range***. *See also* ***buy on opening***.

buy on opening Buying contracts on a financial futures market at a price within the ***opening range***. *See also* ***buy on close***.

buyout The purchase of an entire company.

buy recommendation Recommendation to buy.

Two market analysts today changed their recommendations on A & G shares from attractive to outright buy.

buy side Expression that refers to ***institutional investors*** on the New York Stock Exchange.

BV Abbreviation of ***Besloten Vennootschap***.

BVCA Abbreviation of ***British Venture Capital Association***.

C

CA Abbreviation of ***chartered accountant***.

cabinet crowd Members of the New York Stock Exchange who deal in rarely traded bonds.

cable transfer An alternative term for ***telegraphic transfer***.

CAD Abbreviation for ***cash against documents***.

call Act of demanding payment for shares or stocks, or repayment of a ***debt***. A lender may advance money on condition that it is repayed on call (without notice).

callable bond Bond that may be called for payment before ***maturity date***.

callable fixture Short-term (3-week to 3-month) loan made by a bank to a ***discount house***. The bank thus has a secure deposit that earns interest, and the discount house has the use of funds for buying short-term bills or bonds. The loan is repayable on demand. *See* ***call money***.

called-up capital Some of money that has been paid to a company by its shareholders. *See also* ***partly-paid shares; uncalled capital***.

call money Type of loan made by a bank, which must be repaid upon demand. It is also known as money at call.

call option Option to by shares, commodities or financial futures at an agreed price on or before an agreed future date.

call over Method of trading on a stock exchange whereby the securities listed are called out in order, and dealers make bids or offers for each ***security*** according to their instructions.

call-over price Price for a security verbally agreed at ***call over***.

call provision Condition attached to a ***bond*** by which the issuer is entitled to redeem the bond at a fixed price after a specified period of time.

call up Alternative term for ***call***, especially with respect to ***partly-paid shares***.

Calvo clause Contract clause regarding foreign investment. It states that, in the event of a dispute, the parties agree to abide by the law of the foreign country.

Canadian Bankers Association Originally formed as a voluntary association in 1890, this bankers' association is unique in that it was specifically chartered by act of the Canadian Parliament in 1900 (amendment to the Canadian Banking Act) to effect greater cooperation among Canadian banks in the issuance of notes, in credit and control, and in various other aspects of bank activity.

cancellation Voiding of an agreement, either in due course (such as the discharge of a bill of exchange or the payment of a cheque) or by defacement or mutilation of a document.

cancellation price Lowest price a unit trust manager can accept for units on any one day, as formulated by the ***Securities and Investment Board.***

C & F Abbreviation of ***cost and freight.***

CAP Abbreviation of ***Common Agricultural Policy.***

cap Interest rate ***option*** that enables the investor to hedge against the possibility of ***interest*** rates rising to the investor's disadvantage. *See* ***hedging.***

capacity Measurement of the ability of a company to produce goods or services.

cap and collar mortgage Mortgage with fixed upper and lower limits of the variable interest rate.

capital Vague term that most often requires a qualification. Unqualified, it usually refers to the resources of an organization or person (*e.g.* equipment, skill, cash).

capital account Part of the ***balance of payments***, which refers to international movements of ***capital***, including intergovernmental loans.

capital adequacy Legal requirement that a financial institution (such as a bank) should have enough capital to meet all its obligations and fund the services it offers.

capital allowances Amounts deducted from a company's ***profits*** before tax is calculated, to take into account ***depreciation*** of capital ***assets*** (such as vehicles, plant and machinery, and industrial buildings).

capital assets Another term for ***fixed assets.***

capital bond Full name ***National Savings Capital Bond.***

capital budget Forward planning of forward capital movement, involving larger sums of money and longer timescales than a ***cash budget.***

capital clause In the *memorandum of association* of a company, that section setting out the details of the company's *capital*.

capital duty Former tax paid by companies on profits from new share issues. It ceased to be levied in 1988.

capital employed Capital that a company uses to finance its assets. It is taken to be the sum of shareholders' funds, loans and deferred taxation.

capital expenditure Expenditure on capital goods, *e.g.* ***fixed assets*** such as plant or on trade investments and ***current assets***. Capital expenditure is classed as below-the-line for accounting purposes. *See also* ***trade investment***.

capital gain Gain made from a capital transaction, *e.g.* the buying and selling of ***assets***.

capital gains tax (CGT) Tax paid on ***capital gains***.

capital goods Goods (such as machines) that are used for the production of other goods. Ships are also sometimes regarded as capital goods.

capital growth Increase in the value of an investment over a period of time.

capital guarantee investment Investment, such as those in National Savings, that cannot fall in value (because of a guarantee given by a bank, building society, government or other institution).

capital-intensive Describing a business in which ***capital*** is the most important and costly factor of production. Thus, an industry in which the major cost is the purchase and maintenance of machinery (***fixed assets***) is capital-intensive.

capitalism Economic and political system in which people are entitled to trade for profit on their own account. It is also known as free or private enterprise. *See also* ***communism***.

capitalist economy Economy in which business is conducted for the profit of the companies and persons engaged in it.

capitalization Term with two meanings:

1. It is the conversion of a company's reserves into share capital by issuing more shares.
2. It is the total amount of capital available to a company in the long term.

capitalization issue Alternative term for ***bonus issue***.

capital/labour ratio Proportion of capital to labour used in an economy.

capital market Market made up of the various sources of ***capital*** for (medium- or long-term) investment in new and already existing companies. In the UK it is centred on the London Stock Exchange and the *Alternative Investment Market* (AIM).

capital outlay Expenditure on ***fixed assets*** such as machinery. *See also* ***capital***.

capital profit Profit generated by selling capital goods (***fixed assets***), rather than by trading.

capital reserves Profits from a company's trading that represent part of the company's capital and so may not be repaid to shareholders until the company is wound up.

capital saturation Situation in a company or industry in which there is such a proportion of capital to labour that any increase in capital would have no significant positive effect on output.

capital stock Value of all capital goods owned by a company, industry or nation, after ***depreciation*** has been taken into account.

capital transfer tax (CTT) Tax paid on the transfer of capital, *e.g.* in the form of a gift or bequest. Capital transfer tax covers the former inheritance tax.

capped mortgage Mortgage with a fixed upper limit to its variable interest rate.

captive fund Fund for venture capital held by a large financial services group. *See* ***venture capital***.

captive market Market in which there is a monopoly of production, allowing the consumer no option but to buy that company's product.

CAR Abbreviation of ***compound annual return***.

car Alternative term for a ***futures*** contract.

card Plastic card embossed with account details and provided with a magnetic strip, used in (usually personal) financial transactions.

carnet Document valid internationally that allows the passage of dutiable goods without duty having to be paid until the goods reach their destination.

carry Money borrowed or lent in order to finance trading in ***futures***. The process of borrowing and lending in this way is known as carrying.

carryforward Tax ***rebate*** that is paid because a company had shown a loss during the previous tax period.

carry over To postpone payment on a bargain traded on a stock exchange from one ***settlement day*** to the next.

cartel Group of companies that come together to monopolize a market, agreeing between them which company presides over which area of operation. Cartels are illegal in the UK and the USA.

cascade tax Tax imposed at each stage of production. *E.g.* a product may pass from one country to the next as each stage of production is carried out, and would thus attract several taxation stages, and the price of the finished product would be higher than if it had been produced in one country.

case of need Particular type of endorsement made on a ***bill of exchange***. It is followed by the name of a person or company to whom the holder of the bill may apply in the event that the bill is not paid.

cash Ready money – coins and notes – or to turn something (such as a cheque) into ready money.

cash against document (CAD) Method of payment for goods for export, whereby the documentation for a shipment is sent to an agent or bank at the destination. These are passed to the consignee, who makes the payment. The consignee is free to take delivery of the shipment when it arrives. Cash against document is a process of payment that is also used by large UK investment houses.

cash analysis Note to a bank listing the denominations of cash required (notes and coins) to make up a large sum, such as that used by a business to make up the wage packets of its employees.

cash and carry Popular term for a wholesale warehouse, from retailers buy their goods and transport them away. More and more frequently, cash and carries are used by members of the general public.

cash and new On a stock exchange, a method of postponing payment on a ***bargain*** until the next settlement day. The investor begins with a bargain for which he or she would like to postpone payment. Towards the end of the ***account***, a deal is made that is opposite to the first (*i.e.* the investor either buys or sells a similar ***instrument***). The original position is then restored by yet another purchase or sale, to be settled on the next settlement day. In effect, the investor negates the original position and then returns to it in the next account.

cash at bank Funds that a person or business has on deposit at a bank. *See also* ***cash in hand***.

cash book In ***book-keeping***, a book in which all receipts and payments are recorded in the first instance.

cash budget Forward plan of day-to-day income and expenditure.

cash card Plastic card that allows the holder, by using a ***personal identification number*** (PIN), to withdraw cash from his or her bank or building society account through a ***cash dispenser***. It may also allow access to such facilities as a display of the account balance and ordering bank statements and cheque books.

cash cow Product that continues to provide a healthy ***revenue*** after its initial launch, with relatively little extra investment.

cash deal Agreement or transaction concluded with a cash payment; on the stock exchange, a deal to be completed on the next trading day.

cash dealings Stock exchange deals that must be settled on the following day. Such bargains are said to be for cash settlement rather than account settlement.

cash discount Reduction in the price of goods in return for payment in cash.

cash dispenser Machine that issues cash to customers of a bank or building society, usually by inserting a ***cash card*** and using a ***personal identification number*** (PIN). It is also called an automated teller machine (ATM).

cash dividend ***Dividend*** paid in cash (rather than as shares).

cash float In a bank, money a cashier has to cash customers' cheques or to change money from one denomination to another. In a shop, it is money a cashier has to give customers change.

cash flow Movement of money through a company from the time it is received as income (or borrowing), to the time it leaves the company as payments (*e.g.* for raw materials, salaries, etc.). A negative cash flow is the situation in which there is too little money coming in to pay for outgoings. Conversely, a positive cash flow occurs when a company receives income before it is due to pay outgoings. *See also* ***discounted cash flow***.

cashier Person who receives and issues cash, and usually keeps records of transactions. In a bank, a cashier at a counter is also called a teller.

cashier's check Another term for a ***bank cheque***, and a US term for a ***bank draft***.

cash in advance Method of payment in which the purchaser pays for goods or services before delivery.

cash in hand Funds held as cash (notes and coins) as opposed to those on deposit in a bank (***cash at bank***).

cash investment Investment that provides immediate or short-notice withdrawal of funds at minimum risk; the funds invested are guaranteed. They include a ***current account*** or ***deposit account*** at a bank, National Savings and various building society accounts.

cash limit Term with four meanings:

1. It is the maximum amount provided by a loan or overdraft.
2. It is the maximum amount that can be withdrawn from a ***cash dispenser***.
3. It is the maximum amount stated on a ***cheque guarantee card***.
4. It is the maximum amount a business can spend in a specified time.

cash management Type of bank account available to business clients, which offers services such as debt collection and cash flow services.

cash on delivery (COD) Distribution system whereby the person in receipt of goods makes payment for them on the spot to the deliverer. Such a system is operated by the UK Post office, where it is the postman who takes receipt of payment.

cashpoint Alternative term for ***automatic telling machine*** (ATM) or ***cash dispenser***.

cash position State of the finances of a person or business at a given time, particularly whether there are funds available (cash positive) or unavailable (cash negative).

cash price Price at which goods may be bought using cash. The price paid in cash is usually different from the ***hire purchase*** price in that the latter normally includes interest.

cash purchase Purchase that has been made in cash. *See also* ***hire purchase***.

cash ratio Amount of reserves a bank considers it necessary to maintain, calculated with reference to the bank's turnover.

cash settlement Payment for ***cash dealings***.

cash with order (CWO) Terms of an agreement by which goods are supplied only if payment is made in cash at the time the order is placed.

CAT Abbreviation of ***computer-assisted trading***.

CATS Abbreviation of ***Certificate of Accrual on Treasury Securities***, a form of ***zero-coupon bond***.

caution Term with three meanings:

1. It is any warning.
2. It is an annotation in a bank's records warning that a certain customer should be deal with with care.
3. It is a notice lodged with the Land Registry that places a condition on any pending action.

See also ***caveat***.

caveat Caution or warning.

caveat emptor Latin for "buyer beware". In legal terms this maxim means that a buyer of goods should use his or her own common sense, and that the law is not prepared to aid someone who buys goods foolishly.

caveat subscriptor Latin for "signer beware", meaning that anyone who signs a document is bound by its contents, regardless of whether or not he or she has read it, or understood its legal implications.

CBD Abbreviation of cash before delivery.

CBI Abbreviation of Confederation of British Industry.

CBOT Abbreviation of Chicago Board of Trade.

CCA Abbreviation of ***current cost accounting***.

cedel Agreement among European banks to settle any difficulties in clearing transactions.

cedi Standard currency unit of Ghana, divided into 100 pesewas.

CeFA Professional qualification awarded to financial advisers who pass examinations set by The ***Chartered Institute of Bankers*** (CIB).

ceiling Upper limit, particularly a borrowing limit imposed on a bank customer.

census National survey that provides information on population, economics and social matters. In the UK and the USA a national census is taken every ten years.

Census of Distribution Survey taken every five years of wholesale and retail distribution services.

Census of Production Survey taken annually of industrial production and public utility services.

central bank Bank that often carries out government economic policy, influences interest and exchange rates and monitors the activities of commercial and ***merchant banks***. In this way it functions as the government's banker and is the ***lender of the last resort*** to the banking system. In the UK it is the ***Bank of England***.

Central Fund Fund at Lloyd's of London used to pay claims if an underwriter fails financially.

Central Gilts Office (CGO) Computerized book-entry transfer system for gilt-edged stock established in 1986 by the Bank of England and the Stock Exchange. It ensures automatic "same-day" payments for the electronic transfer of stock.

Central Government Borrowing Requirement (CGBR) Amount calculated by deducting private sector borrowing (by public companies and local authorities) from the ***Public Sector Borrowing Requirement*** (PSBR).

Central Moneymarkets Office (CMO) Method of electronic book-keeping, established in 1990, for transactions in negotiable instruments such as cheques and bank drafts. Each member has a unique number and password and is on-line to the CMO from his or her own premises.

central purchasing Practice of making all purchases required by a company through one department.

Central Unit UK Treasury department that co-ordinates economic information from other departments, and manages the government's economic strategy.

CEO Abbreviation of chief executive officer.

certificate Document that proves something, *e.g.* right of ownership or that certain actions have taken place.

certificated Describing something that has documentary evidence to prove that it is genuine.

Certificate of Accrual on Treasury Securities (CATS) In the USA, a ***zero-coupon bond*** issued by the Treasury Department.

certificate of balance Document from a bank or building society showing the account balance of a customer at a particular time.

certificate of bonds Document issued to a registered bond holder confirming that the bonds are registered in his or her name.

certificate of deposit Essentially, a document (originally issued by merchant banks) declaring that a certain sum had been deposited with a bank. Sterling certificates of deposit refer to long-term fixed deposits of sums over £10,000 and therefore offer high interest rates.

certificate of incorporation Document issued to a company when it has completed legal incorporation procedures and satisfied the requirements of the Companies Acts.

certificate of origin Import-export document that declares the country of origin of goods.

certificate of tax deducted Document issued by a financial institution such as a bank or building society that identifies a customer (with account number, name and address) and states the gross interest earned and tax deducted in a given period.

certification of transfer Act of signing a transfer deed in order to transfer stocks from one owner to another. The transfer is further made official by reporting it to the registrar.

certified accountant Accountant who has passed the examinations of the Association of Certified (and Corporate) Accountants.

certified cheque (US **check)** ***Bank draft*** or a customer cheque guaranteed by the bank on which it is drawn (also sometimes called a marked cheque).

certified copy Copy of a document that is certified as being identical.

certified public accountant Accountant who has passed US professional accounting examinations.

cesser Legal term meaning to stop.

cesser of action The situation in which one court has the proceedings taking place in another court halted.

CET Abbreviation of ***common external tariff***.

ceteris paribus Latin for "other things remaining equal". It is used in economic analysis to study the effects of economic variants while assuming that other factors remain the same.

Cge Pd Abbreviation of carriage paid.

CGBR Abbreviation of ***Central Government Borrowing Requirement.***

CGT Abbreviation of ***capital gains tax.***

CH Abbreviation of ***corporate hospitality.***

chairman A person who chairs a meeting, also called a chairperson or merely "chair", or the most senior director of a company, full title Chairman of the ***Board of Directors.***

chamber of commerce Organization that promotes and represents the interests of those involved in commerce in a particular geographical area.

champerty Illegal practice of paying the ***costs*** of a court case in which one is not involved, in return for a proportion of the ***damages.***

CHAPS Abbreviation of ***Clearing House Automated Payment System.***

Chapter 11 Clause in US company law that enables a company to continue to operate after it has been declared bankrupt (under the direction of the court), so that it may find a way to pay its creditors. The rough equivalent in Britain is ***administration.***

charge Term with four meanings:

1. It is a sum of money that must be paid on goods or services or the act of requesting that sum.
2. It is an obligation to meet a debt.
3. It is a fee charged by a bank for its services and deducted (usually quarterly or half-yearly) from the customer's account, usually called bank charges.
4. It is a legal interest in land agreed to by a borrower to secure a loan that gives the chargee (often a bank) a priority right to repayment when the land is sold.

chargeable Something that may be charged for, most usually a sum of money on which ***tax*** is liable to be paid.

chargeable asset Asset that is liable to give rise to a charge for ***capital gains tax*** (CGT).

chargeable gain Gain, or more specifically capital profit, on which tax is payable.

charge account Alternative term for ***credit account***.

charge card Plastic card similar to a credit card. However, most charge cards may be used only at specific retail outlets or chains. It is also called a store card.

charge off Alternative term for ***write off***.

charges forward When goods are delivered, a notice that all charges must be paid at the time the goods are delivered.

charges register Part of the certificate issued by the UK Land Register that details all ***mortgages*** and ***charges*** in respect of a certain piece of land.

charging order Court order that allows a debtor's land, stocks, shares and interest under a trust to be "earmarked" for the creditor. If the debt is not repayed, the goods become the property of the creditor.

charity card Another name for an ***affinity card***.

charter Term with two meanings:

1. It is the granting in writing of a title, right or privilege.
2. It is the practice of hiring out a ship or aircraft for commercial or private use.

chartered Term applied to a person or institution that has been granted a ***charter***, such as a chartered accountant or chartered company.

chartered accountant In England and Wales, an accountant who has passed the examinations of the Institute of Chartered Accountants and is either an associate or fellow of the Institute. In Ireland and Scotland, a chartered accountant is a fellow or associate of the Institute of Chartered Accountants in Ireland, and Scotland, respectively. The main difference between a chartered accountant and a certified accountant is that the training of the former normally involves a period of time working with a firm of accountants and that of the latter does not.

chartered bank In the USA and Canada, a bank that has a charter as its authority to operate.

Chartered Banker Monthly magazine for associates and fellows of The ***Chartered Institute of Bankers***, first issued in 1995.

C

Chartered Institute of Bankers, The (CIB) Organization founded in 1879 and chartered in 1987 for members of the banking profession throughout the world. It holds examinations for Associateship of the Institute (ACIB) and the Institute's Council can elect senior Associates to a Fellowship (FCIB).

Chartered Institute of Bankers in Scotland, The Organization founded in 1875 and chartered in 1976 and 1991 for memebers of the banking profession in Scotland. Through examinations or election, members can become Associates of The Chartered Institute of Bankers in Scotland (ACIBS) or Fellows of the Institute (FCIBS).

chartist Stock market or economic analyst who believes that trends (*e.g.* in price movements, etc.) follow recognizable patterns and so predicts future trends with the aid of charts. *See also* ***fundamental market analyst***.

chattels Moveable property, as opposed to ***fixtures*** (property that cannot be moved).

cheap jack Person who buys goods at very low prices (*e.g.* from bankrupt companies or goods that are of poor quality) and sells them at below normal price, sometimes in the street or on a market. *See also* ***caveat emptor; mock auction***.

cheap money Alternative term for ***easy money***.

check US spelling of ***cheque***.

checking Computer process that takes place on the London Stock exchange between trading sessions, by which the records of brokers and market makers are reconciled. *See also* ***reconciliation***.

checking account US term for a ***current account***, increasingly used in the UK to denote a building society account with cheque-book facilities.

check sample Sample taken from a consignment of goods and examined to determine whether or not the consignment is acceptable.

cheque The most familiar form of ***bill of exchange***. A cheque is used to transfer funds from a bank to someone else and is the usual way of withdrawing money from a current account.

cheque account Bank account whose holder uses ***cheques*** to draw or transfer funds. The most common type is a ***current account***.

Cheque and Credit Clearing Company London-based organization, a part of the *Association for payment Clearing Services* (APACS), founded in 1985 to clear interbank cheques and paper credits in

England and Wales. (Scotland and Northern Ireland have their own clearing arrangements.)

cheque book Book of 25 or 30 blank cheque forms (or up to 500 forms for a business account). Many banks allow customized cheques to be printed.

cheque book register Bank record of cheque books issued to account holders.

cheque card Plastic card with a magnetic stripe and bearing the holder's name, signature and account details which guarantees payment of cheques up to a certain value (between £50 and £250). Cards with a £50 limit were nicknamed bard cards because they included a drawing of William Shakespeare. Higher-denomination cards have a hologram. Some cheque cards have additional functions, such as acting also as a *cash card*, *credit card* or *debit card*.

Cheque Card Policy Committee Organization, a part of the *Association for Payment Clearing Services* (APACS), that defines the permissible designs of *cheque cards* issued by its members. It also administers the *eurocheque* scheme in the UK.

cheque guarantee card Another name for a *cheque card*.

chequeless (US **checkless**) **society** Future society in which the use of cheques has been superseded. The imminence of the chequeless society may be closer than many people think.

cheque rate Charge made by a bank for issuing a cheque or draft in a foreign currency.

Cheques Act Act of Parliament passed in the UK in 1992 that sanctioned the making of cheques non-transferable by writing or printing the words *account payee* across the cheque.

chief accountant Accountant within a business who deals with all company accounting and the provision of financial information to managers and *directors*, in particular the financial director.

child allowance Payment made in cash by the Department of Social Security in the UK to parents of each child they are supporting. There is an additional allowance payable to one-parent families.

Chinese fire drill Popular term for total confusion.

Chinese Wall Artificial barrier erected in any business where confidentiality between departments is a legal necessity. The Chinese

Wall has become necessary since the ***Big Bang*** changed the London Stock Exchange to a ***dual capacity*** system in 1986. The purpose of the Chinese Wall is to prevent ***insider dealing***. *See also* ***underwriter***.

Chinese water torture tactic Popular term for the gradual ***takeover*** of a company by building up a majority shareholding from shares bought on the open market.

chip card Kind of debit card that contains a computer microchip which stores details of card transactions. It is also called a memory card or smart card.

CHIPS Abbreviation of ***Clearing House InterBank Payments System***.

choice price On futures markets, refers to a situation which, when comparing different market-makers' bid-offer spreads, one finds identical bid and offer price. This price is known as the choice price. *See also* ***backwardation***.

choses-in-action Legal term for a right which cannot be enforced by physical possession, e.g. a copyright or debt. *See also* ***choses-in-possession***.

choses-in-possession Legal term for an asset which can be secured by physical possession, e.g. a book. *See also* ***choses-in-action***.

churning Informal term for the practice of buying and selling stocks and shares solely in order to generate higher ***commission*** income.

CIB Abbreviation of The ***Chartered Institute of Bankers***.

Cie Abbreviation of Compagnie (French for Company).

CIF Abbreviation of ***cost, insurance and freight***.

circuit breaker A mechanism that could halt trading in the stock, futures and options markets when prices fall too far in one trading session.

circular letter of credit ***Letter of credit*** from a bank instructing other banks to pay the holder the sum stated on the production of satisfactory proof of identity.

circulating capital Money used by a company to invest in ***assets*** for resale. When such assets have been sold, the capital raised returns to the company.

City Name given to the financial district of London, situated in the City of London. It covers an area of roughly one square mile and for this reason is also known as the Square Mile.

claim form Document issued by a bank to one of its branches to claim money for an unpaid cheque.

clause Condition of an agreement, most often used in reference to a **contract**.

claw back Demand by the ***Inland Revenue*** that a person or company returns money paid by the Revenue in the form of a tax ***rebate***. A claw back most often occurs because of the changed status of the person or company involved.

clean bill ***Bill of exchange*** that has no documents or special conditions attached.

clean float Floating exchange rate that is completely uncontrolled by the central bank. *See also* ***dirty float***.

clean price Price of a ***gilt-edged security*** excluding any interest that has accumulated since the last payment of a dividend.

clear Term with three broad meanings:

1. To clear is to have something authorized.

The goods cleared customs with no problems.

It took five days to clear the cheque with the bank.

2. It is to sell goods in order to make room for new ***stock***.

They are having a sale; everything is reduced to clear.

3. It is a period of so many days, or a sum of money on which there is nothing to be paid.

He was told that it would take three clear days before the sum was paid into his account.

This year the company made a clear profit.

clearance Term with three meanings:

1. It is the receipt of money from a bill or cheque. Money is not transferred into an account until a cheque payed into it has been cleared (*see* ***clearing***).
2. It is the completion of necessary formalities before goods can enter or leave the country (such as customs ***duty***).
3. It is the completion of necessary formalities before an aircraft or ship may depart.

cleared funds Balance of a bank account assuming that all cheques paid in the credit of the account more than three working days previously have been cleared.

clearing Practice of organizing the payment of financial instruments such as cheques. In the UK, commercial banks are usually members of the ***Banker's Clearing House***, which settles their daily balance.

clearing account Another name for a **current account**.

clearing bank Bank that is a member of a clearing house (*e.g.* in the UK, the ***Banker's Clearing House***) to facilitate the passing and clearing of cheques *See* ***clearing house***.

clearing house Institution that specializes in clearing debts between its members. The best known type is a banker's clearing house, which clears cheques between the major banks.

Clearing House Automated Payment System (CHAPS) Organization founded in 1985, a part of of the ***Association for Payment Clearing Services*** (APACS), that provides a guaranteed same-day electronic transfer of sterling funds within the UK.

Clearing House InterBank Payments System (CHIPS) US organization founded in 1970 that provides on-line electronic transfer of funds in US dollars, mainly for international transactions.

clearings Cheques, drafts, etc. presented by a bank to a clearing house.

clerk In the UK, a person who deals with records of some kind, usually in an office. In the USA, the term is used in the more general sense of anyone dealing with customers, *e.g.* a salesperson in a retail store.

client account Bank account used by a professional practitioner (such as a solicitor) to hold money on behalf of (*i.e.* that belongs to) clients.

close Term with three meanings:

1. On a financial ***futures*** market, it is the thirty seconds before trading closes for the day.
2. It is sometimes used to refer to the ***closing price***.
3. To close a ***position*** is to cover an open position on a futures or options market by making a further transaction.

close company Company whose shares are held privately, by a few individuals (usually not more than five people), and not traded on a stock exchange. The US alternative is closed company or closely-held company.

closed Something that is not open to such things as ***risk*** or the general public.

closed company US alternative term for ***close company***.

closed economy Economy that is self-sufficient in that it makes neither imports nor exports.

closed-end fund Alternative term for ***investment trust***.

closed indent Order for goods placed with an agent abroad that specifies the supplier from whom the goods are to be obtained.

closely-held company US alternative term for ***close company***.

closing Action that ends something, *e.g.* a day's trading or an auction.

closing bid Last bid at an ***auction***, or more generally, the bid that is successful.

closing price Price of shares at the close of trading each day on a stock exchange.

closing purchase Purchase of an option that closes an open ***position***.

closing range On a financial futures market the highest and lowest prices recorded during the close. *See* ***financial futures***.

closing rate Rate at the close of business for the day for the foreign exchange of spot currency.

closing sale On an ***options*** market, transaction in which an option is sold in order to close a ***position***.

closing the sale Persuading a customer or client to commit to a purchase.

club money Relatively inexpensive bank loans to ***discount houses***, which are thereby encouraged to purchase a large number of (competitively-priced) bills.

CME Abbreviation for Chicago Metals Exchange.

CMEA Abbreviation of ***Council for Mutual Economic Assistance***.

CNAR Abbreviation of ***compound net annual rate***.

Co Abbreviation of ***company***.

c/o Abbreviation of cash with order.

COD Abbreviation of ***cash on delivery***.

code System of symbols, letters or numbers. *See* ***sorting code.***

Code of Banking Practice Voluntary code of standards introduced in 1992 and revised in 1994 and 1997 by the ***Association for Payments Clearing Services*** (APACS) and the ***British Bankers' Association*** (BBA). It defines good banking practice for banks, building societies and other card issuers in the UK.

coemption Legal term for ***cornering the market.***

coin Metal token that is ***legal tender.*** The making of ***counterfeit*** money is called coining.

coinage System of money in use in a country.

coin of the realm Coins that are ***legal tender*** in the UK. They are the penny (1p), two pence (2p), ten pence (10p), twenty pence (20p), fifty pence (50p), one pound (1£) and two pounds (£2). There is a limit to the total amount that can be tendered in coins: ***bronze coins*** up to 20p; 5p and 10p coins up to £5; and 20p and 50p coins up to £10.

cold call Sales practice of approaching a potential customer, either by telephone or in person, without any prior introduction.

collateral Informal term for ***security*** put up against a loan.

collecting bank Bank which accepts a cheque for credit of an account. It is also called a remitting bank.

collection order Instruction from a customer to a bank about the presentation and payment of a specified document.

collective Group of people working together towards a common aim.

collective ownership Ownership of *e.g.* a business or property with all the gains being equally divided among the members of the collective.

collectivism Economic system in which all factors of production are owned by the community and controlled largely by the state. *See also* ***communism.***

colon Standard currency unit of Costa Rica (divided into 100 centimos) and El Salvador (divided into 100 centavos).

co-manager Bank that ranks second to the ***lead manager*** in the selling of a new issue.

combat pay US term for ***danger money.***

come to market US term for a ***new issue***.

COMECON Acronym for ***Council for Mutual Economic Assistance***.

COMEX Acronym for Commodity Exchange of New York.

commercial Describing thing or person associated with business or commerce. The term has also recently come to mean a product that will sell well.

commercial attaché Diplomat who specializes in representing the commercial interests of his or her country.

commercial bank Bank that concentrates on cash deposit and transfer services to the general public, often to be found on the High Street. It may be a joint-stock bank or a ***private bank***. *See also* ***Big Four***.

commercial bill ***Bill of exchange*** that is not a ***Treasury bill***.

commercial code Code that is used by international traders in order to reduce the cost of sending faxes, telexes and cables.

commercial paper Corporate debt in a tradeable form. In the USA, the commercial paper is a short-term, non-bank market in which firms lend money to each other without the intervention of a financial intermediary.

commercials Shares in a commercial company, usually a seller of consumer goods. *See also* ***industrials***.

commercial undertaking Another name for a firm or business.

commercial year Period (360 days) used by banks to calculate discounts.

commission Money paid to an ***agent*** or other intermediary, usually calculated as a percentage of the sum involved in the transaction.

The salesman received 5% commission on each sale he made.

commission agent Agent who is paid a ***commission***, usually calculated as a percentage of the value of sales.

commission of current account ***Bank charge*** for having a ***current account***, usually invoked only if the account is not kept in credit.

commitment fee ***Bank charge*** for keeping loan facilities available to a customer (even if they are not used).

C

commitment window The amount of time an employee is prepared to spend in the service of one company.

committed facility *Bank loan* available if required up to a certain maximum amount at an agreed rate of interest pegged to the ***London Inter Bank Offered Rate*** (LIBOR).

committee of inspection Committee made up of a bankrupt company's creditors to direct the company's ***winding-up***, either in the hands of a receiver or a liquidator. *See* ***liquidation; receivership.***

commodity Term with two meanings:

1. In economics, it is any tangible good that is traded.
2. It is raw materials and foods, especially such goods as cocoa, coffee, jute, potatoes, tea, etc., which may also be traded.

commodity broker Broker who deals in ***commodities***, usually in a ***commodity market.***

Commodity Credit Corporation (US) The Commodity Credit Corporation (CCC) was organized October 17, 1933, pursuant to Executive Order No. 6340. This agency was managed by and operated in close affiliation with the Reconstruction Finance Cooperation up to July 1, 1939 as an agency of the United States. On that date, the CCC was transferred to and made part of the US Department of Agriculture, pursuant to the President's Reorganization Plan 1.

commodity exchange ***Commodity market*** on which ***actuals*** and ***futures*** are traded.

commodity market Market on which ***commodities*** are traded.

common Describing something that happens very frequently, or that applies equally to a number of people, without exclusion or differentiation.

Common Agricultural Policy (CAP) A ***European Union*** agreement on farming that aims to protect the farmers of member countries by *e.g.* subsidizing their produce and setting minimum prices.

common external tariff (CET) Import tariff charged by all members of a trading community (*e.g.* the EU) on goods being imported from non-member countries.

communism Political and economic system whereby all factors of production are owned and controlled by the state. *See also* ***capitalism.***

Community Reinvestment Act of 1977 (US) An act passed to further a congressional intent that banks meet the credit needs of their local communities (a form of affirmative action programme for neighbourhoods or communities) and to encourage investment in the immediate communities served by depository institutions. Banks face stiff penalties for failure to comply with local lending standards.

company Enterprise that has been legally incorporated to produce certain goods or services, or to transact any other type of business.

company account Bank account opened in the name of a company, with certain employees empowered to sign cheques. *See also* ***personal account***.

Company's House Formal name Companies Registration Office, the location of the office of the Registrar of Companies, in Cardiff, Wales, containing a register of all UK companies. The register lists a company's directors and shareholders, with copies of the latest ***balance sheets***.

company doctor Person who is brought into a company, usually at board level, that is on the brink of liquidation. A company doctor often has powers to administer very strong medicine in order to put the company back on its feet.

company secretary Someone who is responsible for ensuring that his or her company complies with company law.

comparative advantage State of being more efficient in one activity than in another, relative to a different country. *E.g.* a country is able to produce cars twice as efficiently as another, but produces aeroplanes ten times more efficiently. In a free market, this country would export aeroplanes and import cars and it is said that, in the production of aeroplanes, it has a comparative advantage over the other.

compensation Usually a sum of money paid in lieu of something lost.

She received substantial compensation for the injuries she sustained in a road accident which prevented her from working for a full year.

competition Effort directed towards doing better than someone else, especially that among rival companies in the same market.

When they entered the market, Nutbrown Productions found themselves in direct competition with several much larger companies.

competition analysis The process of gathering and assessing information about one's corporate competition.

complements Two goods that are related in such a way that when ***demand*** for one increases, demand for the other rises at the same time.

E.g. cameras and photographic film are complements, as are cars and petrol.

completion The finish of something, such as a job or contract.

compliance cost Cost to a company of complying with a regulation, such as keeping records of ***value-added tax*** (VAT) for the Customs and Excise.

composite currency peg Type of ***exchange rate*** system in which a country pegs its currency to a ***basket of currencies*** of its main trading partners.

composite rate tax (CRT) A rate of tax (3% below the basic rate) in the UK between 1951 and 1991 that banks and building societies deducted from the interest paid to investors. Taxpayers now have to pay the full basic rate of income tax on the interest, which is deducted by the bank or building society.

compound Term with two meanings:

1. It is to agree with creditors to settle a debt by paying only part of it.

He compounded his debts with his creditors.

2. It is to add something to a thing that is already there. *E.g.* compound interest is calculated by adding each interest payment to the capital sum and taking this new total as the basis for the next reckoning.

compound annual return (CAR) Total return on a sum invested or lent over a period of a year, including the return on ***interest*** previously accrued. *See also* ***compound net annual rate***.

compound interest Rate of interest calculated by adding interest previously paid to the capital sum plus previous interest payment. *See also* ***simple interest***.

compound net annual rate (CNAR) Return, after deduction of tax at the basic rate, of interest from a deposit or investment that includes the return on interest previously accrued. *See also* ***compound anual return***.

Comptroller of the Currency (US) The Office of the Comptroller of the Currency was created by act of Congress approved February 25, 1863 (12 Stat. 665), as an integral part of the National Banking System. The Comptroller is required by law to report directly to Congress annually. The most important functions of the Comptroller of the Currency relate to the organization, operation and liquidation of national banks.

compulsory liquidation Liquidation of a company that has become insolvent. In this case, the Official Receiver is initially in charge of the disposal of the company's assets. *See* ***insolvency; receivership.***

computer-assisted trading (CAT) Method of trading in which brokers and traders use computers on, *e.g.*, the foreign exchange market or the stock exchange.

con Popular abbreviation for ***confidence trick***.

concealed unemployment *See* ***disguised unemployment.***

concern Alternative term for a business or company.

When he left the business, it was still a going concern.

concert party Group of people who come together secretly to act "in concert", that is, to orchestrate a market in the group's favour. *E.g.* two or more people my form a concert party to buy shares in a company in order to effect a takeover. Such action is illegal.

concession Term with two broad meanings:

1. It is the right to use someone else's property as part of a business.
2. It is an allowance made to someone who would otherwise be charged.

conditional Something that is not certain but depends on an event or situation, such as a conditional bill of sale.

conditional bill of sale ***Bill of sale*** by which the owner of the goods transferred retains the right to repossess them.

conditional endorsement Endorsement on which the endorser has added a condition, which has to be fulfilled before the endorser receives the proceeds of the bill. The condition does not affect the ***paying banker***, who can ignore it.

Confederation of British Industry (CBI) Independent organization established in 1965 by combining the British Employers Confederation, the Federation of British Industry and the National Association of British Manufacturers. It represents industry in consultations with the government and propotes the activities of industry in the UK.

conference line Term with two meanings:

1. It is a service available to corporate telephone users, which allows several callers in different locations to talk to each other at the same time.

2. It is a group of shipping companies that have agreed on freight rates and passenger fares. Conference line shippers usually charge lower rates than non-conference lines.

confidence Feeling of certainty or security. *E.g.* confidence in a company's ability to produce goods is extremely important if it is to find ***investment***.

confidence trick Business deal (or any form of agreement) in which one person gains another's confidence and proceeds to do the unexpected, *i.e.* to trick him or her.

conglomerate Very large public company that is extremely diverse and probably international in its operations.

conman Informal term for someone who plays ***confidence tricks*** – a confidence trickster.

consideration In most forms of ***contract***, the agreement is made binding by the promise or payment of a sum of money or other favour from one party to the other. Such a payment or favour is known as a consideration. The term is also used informally to mean any kind of payment.

If you want to buy a car, he'll find the one you want for a consideration.

consignment Shipment of goods sent to someone (*e.g.* an agent), usually so that he or she may sell them for the consignor.

consistency concept In ***accounting***, a concept whereby accounts for one period are constructed on the same principles as for another.

Consol Abbreviation of Consolidated Stock or Consolidated Loan, a form of fixed-interest government security that has no ***redemption date***.

consolidated accounts If a company has subsidiary companies, each subsidiary has its own set of profit and loss accounts, but these must also be consolidated to form accounts for the whole group. These are known as consolidated accounts. *See also* ***profit-and-loss account***.

Consolidated Fund Essentially the bank account of the UK Exchequer, controlled by the Treasury and held at the Bank of England. Taxes are paid into the consolidated fund and money for government expenditure is drawn from it.

consolidated tape Ticker tape that brings information regarding transactions that are listed on the New York Stock Exchange, but transacted on any of the regional US exchanges.

consolidation Term with three meanings:

1. In shipping, it is the practice of putting together goods for shipping to the same destination.
2. In *accounting*, it is the practice of putting together the accounts of *subsidiary companies* of a group, to calculate overall results for the group as a whole.
3. In share dealings, it is the practice of combining a number of low-priced shares, to produce a realistically marketable *lot*. *See also* ***split***.

consortium Group of companies that come together to bid for a certain project. It is usually dissolved after that one project is complete. It is similar to a ***syndicate***, only more short-term.

consortium bank Bank owned mainly by several other banks, often set up to establish an office overseas.

constitution Set of rules and details of aims, laid down by a society or club.

constructive dismissal The imposition of terms of general conditions to an employee's work situation with the intent of forcing an employee to resign.

constructive industry Companies and people involved in ***secondary production***, *e.g.* manufacturing.

consumable Describing something that is used up (*e.g.* computer printer ink, degreasing solvents, welding rods) in a business or industry, as opposed to things (*e.g.* raw materials) that are incorporated into a product.

consumables Goods that are ***consumable***.

consumer Person who buys goods for consumption.

consumer advertising Advertising directed at the consumer. This form of advertising may be either informative or persuasive. *See also* ***informative advertising; persuasive advertising.***

consumer banking Alternative term for ***retail banking***.

consumer credit Personal credit, such as a ***bank loan*** or incorporated into a ***hire-purchase*** agreement.

Consumer Credit Act Act of Parliament passed in the UK in 1974 that safeguards people who take out personal credit worth up to £15,000. It covers ***bank loans***, ***credit cards***, ***credit sale agreements***, ***hire-purachase***

agreements and ***mortgages*** (bank ***overdrafts*** are excluded). *See also* ***annual percentage rate; cooling-off period.***

consumer credit agreement Personal credit agreement, limited to a maximum borrowing of £15,000. *See* ***Consumer Credit Act.***

consumer durable Consumer goods of some technological sophistication that yield utility over a period of time. *E.g.* clothing, cars, washing machines, etc.

consumer goods Goods that are consumed in use, either over a short period (*e.g.* foodstuffs), or over a longer period, such as motor vehicle tyres (or even the motor vehicles themselves). *See also* ***consumer durable.***

consumer price index US term for ***retail price index.***

consumption Act of consuming, *i.e.* using goods or services that are thereby damaged or used up and cannot therefore be re-sold.

conspicuous consumption Consumer trend that involves the consumer buying goods (usually status symbols, such as sports cars, etc.), deriving satisfaction, not from consumption of the goods themselves, but from being seen by other people to own them.

contango Stock exchange term for a delayed settlement of a bargain from one account to the next. A ***premium*** is payable. The term is also used more frequently in futures trading to mean the opposite of ***backwardation.***

contemptuous damages Damages awarded if the court agrees that the defendant was at fault, but believes that the loss or injury caused was so minor that the case should not have been brought.

contingency Something that is liable, but not certain, to happen at some time in the future. *See also* ***contingent.***

contingent Something that depends on an uncertain event taking place.

The bank's willingness to lend the company money is contingent upon our breaking even at the end of this financial year.

continuation Alternative term for ***contango.***

continuing security Security obtained by a bank to secure a loan that continues to be security for further advances.

continuous credit account Another name for a ***budget account.***

contra Latin for the "opposite side". *See also* ***per contra.***

contra account Account that is credited or debited against another account.

contract Term with two meanings:

1. It is a legally binding agreement between two or more parties.
2. It is to form such an agreement.

contract bond Alternative term for ***performance bond.***

contract in In general, to make an agreement to join some scheme (and participate in its benefits). In particular, it is the decision of a company to make contributions towards the state pension scheme for its employees. If a company does contract in in this way, it is also able to provide extra pensions by using private schemes. *See also* ***contract out.***

contract out In general, to make an agreement to forego some activity (and its possible benefits). In particular, the term refers to a company that believes it can provide sufficient pension cover for its employees more economically using a private scheme than using the state pension system. In this case, the company is required by law to provide at least the minimum payments of a state pension. *See also* ***contract in.***

contract size Size (*i.e.* weight) of a futures contract, so as to ascertain its value. Contract sizes are all fixed, *e.g.* COMEX gold is 100 oz.

contra entry In double-entry ***book-keeping*** an item that is entered to balance out another. Its purpose is to negate the original item, often because that entry was made in error.

contra proferentem rule Nickname for the following Latin maxim: *verba chartarum fortuis accipiuntur contra proferentem* – the words of the contract are constued more strictly against the person proclaiming them. In effect, the contra proferentem rule means that if a contract is ambiguous, it will be construed in a way that is the least advantageous to the party that drew up the contract.

contrarian Informal term for a speculator in stocks and shares who goes against short-term trends. *E.g.* a contrarian may decide on a buying policy in a ***bear market.***

contribution Money paid as an addition to another sum.

con trick *See* ***confidence trick.***

controlled economy Economy in which the government tries to control elements of economic activity by legislating for key areas rather than taking direct charge of the factors of production. *See also* ***planned economy***.

controlling interest Sufficient holding of voting shares in a company (more than 50%) to give a single shareholder control of the company. Legally, a director has a controlling interest if he or she owns more than 20% of the voting shares.

control of the money supply System established by the Bank of England in 1981 to control the amount of liquidity in the banking system, thereby influencing interest rates. Banks are required to keep an average of 5% of eligible liabilities as bills with the London Discount Market.

convenor Person who calls (convenes) a meeting. The term is often used for the person in a trade union who organizes union meetings, and is the senior elected union representative at a particular site.

conventional option Alternative term for ***traditional option***.

conversion Term with two meanings:

1. It is the changing of one thing into another that is equivalent.
2. In a legal context, it is interference with the property of someone else, so as to deprive him or her of the right of ownership.

convertible Describing something that is easily capable of ***conversion***. The term has the more specific meaning of loan stock, bonds and debentures that are easily converted into ordinary shares. These are known as convertibles, or, in the USA, converts.

convertible bond Also known as convertible loan stock or convertible, a bond that is offered at a fixed, low rate of interest with an option to convert the bond into an equity share.

convertible currency Currency that is easily exchangeable for another currency.

conveyance Transfer of ownership of land or other property.

cooling off period Period of ten days (in the UK) during which a person who has agreed to a certain form of contract (such as a ***credit sale*** or ***hire-purchase*** agreement) may withdraw from that agreement and have his or her money repaid. Such a period exists in order to minimize the effects of hard selling that some companies or their agents undertake.

co-operative Group of people who come together to produce goods or services and who share all profits.

co-operative society Society of consumers and producers (or retailers) who share the profits of their co-operation.

copy Term with two meanings:

1. It is to reproduce something.
2. It is text, or some form of written material, such as that produced for an advertisement or newspaper.

copyhold Alternative term for ***freehold***.

copyright Legal term for the right of ownership of an author over his or her own work. Copyright extends for a term of 70 years after the author's death.

copywriter Person who writes advertising ***copy***.

cordoba Standard currency unit of Nicaragua, divided into 100 centavos.

Corn Exchange London commodities exchange that deals in such commodities as cereals and animal foodstuffs.

corner the market To build a virtual ***monopoly*** in particular goods or services, so that the monopolist is able to dictate ***price***.

corp Abbreviation of ***corporation***.

corpocracy If a company is involved in several mergers, its management is at risk of becoming cumbersome and confused. The resulting corporation thus labours under a large and inefficient bureaucracy and is known informally as a corpocracy.

corporate To do with a ***corporation***.

corporate bond Bond issued by a company, which most frequently happens in the USA.

corporate culture Culture that grows up within a company, among its employees. Corporate culture embodies such factors as dress, its employees' attitudes towards working and their expectations, and the style of working relationships.

corporate finance Funding for a business or large corporation, usually from a bank.

corporate hospitality (CH) Hospitality extended to a company's most favoured clients (or potential clients) in the form of entertainment, *e.g.* tickets to the theatre or to prestigious sporting events.

corporate identity Identity of a company as displayed in the visual images it uses, *e.g.* its logos and colours.

corporate image Image that a company presents to the general public. Some large companies spend large sums in an attempt to improve their corporate image.

corporate licensing Alternative US term for merchandising.

corporate planning Activity undertaken to plan the future aims of a company, covering such subject areas as new products, sales targets and production targets.

corporate raider Someone who buys enough shares of ***target*** company to take it over or to sufficiently influence the management to make changes that improve the share value of the company. The raider can then sell the shares at a profit.

corporate veil Protection against liability that is afforded to multiple shareholders in a company as opposed to one single owner. *See also* ***limited liability***.

corporate venturing Practice of a company providing ***venture capital*** for another. Corporate venturing is usually undertaken to give the investing company a potential foothold in a new (or related) market or field, or to lay the foundations for a possible ***takeover*** at some future date.

corporation Large ***company***, usually with several ***subsidiary companies***. In the USA, it is a company that has been incorporated under US law. Therefore, the term is a virtual synonym for company. Often it is abbreviated to corp.

corporation tax (CT) Tax levied on a company's profits. *See also* ***advance corporation tax***.

correspondent bank When a transaction is initiated at a foreign branch of a bank, the home branch to which the instructions are sent is known as the correspondent bank. *See also* ***originating bank***.

corset Restriction applied by the Bank of England on the amount of credit a bank can extend to its customers, usually in an attempt to control inflation.

cost Amount of money that has to be expended to acquire something, in most cases its price.

cost accountant Accountant who specializes in reckoning the ***cost*** of manufacturing a unit of a product, taking into account such variables as cost of raw materials and ***labour***, and thereby making a ***projection*** of probable cost at the planning stage of a project. This in turn enables the manufacturer to ***tender*** a price to a prospective buyer.

cost accounting Work undertaken by a ***cost accountant***.

cost analysis Examination of the ***cost*** of producing a particular product, normally undertaken before the project is begun.

cost and freight (C & F) When exporting goods, a contract in which it is agreed that the exporter pays all costs up to the delivery point except for insurance. *See also* ***cost, insurance and freight; cost, insurance, freight and interest.***

cost centre Particular operation within a business that is charged separately for its own expenses (so that its cost can be accurately assessed). *See also* ***overheads; unit cost.***

cost-effective Describing something that gives value for money. It is often used as a relative term.

costing Practice of working out how much a product will cost to produce, taking into account costs such as raw materials, labour, overheads, etc. A frequent alternative term is costing-out.

costing-out *See* ***costing***.

cost, insurance and freight (CIF) Foreign trade contract stipulating that the exporter pays all costs up to the point of delivery, including insurance of goods in transit. *See also* ***cost and freight; cost, insurance, freight and interest.***

cost, insurance, freight and interest (CIFI) Export contract, by which the exporter is bound to pay all costs to delivery, along with insurance on goods in transit and interest on the value of the goods. *See also* ***cost and freight; cost, insurance and freight.***

cost minimization Practice of seeking the minimum cost at which a company is able to produce the output it requires.

cost of funds Cost incurred by banks in borrowing on the ***money market***, which determines the interest rate it charges to its borrowers.

cost of living In national terms, the amount of money each person has to spend in order to buy food and accommodation. *See also* ***retail price index.***

cost-plus System of charges whereby the buyer pays the cost of the item plus a commission to the seller.

Peter decided to charge for the goods on a cost-plus basis.

cost-push inflation Theory that inflation is caused by increases in the cost of manufacturing process, thus pushing up overall prices to the consumer.

cost unit One article, to which a cost may be ascribed for ***accounting*** purposes. Cost units may include simple articles such as raw materials (*e.g.* a plank of wood), or articles in production (although these are more complicated in that they require the accounting to take into account direct and indirect costs). *See also* ***cost centre***.

costs Term with two meanings:

1. It refers to expenses incurred during a court case.

Bill was fined £200 and ordered to pay costs.

2. It is the sum of the cost of each item used during production of goods or services.

Council for Mutual Economic Assistance (COMECON or CMEA) Group of Communist bloc countries that combined in 1949 with the aim of producing a self-sufficient economic bloc that could be co-ordinated from a central point (and to consolidate Soviet influence in the area). Its members were: Bulgaria, Cuba, Czechoslovakia, East Germany, Hungary, Mongolia, Poland, Romania, USSR, and Vietnam. In 1991 it was succeeded by the Organization for Economic Cooperation (OIEC).

Council of Economic Advisers (US) An agency within the Executive Office of the President that analyzes the national economy and its various segments, advises the President on economic developments, appraises the economic programmes and policies of the federal government, recommends policies for economic growth and stability, and assists in preparation of the annual Economic Report of the President to Congress.

counter Term with two meanings:

1. It is a (figurative) table across which goods are bought and sold.
2. It is a prefix meaning against (as in, *e.g.*, counterinflationary).

counter automation Computer system that gives bank cashiers real-time access to a customer's account details (whether or not the account is held at that bank).

counterbid Bid that is made (*e.g.* during a takeover battle or an auction) against a previous bid, going one better.

counter cheque Cheque written on a blank cheque form obtained over the counter of a bank, and not from the account holder's cheque book. It is also known as a window cheque.

counterclaim Claim for damages made by a defendant against a plaintiff, in the hopes that the counterclaim will offset any ***damages*** payable to the plaintiff in the first action. *See also* ***set-off***.

counterfeit Describing something (particularly money) that is forged.

counterfoil Document kept as a record of a transaction, often attached to (and then detached from) a bond, certificate or cheque.

countermand Formal term for stopping a cheque. *See* ***stopped cheque***.

countermarketing Willful destruction of the reputation or credibility of a product, either by a competing firm or by a consumer action group.

Anti-smoking groups have recently launched a biting countermarketing strategy against tobacco products.

countermove Tactical action taken in response to moves made by an opponent, *e.g.* during ***takeover*** battle.

counter-offer Offer (*e.g.* of a price on a property) made in response to a previous offer.

Both companies wanted the premises so badly that counter-offer after counter-offer was made, until the final price was astronomical.

countersign To sign a document that has already been signed by someone else.

Please would you ask Mary to countersign this contract before I return it.

countervailing credit Alternative term for ***back-to-back*** credit.

coupon Term with two meanings:

1. It is a document attached to a bond, that must be detached and sent to the paying party in order for the bond holder to receive ***interest*** payments. Each payment is detailed on the coupon for each payment period.
2. It is an alternative term for interest that is payable on a ***fixed-interest security***. *See also* ***cum coupon; ex coupon***.

coupon bond Alternative term for ***bearer bond***.

covenant Term with two meanings:

1. It is broadly any form of ***agreement***.
2. More specifically, it is an agreement taken out between two parties, stating that one party agrees to pay the other a series of fixed sums over a certain period of time. If the covenant covers a period longer than six years, then the payer is entitled to ***tax relief*** on the payments.

cover Term with several meanings:

1. It is any form of ***security*** (*i.e.* collateral).
2. It is used in financial futures markets to the buying of contracts to offset a short position.
3. It describes the number of times a company could pay its dividends to shareholders from its earnings.

This year's annual report shows that C & F White plc are three times covered.

4. It is to make enough money in selling products or services to pay for their production.

I am pleased to say that last year we more than covered our costs.

5. It is the amount of money an insured person stands to receive from an insurer should he or she make a claim.

Tim has £600,000 insurance cover for his small art collection.

6. It is the constituent amount put up as ***margin*** per unit of quotation on a futures contract, which combined will dictate the margin.

covered bear Dealer who sell ***shares*** or ***commodities*** he owns, hoping to buy them back later at a lower price (*i.e.* he or she is not taking the risk of ***short selling***). He or she is also known as a protected bear.

covered interest arbitrage System in which money borrowed in one currency is converted into another and then invested, before selling it for a future delivery against the first currency. *See also* ***arbitrage***.

CPA Abbreviation of certified public accountant.

CPP Abbreviation of ***current purchasing power (accounting)***.

crash Term with two meanings:

1. It is an informal term for a very severe drop in prices on securities, financial and commodities markets. The most famous was the Wall Street Crash of 1929, which led to the 1930s depression; the largest

in recent years was the worldwide drop in share prices on 15 October 1987.

2. It is an informal term for a computer failure. In the USA, this is also known as a brownout.

crawling peg Form of fixed ***exchange rate***, in which the rate is allowed to fluctuate according to supply and demand, but within certain specified minimum and maximum limits. It is also known as a sliding peg. *See also* ***adjustable peg***.

creative accountancy *See* ***number fudging***.

credit Term with several meanings:

1. It is a loan of money.

Andrew found it difficult to obtain credit from any bank.

2. It is to add a sum to an ***account***.

My bank credits my account with interest automatically.

3. In book-keeping, it is a ***balance*** that shows a profit.

When he had rationalized his extremely complicated personal finances, he found that he was in credit after all.

4. It is the financial standing of a person or company.

Their credit is very good, so you may feel confident about lending them money.

credit account Account offered by ***retail*** stores and chains, which allows a customer to buy goods on the spot (usually by means of a plastic card) and to pay for them at the end of the accounting period or in ***instalments***. Some credit accounts also pay ***interest***.

credit advice Document from a bank telling a customer that specified funds have been credited to his or her account.

credit agency (US **credit bureau)** Company that gathers information on the credit-worthiness of individuals and companies, and distributes this information to those providing credit facilities.

credit balance In accounting, balance showing that more money has been received than is debited and so the account is in ***credit***.

credit broker Person who introduces someone wanting credit to someone who can provide it. Some retailers who sell goods by means of ***credit sale agreements*** are licensed credit brokers.

C

credit bureau Alternative term for ***credit agency***.

credit card Plastic card that enables the user to buy goods on *credit*, paying outstanding sums on his or her account in monthly instalments.

credit clearing Organization, a part of the Cheque and Credit Clearing Company, that deals with the *clearing* of credits paid over the counters of branch banks (which usually takes three working days).

credit crunch Situation in which *short credit* becomes scarce and thus more expensive than *long credit*.

credit entry Item of *credit* recorded in a *ledger* for accounting purposes.

credit freeze Action by banks to restrict the extension of credit to customers. It is aso known as credit squeeze.

credit limit The maximum sum that a person is prepared to lend to another.

At Christmas I spent right up to my credit limit.

credit note Document, often printed in red, issued to confirm the transfer of credit from one account to another. Also a note or document confirming the availability of funds for a future purchase.

creditor Person or company to whom money is owed.

credit rating Rating assigned to a person or company in order to indicate creditworthiness.

credit reference Record of the past reliability of a borrower, usually provided by a bank, to enable the borrower to obtain further credit.

credit sale agreement Contract that permits a buyer to pay for goods received by means of instalments paid over a period. Unlike a *hire-purchase* agreement, it confers ownership as soon as the contract is signed.

credit scoring Method of assessing a company's or person's ability to make loans.

credit squeeze Alternative term for *credit freeze*.

credit transfer Method of paying money into another person's bank account (usually by *giro*).

credit union (UK) Non-profit making mutual organization that offers facilities for savings, makes small loans, and may provide basic personal insurance within a local area.

(US) Member-owned, democratically governed, non-profit cooperatives that provide financial services to members and whose earnings are returned to members. Over sixty million Americans are members of credit unions.

creditworthy Describing a person who, from his or her record, is deemed willing and able to pay back credit. Thus, a creditworthy person finds it easier to borrow (and to borrow larger sums) than someone who is deemed to be a credit risk.

creeping takeover Gradual increase in a shareholding through open purchase on the stock exchange with the aim of accumulating enough shares to make a ***takeover bid***.

CREST Electronic (and therefore paperlesss) system introduced by the Bank of England for processing shares for the securities market. It includes registration, purchases, sales and the payment of dividends as they become due.

CRT Abbreviation of ***composite rate tax***.

cross Term with two meanings:

1. It is to mark a ***cheque*** with two parallel lines to prevent the cheque being cashed over the counter, thus ensuring that the cheque is paid into a bank account.
2. It is the practice of buying and selling the same block of ***shares*** or ***futures*** contracts simultaneously by the same broker.

cross-border accord Agreement made between two neighbouring countries, often with regard to trading.

crossed cheque Cheque that is scored across with two parallel lines, often also with the words ***account payee*** or & Co (and company). This indicates that the cheque must be paid into a bank account. *See also* ***uncrossed cheque***.

cross-firing Fraud that involves opening two or more accounts at different banks. Money withdrawn from the first bank is backed by a cheque drawn on the second bank, and so on.

cross guarantee Guarantee required by a bank from a parent company when making a loan to one of its subsidiary companies.

crossing *See* ***cross***.

cross rate Rate at which one currency may be exchanged for a second, expressed in terms of a third currency.

crowd The people who wish to trade in a particular option or future, so named because to do so, they must gather around the relevant ***pitch***.

crown Standard currency unit of Denmark, Norway and Sweden, more properly called ***kroone*** or ***krona***. The crown was also a British coin worth 5 shillings (25p), hence the name half-a-crown for the former coin worth 2 shillings and 6 pence (12½p).

cruzeiro Standard currency unit of Brazil, divided into 100 centavos.

crown jewel tactic Strategy undertaken by a company that is threatened by ***takeover***, in which it sells, or offers to sell, the best part of its business to someone other than the ***raider*** (*e.g.* a ***white knight***), in order to make the target seem less desirable.

CT Abbreviation of ***corporation tax***.

CTT Abbreviation of ***capital transfer tax***.

CUG Abbreviation of closed user group.

cum coupon ***Security*** that is passed from one holder to another with ***coupon*** (enabling the holder to claim ***interest*** payments) attached. *See also* ***ex coupon***.

cum dividend Shares that are sold with the right of the new holder to claim the next ***dividend*** payment. It is sometimes abbreviated to cum div. *See also* ***ex dividend***.

cum new Shares that are sold with the right to claim participation in a scrip or rights issue. *See also* ***ex new; scrip issue***.

cumulative preference share Kind of ***preference share*** whose holder can claim any dividends not paid in earlier years, as long as the company has funds to pay them. Even then, eventual payment is guaranteed before payment to holders of ordinary shares.

cupro-nickel Alloy , consisting of 75% copper and 25% nickel, used for modern UK "silver coins" (5p, 10p, 20p and 50p). *See also* ***bronze coins***.

currency Coins and banknotes that are used as ***legal tender***.

currency bond ***Bond*** issued in a foreign country. It is repaid in the appropriate foreign currency.

currency clearings Clearings that take place daily in London in eight foreign currencies (Australian dollar, Canadian dollar, Deutschmark, Dutch guilder, French franc, Italian lira, Japanese yen and US dollar), managed by the Currency Clearings Committe, a part of the

Association for Payment Clearing Services (APACS).

currency contract period Following the devaluation of a currency, the time during which contracts negotiated before the devaluation become due.

currency exposure Risk of holding assets in a foreign currency. The risk is incurred because its value, relative to that of the host nation's currency, may fall. It is possible to hedge against currency exposure by selling foreign currency on the ***forward markets***. *See* ***hedging***.

currency gyration *See* ***floating exchange rate***.

currency inconvertibility Situation that arises when a company cannot change ***local currency*** into a ***convertible currency*** in order to transfer funds out of the country.

currency note ***Banknote*** of a country in which it is ***legal tender***.

currency option contract Contract that allows the purchaser of the option the right (if he or she wishes) to trade in a foreign currency at a pre-set exchange rate within a specified time period.

currency swap Transaction where one currency is exchanged for another at a fixed rate.

current Describing continuing state of affairs that is occurring or relevant at the present time, and is expected to remain so in the near future.

current account Term with two meanings:

1. It is the most common type of bank account for personal use, which usually pays no interest but funds may be accessed immediately by writing a ***cheque***. In this sense it is also known as a cheque account or, in the USA, a checking account.
2. It is part of the balance of payments, which refers to national ***income*** and ***expenditure***, including ***visible trade*** and ***invisible trade***.

current asset Asset that is used by a company in its day-to-day operations, *e.g.* raw materials, etc.

current assets ratio Slightly different to the ***acid-test ratio***, the current assets ratio is the ratio of a company's assets including its stock-in-trade, to its current liabilities.

current balance Balance of a bank account at the close of business.

C

current cost accounting (CCA) Also known as inflation accounting, a method of accounting that takes changes in prices due to ***inflation*** into account, adjusting values of assets, costs, etc.

current expenditure Expenditure on assets for resale, such as raw materials rather than on fixed assets. It is also known as above-the-line expenditure. *See* ***fixed asset***.

current liability Money owed (by a company or individual) that should be paid within a year of the date on the balance sheet. *See also* ***long-term liability***.

current purchasing power accounting (CPP) Method of accounting that has been advocated since the 1970s, and which involves stating all accounts in terms of a unit of purchasing power, calculated from a price ***index***. Current purchasing power accounting has not yet become a common method.

current ratio Test of ***liquidity*** made by dividing a company's ***current assets*** by its ***current liabilities***. It is also called current assets ratio or working-capital ratio.

current yield ***Dividend*** calculated as a percentage of the price paid for each share.

curriculum vitae Latin for "course of life". It is a document that relates (most usually in tabular form) the education, qualifications, and career of a person. It is known in the USA as a resumé.

custodian bank Bank that provides independent collective investment services for ***unit trust*** companies. It holds their cash and securities, and ensures compliance with regulations.

custodier Role of a bank as provider of safe keeping for assurance policies, deeds, securities, wills, and so on of its customers.

Customs and Excise UK Government department charged with levying indirect taxes, including ***value-added tax*** (VAT) and ***customs duty*** on goods imported into the UK or produced in the UK for home consumption (***excise duty***). It full name is Board of Customs and Excise.

customs barrier High level of customs duty that makes trade difficult. It is also known as a tariff barrier.

customs duty Duty levied on imports by the ***Customs and Excise***, either as a protectionist measure, or simply to raise revenue.

cut a deal To agree on the basic principles of an agreement. Negotiation or finalization of details usually follows.

CWO Abbreviation of cash with order.

cyclical unemployment Unemployment caused by movements in the trade cycle, *e.g.* during a ***recession***.

cyclicals Shares in companies that are involved in basic industries, such as the provision of raw materials, metals, etc. They are so called because their prices on the stock market tend to rise and fall with the business cycle.

D

DA Abbreviation of ***deposit account*** or ***discretionary account.***

D/A Abbreviation of ***documents against acceptance.***

daisy chain The practice of buying and selling the same stocks or shares several times, usually to make it appear that there is more activity in their trading than there really is.

dalasi Standard currency unit in The Gambia, divided into 100 bututs.

damages Civil court award of monetary compensation for loss or injury.

danger money Extra money that is paid as ***wages*** to employees carrying out dangerous work. In the USA it is also known informally as combat pay.

dangling debit Method by which a firm creates a goodwill account by writing off goodwill to reserves. Funds in a goodwill account are excluded from shareholders' funds.

data Items of information, particularly in computer applications.

data acquisition Purchase of data, computing software, etc.

database Data organized to allow easy access to the most up-to-date information and its collation with older data. The term is generally applied to electronic storage devices (*i.e.* computers), which can store, organize and search for data more rapidly than was hitherto possible.

data processing Sorting and organization of data in order to produce the desired information, generally according to standard procedures.

Data Protection Act Act of Parliament in the UK of 1984, which is intended to protect the consumer against misuse of personal information about him or her stored in a computer system. Information covered by the ***Consumer Credit Act*** is, however, exempt.

data security Protection of data from electronic criminals. Data security generally entails the production of programs intended to deny unauthorized persons access to a database by means of passwords and other identification procedures. Maximum security is obtained by encryption, in which information is held in a coded form. *See* ***electronic crime.***

date The day, month and year. In the UK these are usually recorded numerically in that order (*i.e.* 1:2:98 is 1st February 1998). However in Europe and the USA they are recorded in the order month, day, year (*i.e.* 1:2:98. is January 2nd 1998). The potential for confusion is vast.

dated stock Stock that has a fixed maturity date, as opposed to undated stock.

datel service British Telecom service that enables the transmission of computer data via telephone lines.

dawn raid Buying of a significant number of a target company's shares at the start of the day's trading, or before the market becomes aware of what is happening, often at a price higher than normal. The purpose of a dawn raid is to give the buyer a strategic stake in the ***target*** company, from which the buyer may launch a ***takeover bid***.

day book Ledger in which transactions are listed on a daily basis prior to transfer to ledgers that deal with transactions on a subject basis. It is usual to keep separate purchase and sales day books.

daylight overdraft Situation that occurs when a bank allows a customer's account to go into the ***red***, on the understanding that the debt will be repaid by the end of the day. *See also* ***float***.

day order Order given by an investor to a ***stockbroker*** which is valid only on the day it was given. A day order also specifies a price limit on the transaction envisaged. If not completed on the day in question, the transaction is automatically cancelled.

days of grace Period of three days still permitted in the UK for the payment of any ***bill of exchange*** except ***bills of sight***. Days of grace have been abolished in most other countries.

day-to-day loan Alternative term for overnight loan or day-to-day money, borrowed particularly by a financial institution which is temporarily illiquid. The money is lent to companies wishing to be paid ***interest*** on money earned in the previous day's trading. ***Interest rates*** on day to day loans are high and variable.

DCE Abbreviation of ***domestic credit expansion***.

DCF Abbreviation of ***discounted cash flow***.

dead cat bounce Brief rise in the stock ***index*** of a falling market. The term refers to the supposed ability of a cat always to land on its feet: if a falling cat bounces, it must be dead. *See also* ***bottoming out***.

D

deadheading US term with two meanings:

1. It is the promotion of a junior member of staff over the heads of more senior members.
2. It is the movement of a company vehicle from one location where it is not needed to a location where it is, and using it to transport employees at the same time.

dead-in-the-water Describing a project that has failed completely, often before it is properly underway.

dead security Security backed by an exhaustible industry (such as mining), which is thus a poor risk for a long-term loan.

deadweight ***Debt*** that is not covered by or incurred in exchange for real assets. *E.g.* the part of the National Debt taken on to pay for war is a deadweight debt.

deal Agreement or transaction; in particular, any bargain made on a stock market.

dealer Anyone who is engaged in trading on a financial market.

dealing Activity of dealers.

dealing for the account Speculative stock market trading in which shares are bought and sold in the very short term. Because accounts do not have to be settled until ***account day***, it is possible for a dealer to buy thousands of pounds worth of stock without having to pay for them. If the stock is then sold before account day, the dealer can keep any ***profit*** resulting from price fluctuations while the stock was held. Conversely, ***bears*** may sell stock which they do not actually possess in the belief that they will be able to buy back the stock at a lower price as the market falls. This practice is known as selling short.

dear money Money is said to be dear when it is difficult to find investment or loans and the interest rate for borrowing is consequently high.

death of an account holder Notification to a bank that a customer has died removes the authority of the bank to debit the customer's acocunt (*e.g.* to pay cheques or direct debits). The account is thus stopped and any cheques drawn on it are returned marked "drawer deceased".

death valley curve Period of time during which a start-up company uses venture capital at an extremely fast rate, to the point where it is using equity capital to fund overheads, an unhealthy state of affairs.

death valley days Nickname for "dry" periods on the financial markets – days on which little trading takes place. *See also* ***valium picnic***.

debenture Long-term loan to a company made at a fixed rate of interest and usually with a specified ***maturity date***, generally between 10 and 40 years. Debenture holders are numbered with the company's creditors, and in the event of ***liquidation*** have preferential claims on the firm. Debentures may be treated as tradeable ***securities***.

debenture capital That part of a company's capital that is issued in the form of ***debentures***.

debenture issue Issue of ***debentures***, whether secured or unsecured, by a company wishing to raise loan capital. The debenture-holders become the company's principal ***creditors*** and have the right to preferential repayment of their loans in the event that the firm encounters financial difficulties. *See also* ***loan capital***.

debenture stock ***Debentures*** may be divided into units and traded on the exchange. These securities are known as debenture stocks.

debit A sum owed by or a charge made on a person.

debit balance In accounting, balance that shows a ***debit***.

debit card Plastic card issued by a bank to its customers which may be used in place of a ***cheque*** book. By accessing the bank's electronic records, the debit card makes ***direct debit*** of an account possible.

debit entry Item of ***debit*** recorded in a ledger for accounting purposes.

debit note In ***accounting***, notification sent to a customer that the supplier is about to debit the client's account with a certain sum. Debit notes are normally issued in unusual situations, *e.g.* when a client has been charged too little for goods received.

debit side In ***accounting***, the side of a ***ledger*** on which debits are listed. Hence, in informal use, it is the negative points in an argument.

debt Sum of money, or value of goods or services, owed by one person, group or company to another. Debt arises because the seller allows the purchaser ***credit***. Assignable debts may be transferred in whole from one person to another. In commerce, the term is also used to describe the whole of a company's borrowings.

debt bomb Financial repercussions envisaged if a major international debtor were to default.

There was general concern on the money markets as the economy of two of the debt bomb nations showed a marked deterioration.

debt collection agency Firm that charges a ***commission*** for collecting its clients' outstanding debts.

debt discounting Purchasing a debt at a discount, usually from a trader such as an exporter.

debt factoring Purchasing of a company's debts (at a discount) by a factor. *See* ***debt discounting; factoring***.

debt-for-equity Substitution of an ***equity*** stake for a debt that is proving difficult to recover, despite the good prospects of the borrower.

debt forgiveness In international finance, writing off part of a nation's debt, or selling the debt to a third party for a large discount.

debtor (Dr) Person or company that owes money, goods or services to another.

debt rescheduling When a debtor has difficulties making repayments, a method by which the lender defers interest or repayments, extends the loan period, or agrees to a completely new loan.

debt servicing Payment of ***interest*** on a debt.

debtnocrat Bank official who specializes in high-level lending, often to developing nations.

debt-to-equity ratio A company may finance itself through borrowing or through shareholder investment, depending on current interest rates. The proportion of each is known as debt-to-equity ratio, or ***gearing***.

debut Arrival on the stock market of the shares of a new company and the first day's trading in that company's stock.

deceased partner Normally a partnership is dissolved when one of the partners dies. But the partnership agreement may allow for the business to continue trading and the value of the deceased person's share is passed to his or her nominee. If a partnership's bank account is overdrawn when one partner dies, the account is closed and another opened in the names of the surviving partners, so that the deceased person's estate remains liable for part of the debt.

decentralization Distribution of the constituent parts of a company or government to a variety of geographical locations. The advantages include the availability of cheaper labour (that is likely to be initially offset by the cost of relocating key personnel), increased efficiency and, in the case of government, the provision of incentives to industry to consider non-metropolitan locations.

decimal currency Currency system whose standard unit is subdivided into 100 parts, as used by nearly every country in the world. Decimal currency was introduced in the UK in 1971.

declaration of solvency Formal statement by a company's directors that it is seeking voluntary liquidation but that it expects to pay its creditors within at least 12 months.

decontrol Alternative term for ***deregulation***.

de-diversification Shedding of interests and companies acquired by a corporation in the process of ***diversification***, so as to reduce the variety of business in which the company engages.

deduction Money legally deducted from wages and salaries at source and allotted to pay taxes and (in the UK) National Insurance contributions.

deductions at source *Income tax* deducted by an employer from an employee's pay before he or she receives it, or the deduction of income tax from interest earned by, *e.g.*, a building society account. The sum deducted is then paid by the company to the Inland Revenue. Deduction at source helps to prevent ***tax evasion***.

deed Document that records a transaction and may bear the seals of the parties concerned to testify to its validity.

deed of covenant Document that formalizes the transfer of income from one person to another or to an institution in order to reduce income tax payable. It is often done to make donations to a charity; the donor deducts basic rate tax (often then getting tax relief) and the charity claims the tax deducted.

deed of partnership Agreement that forms the basis and terms of a partnership between two or more people.

deed of transfer Legal document that gives authority to registrars of securities to transfer them from the seller to the buyer.

deep market Financial market where many transactions can occur without affecting the price of the underlying financial instrument.

deep-pocket view Theory that some ***subsidiaries*** may have access to more funds than an independent firm of similar size. The deep-pocket view argues that the subsidiary may call upon the greater resources of its parent company to engage in competition with independents in its sector.

de facto By virtue of existence, rather than any legal right. *E.g.* the de facto owner of a property may be the person in occupation, whether or not he or she has legal title to the land.

default Failure to comply with the terms set out in a ***contract***. Legal proceedings generally follow if the matter cannot be settled amicably.

default notice Notice issued by a lender to a borrower who is in default on a loan subject to the Consumer Credit Act (1974). If the notice is not complied with, the lender can seek an ***enforcement order***.

defeasance Condition built into the wording of a deed that renders the deed void if the condition is complied with. The term is also used for any annulment or act that renders something null and void.

defence bond Bond issued by the UK government to cover spending during and immediately after World War II. Defence bonds were first issued in 1939 and discontinued in 1964.

defensive stock Shares in companies that are not affected by economic cycles, because they produce necessities, *e.g.* food.

defensive tactics The strategy used when a "player" feels threatened by aggression. Thus the subject of a hostile ***takeover*** bid sometimes arranges defensive tactics with the aim of making the takeover more difficult, *e.g.* pushing up its own share price. Examples of defensive tactics are the ***Lady Macbeth strategy*** and the ***poison pill***.

deferment Postponement, *e.g.* of a payment.

deferred asset Expense incurred that does not match the income it will provide in the same accounting period. It is also termed a deferred debit.

deferred coupon note Type of ***bond*** on which interest is due after a specified date.

deferred credit Income received before it is earned in a given accounting period, such as a government grant. It is also termed a deferred liability.

deferred futures Futures contracts that are farthest away from ***maturity***. *See also* ***nearby futures***.

deferred liability Liability that does not fall due until after a period of a year.

deferred ordinary shares Category of shares, usually issued to a company's founders, entitling them to special dividend rights.

deferred taxation Tax for which a person or company is liable, but which has not yet been considered or demanded by the Inland Revenue.

deficit Excess of ***expenditure*** over ***income***, or ***liabilities*** over ***assets***.

deflation Persistent decrease in prices, generally caused by a fall in the level of economic activity within a country. Deflation should not be confused with ***disinflation***.

deflationary gap The difference between the actual level of ***investment*** and the level necessary to restore full employment.

defray To settle an ***account*** or to lay out money in payment for goods or services.

defunct Describing a company or organization that no longer functions as such.

degearing Reduction of ***risk*** or ***leverage***. Examples include cutting ***borrowing*** and reducing ***exposure*** to forces which a company or ***dealer*** cannot control. *See also* ***hedging***.

dehoarding Putting back into circulation money (or goods) that have been unavailable for business or commercial use.

de-industrialization Decline in the relative importance of manufacturing. *See also* ***sunrise industry; sunset industry***.

delayed payment surcharge Extra payment (in addition to interest) that is charged while a debt is outstanding.

del credere (agent) Person who accepts goods on consignment from exporters, agreeing (in return for an additional ***commission***) to pay for them in the event that the original purchaser defaults.

delegation Term with two meanings:

1. It is a body of accredited representatives to a gathering (*e.g.* a conference).
2. It is to cede responsibility to other, usually junior, members of staff.

delegatus non potest delegare Latin for a "delegate cannot delegate", a principle that precents a contractor from subcontracting part of the work.

delivered pricing Practice of calculating a price of goods for sale that includes the cost of delivery.

delivery Handing over of ***property*** or monetary ***assets***. In the City the term has two more specific meanings: it describes a transfer of ***securities***, and the receipt of the financial instrument or cash payment specified in a financial ***futures*** contract. *See also* ***cash on delivery; delivery note***.

delivery note Broadly, a note advising a recipient of the intended delivery of goods. In the ***securities*** market, however, a delivery note requests the delivery of a security.

delivery of bill Tranfer of possession of a bill (or a cheque) from one person to another or his or her agent.

delta Stock exchange classification of shares that are traded on the Alternative Investment Market. They are generally relatively inactive and stable shares in small companies. *See also* ***alpha; beta; gamma***.

demand Term with two meanings:

1. It is the desire for possession of a particular good or service at a specific price expressed by those able and willing to purchase it.
2. It is a request, such as a request for payment of a ***debt***.

demand bill ***Bill of exchange*** to be paid on demand, also called a demand draft. Examples include a cheque and a draft drawn by a bank on itself or its head office.

demand deposit Deposit of a sum of money with a bank, building society or other financial institution that may be withdrawn at a moment's notice. It is also called a sight deposit.

demand draft *See* ***demand bill***.

demand-pull inflation Theory that demand is caused by excess of demand over supply, thus pulling prices up.

demerger Spltting up of a large company or group of companies into smaller independent ones, or the selling off of a group's subsidiaries. It is usually done to improve the value of the company's shares.

demonetization Term with two meanings:

1. It is the process of removing a particular coin or note from circulation and declaring it to be illegal tender. In the UK, the farthing, half-penny, three-penny and six-penny coins, and the pound note, have all been demonetized.
2. It is the abandonment of the use of a precious metal (gold or silver) as a monetary standard. *See* ***gold standard***.

denar Standard currency unit of Macedonia, divided into 100 deni.

denationalization The ***privatization*** of a previously nationalized industry by floating the company involved on the stock exchange and selling shares to members of the public or institutions. In the UK, denationalized industries include British Telecom, British Gas, British Airways and British Rail.

denomination The face value of something, *e.g.* the unitary classification of coinage, or the nominal value of ***bills*** and ***bonds***.

The US government issues Treasury bonds in denominations of $10,000.

Department of Trade and Industry (DTI) Government department in the UK that advises on and controls business and finance.

depauperization Relief of poverty (generally through economic growth).

deposit Goods or money placed with a bank or other financial institution, or an initial payment made on an item to reserve it, or an initial payment for something being bought on ***hire purchase*** or by means of a ***credit sale agreement***.

deposit account Bank account that pays ***interest***, but sometimes notice has to be given before funds may be withdrawn.

depositor Person who makes a ***deposit***.

deposit protection schemes Schemes that protect personal deposits (but not company deposits) in banks and building societies. Both schemes cover up to 90% of deposits up to a maximum of £20,000 deposited.

deposit rate ***Interest rate*** paid by a bank on a ***deposit account***.

deposit receipt *See* ***deposit slip***.

deposit rundown Larger than normal withdrawal of funds from a bank or other financial institution, usually in the belief that extra funds are going to be needed for some forthcoming crisis.

deposit slip Document that records the time and place of a deposit and its value. It is also termed a deposit receipt.

depository Secure place where money or goods are stored (deposited). Depositories may be distinguished from banks in that they do not transact other financial business and do not necessarily offer ready access to the assets stored. *See also* ***deposit***.

depreciation Progressive decline in real value of an ***asset*** because of use or ***obsolescence***. The concept of depreciation is widely used in ***accounting*** for the process of writing off the cost of an asset against profit over an extended period, irrespective of the real value of the asset. *See also* ***historical cost accounting***.

depreciation rate Rate at which ***depreciation*** occurs or is applied for accounting purposes.

depression Major and persistent downswing of a trade cycle, characterized by high unemployment and the under-utilization of other factors of production. A less severe downswing is known as a slump or recession.

deregulation Removal of controls and abandonment of state supervision of private enterprise. The most notable recent instance of deregulation is that of the London Stock Exchange (commonly termed the ***Big Bang***).

derivative Transferrable high-risk security such as a ***future*** or an ***option***.

derivative-based funds Type of ***unit trust*** linked to the performance of derivatives (futures and options), and therefore high-risk investments.

designated investment exchange (DIE) Foreign investment exchange that has equivalent operating standards to home exchanges, as acknowledged by the ***Securities and Investment Board*** (SIB).

designated market maker ***Market maker*** who undertakes to be present on the trading floor of the stock exchange and to maintain up-to-date two-way prices in return for certain concessions.

Desk, The Colloquial name for the Securities Department of the New York Federal Reserve Bank.

detinue Legal term meaning action to recover something that has been detained.

Deutschmark (DM) Standard currency unit of Germany, divided into 100 Pfennigs. It is often termed simply Mark.

devaluation Reduction in the relative value of a ***currency***. The devaluation may be relative to an absolute value (*e.g.* the ***gold standard***) or to other relative values (*e.g.* other currencies). The pound sterling was devalued against the US dollar in 1949 and again in 1967. *See also* ***revaluation***.

develop To begin to realize the potential of, *e.g.*, a product or company.

developing country Country that is beginning to industrialize, but which is still too poor to do so without ***foreign aid***. Developing countries are characterized by improving standards of health, wealth (standard of living), education, capital investment and productivity, and by a broadening of the economic base.

development aid Financial and material aid to a ***developing country***.

development area Economically depressed area suitable for reindustrialization. Development areas are designated by the state and incentives are provided to help to attract new businesses to the area, to encourage the relocation of existing businesses, and to enhance the prospects for employment.

development capital Funds made available (to ***venture capital*** companies and other specialists) through investment in ***equities*** and ***loan capital***.

development expenditure Money spent by a company on ***research and development***. Development expenditure may be tax deductible.

diarizing Keeping a written or computerized record of actions to be taken in the future. For example, a bank keeps a diary of customers' ***direct debits*** and ***standing orders***.

DIE Abbreviation of ***designated investment exchange***.

dies non Day that is not counted for some purpose. *E.g.* Saturday and Sunday are not counted as days of the working week. *See also* ***non-business days***.

differential The difference between two values, *e.g.* prices or salaries. *See also* ***wage differential***.

differential pricing Practice that occurs whenever there are varying prices according to differing circumstances. *E.g.* a retailer may charge more for goods or services purchased using a ***credit card*** than for those paid for in cash (or offer a discount on cash sales). The retailer must in law display signs stating that differential pricing applies.

dilution Term with two meanings:

1. It is the reduction in the skill of a workforce overall, as comparatively unskilled workers are recruited in response to a rise in ***demand***.
2. It is a deliberate increase in the number of shares on the market that has the effect of reducing the price of each individual share.

dilution of equity Reduction of individual stakes in a company by the issue of further shares. *See* ***dilution of shareholding.***

dilution of shareholding Reduction in the relative value of a share in the event of a new issue. For example, if a company has a capital of £1,000 in £10 shares, each share represents 1% of the total capital. If a new issue of 5,000 £10 shares is made, a shareholding of £10 represents only 0.16% of the firm's capital. Thus the relative power of each existing shareholder to influence corporate affairs is reduced. *See also* ***rights issue.***

dime Popular term for a US coin worth 10 cents ($^1/_{10}$ of a dollar).

diminishing Something that is declining or falling.

diminishing balance (method) Method of calculating ***depreciation*** by writing off a fixed proportion of the total residual value of an asset each year.

diminishing marginal product Alternative term for ***diminishing returns.***

diminishing returns Concept that suggests that as additional units of one factor of production are added, the relative increase in output will eventually begin to decline. *E.g.* a factory can increase its output by employing more labour, but unless the other factors of production (*e.g.* machinery) are also increased each additional employee will be working with a smaller proportion of the other, fixed, resources available.

dinar Standard currency unit in Algeria (where it is divided into 100 centimes); Bahrain, Iraq, Jordan, Kuwait and Yemen (where it equals 1000 fils); Tunisia (where it equals 1000 millimes); Bosnia-Hercegovinia and Yugoslavia (where it equals 100 paras); Libya (where it equals 1000 dirhans); and Sudan (where it equals 100 piastres).

direct Immediate or unobstructed.

direct action Attempt to take control of a company by purchasing a controlling interest of shares, rather than by negotiation with the company itself. *See also* ***dawn raid.***

direct arbitrage Foreign exchange dealings that are restricted to one centre.

direct costs Costs of materials, items or activities that are directly involved in the production of goods, and without which those goods could not be produced in the short run.

direct debit Practice of debiting a bank account with the sum owed on the authorization of the account holder, but without his or her direct involvement (*e.g.* in issuing a ***cheque*** or making a cash transfer) at the time. The essence is that it is a claim made by a creditor as opposed to a payment made by a debtor. It is a type of ***banker's order***, although the amount to be debited is not specified.

direct expenses Expenses that may be attributed to one or another factor of production. *See also* ***indirect expenses.***

directive European Union (EU) legislation that states what has to be done within a timescale, without defining how it is to be done.

direct labour Members of a company's workforce who are directly involved in the production of goods or services. *E.g.* a welder is part of the direct labour force, whereas an estimator is not.

direct mail Form of advertising and selling. Individual potential customers receive promotional material and information through the post, and order goods that are delivered by post or courier.

director One of the principals of a company, in a ***public limited company*** (plc) appointed by its shareholders. Most companies have a group of directors (the board of directors) who act collectively as the senior management of the company, being responsible to the shareholders for its efficient running and future development. The duties and legal responsibilities of a director are defined in the Companies Acts. They include the compilation of an ***annual report*** and the recommendation of an annual ***dividend*** on shares. *See also* ***board of directors.***

directorate Alternative term for a ***board of directors.***

Director of Savings Official responsible for running the ***National Savings Bank*** and its various accounts, bonds and certificates.

directors' interests Interests in a company's debentures, shares and share options held by the directors of the company, which must in law be disclosed.

directors' valuation In ***accounting***, the right of a board of directors to estimate the value of a firm's shareholding in an unquoted company. The directors' valuation is called for only if the value of the shares concerned has changed since they were purchased. *See also* ***unquoted company.***

direct placement Selling of shares directly to the public without using an ***underwriter.***

direct production System of production that does not use machinery or division of labour. In a true system of direct production, each person makes the things that he or she requires, rather than making them to sell for profit. *See also* ***indirect production***.

direct quotation Quotation of a currency exchange rate in terms of one unit of the home currency; *e.g.* £1 = 3.33 DM.

direct taxation System of taxation whereby companies and individuals pay tax on income directly to the Inland Revenue (or through an employer), as opposed to ***indirect taxation***, in which tax is added to the price of goods and services.

dirham Standard currency unit of Morocco (where it is divided into 100 centimes) and the United Arab Emirates (divided into 10 dinars).

dirty float Partly-managed floating ***exchange rate***, in which the central bank continues to intervene in the market for its own currency.

dirty money Money obtained illegally, generally through unlawful international business activities. *See also* ***black money***.

disaster recovery plan A comprehensive statement of consistent actions to be taken before, during and after a disaster. The plan is designed to provide for the continuity of operations and the availability of critical resources should a disaster occur.

disbursement Payment made on behalf of a client by a banker, solicitor, or other professional person. It is ultimately charged to the client's account.

discharge Term with two meanings:

1. It is to dismiss a member of staff from one's employment.
2. It is to pay a debt such as a ***bill of exchange***.

discharged bankrupt Person discharged from bankruptcy (*see* ***discharged in bankruptcy***). The debts of the person concerned are considered to be settled and, if solvent, he or she can begin again.

discharged bill Bill of exchange that has been paid by the drawer or drawee, or is being held by an ***acceptor***. If a holder renounces rights to the debt against an acceptor, the bill is also deemed to be discharged.

discharged in bankruptcy Occurs when the bankrupt is released from bankruptcy by the court after his or her debts have been paid, or it has been seen that all reasonable efforts have been made to do so.

disclaimer Clause in a ***contract*** that states that one of the parties does not take responsibility for some occurrence. *E.g.* the owners of many car parks advise drivers that they disclaim any responsibility for loss or damage to cars or anything contained in them.

disclosure Revealing of relevant information. The term has two major uses:

1. It is the requirement that a limited company must disclose its financial dealings and position by the publication of accounts, and deposit at Companies House lists of directors and shareholders in the company.
2. It is the requirement that parties to any contract should disclose relevant information. *E.g.* a person holding a life assurance policy must notify the assurers of his or her medical history.

discount In commerce, term with five specialized meanings:

1. It refers to the amount by which a new share issue stands below its par value. *See* ***parity***.
2. It refers to the price of a share whose ***price/earnings ratio*** is below the market average.
3. It refers to the amount by which a currency is below par on the foreign exchanges.
4. It is to make a reduction in the face value of an article (or the price being charged for it), generally in order to make a purchase more attractive to a customer.
5. On financial markets it is the charge made for cashing an immature ***bill of exchange***, the discount being proportional to the unexpired portion of the bill.

discounted cash flow (DCF) Method of assessing a company's investments according to when they are due to yield their expected returns, in order to indicate the present worth of the future sum. In this way it is possible to determine preference for one of a number of alternative investments.

discounted value If a share price falls below its par value, then the lower price is known as its discounted value.

discount house Company whose main activity is the ***discounting*** of ***bills of exchange***.

discounting Act of making a ***discount***. More specifically, it is the practice of selling a debt at a discount to an institution.

discounting bank Bank that specializes in discounting ***bills of exchange***.

discount market That part of the London money markets that involves the buying and selling of short-term ***debt*** between the commercial banks, the ***discount houses*** and the Bank of England, which acts as the ***lender of the last resort***.

discount rate Rate at which a ***bill of exchange*** is discounted. *See* ***discounting***.

discount window Method by which a bank gets short-term funds from a central bank, either by securing a loan or by issuing Treasury bills.

discretionary Something that is not compulsory, but is left to the discretion of the person or authority involved, such as a ***discretionary grant***. It is the opposite of mandatory.

discretionary account (DA) Account into which ***discretionary funds*** are placed.

discretionary fund Sum of money left with a stockbroker, to be invested at his or her discretion. *See also* ***managed fund; unit trust***.

discretionary grant Grant that is not automatically paid, but is made at the discretion of the authority concerned. *See also* ***mandatory grant***.

discriminating monopoly Monopoly in which the monopolist sells its goods or services at two different prices to two or more different sectors. *E.g.* the electricity industry may sell electricity at a cheaper rate to industrial users than to domestic users, in an attempt to prevent the larger industrial users from changing to cheaper forms of power.

disguised unemployment Also known as ***concealed unemployment***, unemployment of those who are not earning and not searching for work. *E.g.* during times of high unemployment, a housewife may wish to work but decides it is not worth trying to find a suitable job. This form of unemployment is "disguised" by the method of calculating unemployment figures in the UK. It can be said not to exist in the USA, where calculation methods enable the authorities to take such cases into account.

dishonour To refuse to accept or discharge a ***bill of exchange*** when it falls due for payment. Cheques are sometimes dishonoured ("bounced") by a bank if there are insufficient funds in the drawer's account to make the payment. *See also* ***acceptance for honour; bounced cheque***.

dishonoured cheque Cheque that a bank refuses to pay, usually because the account on which it is drawn contains insufficient funds or because payment would make the account overdrawn beyond any overdraft limit. *See also* ***bounced cheque***.

disinflation The curbing of ***inflation*** by the adoption of mild economic measures such as the restriction of ***expenditure***. Other measures include increasing ***interest rates*** and the deliberate creation of a budget surplus. Disinflation is a mild form of ***deflation***, which by contrast indicates an uncontrolled fall in prices.

disintermediation Withdrawal of a financial intermediary from a negotiation. The term may also be applied to the flow of funds from lenders to borrowers "off the balance sheet" without the intervention of an intermediary (*e.g.* a mortgage broker).

disinvestment Withdrawal or sale of an investment. Governments and companies sometimes decide to disinvest from nations whose economic or political complexion offends them.

dismissal Notice of redundancy served on an employee.

dispensation notice Instruction to a bank from the holders of a joint account to send just one statement (rather than one to each of the account holders).

disposable income That part of a person's income that he or she may dispose of in any way, *i.e.* what is left after such necessities as accommodation and food have been paid for.

disposables Non-durable goods; those that are consumed during their use. Food, drink, and fuel are all disposables.

dissaving Preference for spending rather than saving.

dissident shareholder One of a group of shareholders who have expressed their discontent with present management performance, and are determined to replace current managers.

dissolution ***Winding up*** of a company, usually by the legal process of ***liquidation***. In the case of a ***partnership***, dissolution may be occasioned by the death or retirement of one or more partners (*see* ***death of a partner***), by ***bankruptcy*** or by the expiry of a specified time period, without recourse to law.

distraint The legally-authorized seizure of ***assets*** to compel a debtor to pay a ***debt***. If the debt remains outstanding, goods obtained by distraint may be sold in order that the ***creditor*** may obtain satisfaction.

distress borrowing Situation in which a company or person is forced to borrow money even when interest rates are high.

distress merchandise Goods and assets made available for sale by a company facing or already consigned to ***bankruptcy***. Most distress merchandise is placed on the market on the orders of an official ***receiver*** in order to provide liquid sums for the payment of creditors. *See also* ***receivership***.

distributable profits Company profits that can be distributed to shareholders as dividends. For a public company, such distribution must not reduce the net assets to less than the sum of the undistributable reserves and the called-up share capital.

distributable reserves Retained company profits that can be distributed to shareholders as dividends.

distribution Term with three meanings:

1. It is the transport, allocation and placement of raw materials or goods to and from the factory to warehouses and shops.
2. It refers to payments made by a company from its profits (*e.g.* ***dividends***).
3. It is the apportioning of a ***scrip issue*** or ***rights issue*** of shares.

distribution slip Document that describes the goods that have been distributed, their location and eventual destination.

distributor Wholesaler; a person or company that acts as an agent in the distribution of goods to ***retail*** outlets.

distributor fund Offshore account that distributes 85% of the income that would be subject to ***corporation tax*** had it been based in the UK.

diversification Extension of the range of goods or services offered into new areas, either material or geographical. By extension the term may also be applied to attempts by local authorities or central government to attract a variety of industries to an area heavily dependent upon a single industry, particularly one in decline.

divestment Sale or ***liquidation*** of parts of a company, generally in an attempt to improve efficiency by cutting loss-making businesses and/or concentrating on one product or industry. Divestment is therefore the opposite process to ***merger***.

divestiture Act of ***divestment***.

RCF plc today announced the divestiture of its unprofitable subsidiary, MG *Ltd.*

dividend A share in the profits of a limited company, usually paid annually. Dividends are usually expressed as a percentage of the nominal value of a single ordinary share. Thus a payment of 10p on each £1 share would be termed a dividend of 10%. Dividends are determined by the ***directors*** of a company and are announced at the end of the ***annual general meeting*** (AGM) of the company. *See* ***nominal value; ordinary share.***

dividend cover Degree to which a dividend payment on ordinary shares is covered by profits earned. Thus a company that declares after-tax profits of £10m and makes a total dividend payment of £2m on ordinary shares is said to be "covered five times". An uncovered dividend, on the other hand, is a payment made at least partly from reserves rather than current profits. *See also* ***after-tax profits.***

divident equalization account *See* ***dividend equalization reserve.***

dividend equalization reserve Also known as the dividend equalization account, a ***reserve*** from which a company may make a dividend payment during periods of low profit or trading loss. The firm pays profits into the reserve during years of significant ***profit***. The purpose is to maintain shareholders' confidence in the company.

dividend limitation Government instructions to companies to limit increases in their dividend payments as part of a prices and incomes policy. Dividend limitation curbs the ***income*** of the shareholders and the management in the same way that wage restraints limit increases in the salaries paid to workers.

dividend mandate Mandate signed by a shareholder and delivered to a company, instructing it to pay dividends directly to a third party (generally into a bank account).

dividend per share (in pence) Expression of a dividend in pence per share rather than as a percentage of the total value of a share. Thus a 10% dividend on a share worth £1 would be termed a "10p per share dividend".

dividend policy Company policy, agreed by the board of directors regarding the allocation of profits between shareholders (in the form of dividends) and ***reserves.***

dividend restraint Policy of minimizing increases in dividend payments, generally implemented by a company wishing to build its reserves for investment and corporate growth.

dividend stripping Method of ***tax avoidance*** that makes it unnecessary for a person or company to receive dividend payments (on which tax is payable). Also called bond washing, the technique involves buying gilt-edged securities ***ex dividend*** and selling them ***cum dividend*** before the next dividend falls due.

dividend tax Form of income tax on share ***dividends***. When in operation, dividend tax is deducted by the company at source.

dividend warrant Order to a company's bankers to pay a specified dividend or interest to a shareholder or other investor.

dividend yield Yield calculated in relation to the current market price of the investment: the dividend divided by the share price. *See* ***nominal value***.

DM Abbreviation of ***Deutschmark***, the German unit of currency.

dobra Standard unit of currency of Sao Tome and Principe, divided into 100 centavos.

documentary credit *See* ***letter of credit***.

documents against acceptance (D/A) Way of paying for exported goods in which the exporter sends a bill of exchange with the shipping documents which is held, on arrival, by an agent or bank which releases the goods when the bill has been accepted.

dollar ($) Standard currency unit of the USA, divided into 100 cents. The economic predominance of post-war USA has made the US dollar the most important medium of international trade. It is also the name of the standard currency units of Anguilla, Antigua and Barbuda, Australia, the Bahamas, Barbados, Belau, Belize, Bermuda, the British Virgin Islands, Brunei, Canada, the Caymen Islands, the Cook Islands, Dominica, Fiji, Grenada, Guam, Guyana, Hong Kong, Jamaica, Kiribati, Liberia, Malaysia, the Marshall Islands, Micronesia, Montserrat, Namibia, Nauru, New Zealand, Puerto Rico, Saint Kitts and Nevis, Saint Lucia, Saint Vincent and the Grenadines, Singapore, the Solomon Islands,Taiwan, Trinidad and Tobago, Tuvalu, the Virgin Islands, the West Indies, and Zimbabwe. These currencies are referred to as Australian dollars, Hong Kong dollars, and so on if there is a risk of confusion with US dollars. All are divided into 100 cents. *See also* ***eurodollar***.

dole Informal term for any variety of social security payments, but particularly ***unemployment benefit***.

dollar gap Shortage of US dollars caused by the flow of US funds and aid to Europe in the immediate post-World War II period.

dollar glut Overabundance of US dollars on international finance markets, leading to a fall in the value of the dollar.

dollar premium Extra charge, above the official exchange rate, sometimes demanded for the purchase of US dollars.

dollar certificate of deposit Negotiable document which proves that a sum in US dollars has been deposited with a bank at a given rate of interest for a particular period (minimum of $25,000 for a minimum of 30 days).

dolphin Informal term for a person who buys shares in new issues and then sells for high profit as soon as trading opens. *See also* ***flip***.

domestic Concerning the internal economy of a nation.

domestic banking Normal banking as opposed to international banking or wholesale banking. It is also termed retail banking.

domestic credit expansion (DCE) Measurement of the growth of a nation's ***money supply*** which allows for changes in the ***balance of payments*** by deducting net foreign currency reserves from the figure for money supply itself. It is thus a measure of domestic ***liquidity***.

domestic economy Internal economy of a nation.

domestic market Market for goods and services that exists within a country, as opposed to the international market that is reached by ***exports***.

domestic production Total production of a good or goods within a nation.

domestic sales Goods sold within the country of origin, as opposed to foreign sales, which are goods sold as ***exports***.

domicile A person's place of residence for legal and tax purposes. A person domiciled in the UK is liable to pay British taxes and is subject to British law.

donation Money or other asset given by a person or organization to another person or organization (such as a charity or political party).

donee Person in receipt of a ***donation***.

dong Standard currency unit of Vietnam, divided into 100 xu.

donor Person who gives a ***donation***.

dormant account Bank account that has not had deposits or withdrawals for some time (at least a year). If the bank cannot contact the account holder, or he or she does not contact the bank, any funds are transferred to a dormant ledger held by the bank.

double bottom In the analysis of share market trends, a term that describes a price that hits a low point equal to the last low point. The prediction is that once two similar low points have been reached, the price will tend to go up. *See also* ***double top***.

double-entry book-keeping Process of recording financial transactions under two parallel headings, ***debits*** and ***credits***. *See* ***balance***.

double-figure inflation Inflation that has reached the rate of more than 10 per cent.

double option Option to either buy or sell.

double or quits Terms offered in a wager or ***speculation;*** the losing speculator offers another wager on the same terms as before, but for twice the money. As a result, the winning speculator either doubles the sum earned or is left in the same position as before. Offering and acceptance of such terms implies that each of the two possibilities has an equal chance of occurring.

double pricing Practice of displaying two prices on goods, usually to show the prospective customer that the price has (apparently) been reduced.

double time Rate of overtime payments to workers that is double the normal hourly rate.

It doesn't worry me that I sometimes have to work on Sundays and Bank Holidays, because I am paid double time.

double top In the analysis of share market trends, a price that rises twice to similar high points. The prediction is that after the double top, the price will tend to fall. *See also* ***double bottom***.

Dow Jones Industrial Average Often called simply the Dow Jones, a security price index used on the New York Stock Exchange and issued by the US firm of Dow Jones & Co.

down and dirty Describing the practice of arranging, for a company in financial difficulties, a refinancing package that would severely dilute the holdings of minor shareholders were they not to participate. *See also* ***dilution***.

downgrade To reduce the status of someone or something. *E.g.* a person downgrades his or her shareholding by selling part of it.

down-market Describing something that is of poor quality and often low-priced.

downside The amount a person stands to lose when taking a risk. *E.g.* the amount by which a share price may fall, or the amount a person is liable to lose by making a speculative investment.

downsize To reduce the size of a company's workforce (*i.e.* making employees redundant), usually to make financial savings.

downstream Describing an economic activity in or close to the ***retail*** sector, *i.e.* one involving the distribution and selling of goods and services. The term is frequently applied to the oil industry, in which context the petrol station is downstream and the oil rig is ***upstream***.

downtick Describing a transaction concluded at a lower price than a similar previous transaction. It is also a small and temporary fall in the price of a share. *See also* ***uptick***.

downturn Point at which something begins to fall; *e.g.* a share price that has been rising and begins to fall, or productivity that is beginning to decline.

DPS Abbreviation of ***dividend per share (in pence)***.

Dr Abbreviation of ***debtor***.

drachma Standard currency unit in Greece, divided in to 100 lepta.

draft Written ***order*** from a customer to a financial institution, requesting that money is paid from the customer's account to a third party (*see* ***bank draft***). To draft is to draw up any document, especially a ***contract***.

dragon Informal term for a newly industrialized eastern country (such as Indonesia, Malaysia and Thailand).

dollar draft ***Cheque*** or ***bank draft*** denominated in US ***dollars***.

draw To write a bill of exchange, cheque or promissory note. The person who does so is the drawer.

drawback Repayment of customs and excise ***duty*** on certain goods to an exporter who has already paid duty on imported raw materials. *E.g.*

drawback may be claimed on tobacco imported to make cigarettes when the cigarettes are then exported. *See also* ***re-export***.

drawdown Sum of money borrowed.

The drawdown on that project was $100,000.

drawee Person or company to whom a ***bill of exchange*** is addressed, *e.g.* the bank ***account*** on which a ***cheque*** is drawn, or the ***acceptor*** of a ***bill of exchange***.

drawer Person who draws a ***bill of exchange***, *i.e.* who orders payment (from the drawee); *e.g.* the person who signs a ***cheque***.

drawer deceased *See* ***death of an account holder***.

drawing account Bank account from which funds may be withdrawn at will. *See also* ***current account***.

drip-feed Steady payment of money at regular intervals. It is usually a pejorative term that implies that the recipient is dependent on the payments. It is often applied to ***foreign aid*** to underdeveloped countries. The term is also used by venture capitalists for ***venture capital*** payments made to a start-up company in stages.

drive Concerted effort.

drop-dead date Date on which it is expected that a troubled company will run out of funds.

drop-dead fee Payment offered to a bidder by the ***target*** of a (usually ***takeover***) bid in an effort to induce the bidder to withdraw the bid.

drop-dead rate Amount demanded by a would-be corporate ***raider*** to withdraw the bid.

drop lock Loan stock issued when a specific ***interest rate*** is reached. The purpose is to convert short-term borrowing into long-term loans. *See* ***loan stock***.

DTI Abbreviation of ***Department of Trade and Industry***.

dual capacity Stock exchange system that makes no distinction between the functions of ***stockbrokers*** and ***jobbers***. One person (called a ***market maker***) may therefore both buy and sells stocks and shares on the ***exchange***. The London Stock Exchange was converted to dual capacity in October 1986. *See* ***Big Bang; single capacity***.

dual control Situation in which two people are required to fulfill a single function. In a bank, two people may have to sign drafts for more than a certain amount, and two officers may hold keys, both of which are needed to open a safe.

dud Informal term for something that is worthless or forged.

She was very angry to find that she had accepted a dud cheque.

due Something that is owed to someone, or something that belongs to someone by right.

Last Friday, my rent for next month became due.

Each year she paid her dues to the trade union.

See also ***due date***.

due date Date on which a ***bill of exchange*** is due to be paid. Instruments not payable on demand, on sight or on presentation are allowed three ***days of grace***.

dull market Market on which little activity is taking place. *See also* ***valium picnic***.

dummy Something that is false and has no substance.

I discovered that it was a dummy company.

dumping Sale of surplus goods overseas at extremely low prices.

Several countries in the Pacific basin have been dumping electronic components onto Western markets.

duopoly ***Market*** in which there are only two competing companies. Because competition between duopolists is particularly fierce and destructive, there tends to be some form of implicit or explicit agreement to share the market, e.g. on a regional basis. *See also* ***monopoly***.

duopsony ***Market*** in which there are only two purchasers of a type of goods or services, but a number of competing suppliers. *See also* ***duopoly; monopsony***.

durable Describing goods that are not consumed by their use but which endure for a reasonable period of time. Some manufacturers of durables incorporate some form of ***obsolescence*** to ensure a continuity of demand. *See also* ***disposable***.

Dutch auction Type of auction in which the seller begins by proposing a high price and gradually begins to lower it until someone agrees to buy.

duty Broadly, any ***tax*** levied by a public authority, particularly that imposed on imports, exports and manufactured goods. *See also* ***Customs and Excise***.

duty-free Describing goods on which no ***duty*** is charged. In the UK, the term is most usually applied to goods which, although sold elsewhere in the UK, are available (from duty-free shops and ports) to those about to enter or leave the country. It is a condition that the goods are for consumption overseas or for personal consumption. The EU wishes to end the practice.

duty-paid Authenticated statement attached to goods on which duty has been paid, to facilitate their passage through customs.

dynamics Analysis of the behaviour of variable elements.

There have been changes in the dynamics of stock exchange trading since Big Bang.

dynamization Giving new dynamism (drive) to a company, generally by importing a new management team.

E

eagle US gold coin. There have been various eagles, weighing up to 1 ounce.

E & OE Abbreviation of ***errors and omissions excepted***.

early bargain Deal struck on the stock exchange after the exchange has closed and considered to be among the first transactions of the following day. Early bargains are also known as after-hours dealings.

early stage investment Funds, usually provided by a ***venture capital*** company, that finance the start-up of a new business.

early withdrawal penalty Penalty charged for withdrawal of funds from a fixed-term investment before the investment matures.

earned income Income received in exchange for labour, rather than derived from investments (the definition does, however, include some pension and social security payments).

earnest money Either part payment (***deposit***) made on goods or services, showing that the buyer is serious about buying; or the ***margin*** on a futures market.

earning Act of generating ***income***.

earning capacity Value of an employee's services to a company. *E.g.* the earning capacity of an advertising sales executive is equivalent to the ***revenue*** he or she brings in. The term is also applied more colloquially to describe the maximum wage that can be earned in a specific job.

earning potential Net present value of a person's expected future earnings. Earning potential is as a key determinant of ***creditworthiness***.

earning power Value of a person's services at a specified time and in a free market. Earning power is indicated by the salary that could be commanded if the person were to change jobs.

earnings Return, monetary or otherwise, for human effort. Broadly earnings may be defined as wages plus any bonuses (*e.g.* for overtime worked). The term is also used to describe the income of a company.

earnings before interest and tax (EBIT) Company's profit before deductions are made for tax and any interest owed.

earnings per share (in pence) (EPS) Method of expressing the ***income*** of a company, arrived at by dividing the annual net income attributable to the shareholders by the number of shares. Earnings per share can then be used to calculate the ***price/earnings ratio*** of a company.

earnings yield Hypothetical figure that provides a reliable measurement of the worth of an investment. It is reached by relating a company's divisible net earnings to the market price of the investment. Sometimes, with reference to fixed-interest ***securities***, the term is used interchangeably with ***flat yield***.

earn-out Employee incentive scheme whereby the employee is offered ***share*** options that give him or her an interest in the company for which he or she works.

EAS Abbreviation for ***Enterprise Allowance Scheme***.

easement Legal term that refers to the right of somebody other than the landowner to use a piece of land without taking anything from it. Right of way is an example of easement. *See also* ***profit a prendre***.

easy market Market in which there are few buyers; prices are therefore low.

easy money Money borrowed at a low rate of ***interest***, usually consisting of funds made available by authorities wishing to encourage economic activity. It is also known as cheap money. *See also* ***tight money***.

EBIT Abbreviation of ***earnings before interest and tax***.

echelon Level in the hierarchy of a company.

He rose very quickly to the higher echelons.

EC Abbreviation of ***European Commission*** and of ***European Community***, now replaced by the ***European Union*** (EU).

ECGD Abbreviation of ***Export Credits Guarantee Department***.

ECI Abbreviation of ***equity capital*** for industry.

econometrics Branch of statistics that uses mathematical models to test economic hypotheses, describe economic relationships, and forecast economic trends. Econometrics is employed to produce correlated quantitative data rather than to prove economic causation.

economic Term with two meanings:

1. It is something that concerns the study of economics.

2. It is something that is cost-effective.

economic cost Total expense involved in undertaking a certain activity. Economic cost includes ***accounting cost*** and ***opportunity cost***.

economic development Per capita increase in national income. Broadly, the rate of economic development is a way of expressing the growth of an economy and can be used to determine the relative growth of a number of competing or allied economies. The rate of economic development is often used as a simple guide to the health of an economy.

economic indicator One of several measurable variables used to study change in an economy. In addition to the variables mentioned above, economists study production indexes, unemployment trends, the amount of overtime worked and levels of ***taxation***.

economic profit Profit calculated in ***accounting*** as the difference between ***income*** and ***cost***. In economics, however, economic profit also takes into account ***opportunity cost***.

economic refugee Person who leaves his or her country for economic (rather than political) reasons. The term embraces both ***tax exiles*** and those who leave a country in which employment prospects are bleak. Irish emigrants to the USA and (in the post-war period) British emigrants to Australia were economic refugees.

economy Term with two meanings:

1. It is the financial and productive apparatus of a nation.
2. It is (the exercise of) frugality.

economy drive Effort to improve the efficiency of a company by cutting unnecessary ***expenditure*** and costs and making better use of resources.

economy of scale Reduction in the average cost of production made possible by the large size of a firm or industry. Internal economies of scale are defined as those enjoyed by a single large company or organization and are, broadly, made possible by the distribution of indirect costs and improvements in technology, which increase the optimum level of output.

External economies of scale are those associated with an industry or location. *E.g.*, a concentration of shipbuilding companies on a river leads to the creation of a large pool of skilled labour which can be drawn on if one company wishes to expand.

econospeak Economic jargon.

ECU Abbreviation of *European Currency Unit.*

ECU Treasury Bill *Treasury Bill* whose denomination is in *ECUs*.

EDP Abbreviation of *electronic data processing.*

EEC Abbreviation of *European Economic Community*, now repalced by the *European Union* (EU).

effective Actual, real or capable of producing a desired outcome.

effective date Date on which a *contract* becomes effective.

effective demand The quantity of an article or service actually purchased at a particular price. *See also* ***pure demand.***

effective exchange rate Average of a country's exchange rate and those of its important trading partners. The currency rates are weighted to take into account the relative levels of trade.

effective yield Yield calculated as a percentage of the price of an investment.

efficiency Measure of the use of resources. High efficiency is achieved by getting the most output from the least input.

EFT Abbreviation of *electronic funds transfer*.

EFTA Abbreviation of *European Free Trade Association.*

EFTPOS Abbreviation of *electronic funds transfer at point of sale.*

EGM Abbreviation of *extraordinary general meeting*, any meeting of company shareholders except the *annual general meeting* (AGM).

EIB Abbreviation of *European Investment Bank.*

elasticity Ability of a bank to meet demands for currency and credit when needed and to reduce their availability when this is needed (*e.g.* when there is overexpansion).

electronic banking Banking activities accessed by using a computer, employing *modems* and telephones.

electronic cottage Popular US term for the home of someone who makes use of computer communications to enable him or her to dispense with travelling to an office.

electronic crime Criminal activities conducted with the help of computers. It generally involves breaking into other computer systems (hacking) via a ***modem***, often by using special programs to run combinations of letters and numbers until a password is discovered. Expert users can then manipulate records and data to their own advantage.

electronic data interchange (EDI) Method by which companies or people communicate with their banks, clients and suppliers using computers. Banks may be ***on-line*** to each other; other users may employ ***modems*** and telephone lines.

electronic data processing Collection, interpretation and transmission of data by electronic means. Most electronic data processing is performed by computers, which receive information inputs from their own keyboards or from other computers, interpret it using computer programs and transmit it electronically via cables (***on-line***) or telephone lines (using a ***modem***).

electronic funds transfer (EFT) Transfer of funds by computer. *See* ***chequeless society***.

electronic funds transfer at point of sale (EFTPOS) Automatic, computerized transfer of funds from a retail customer's bank account to the retailer's bank account using a ***credit card*** or ***debit card***.

electronic mail (e-mail) Service provided by a number of organizations (notably Prestel in the UK and Internet worldwide) that allows two computer users linked by ***modem*** to deposit messages on each other's machines.

electronic point of sale (EPOS) Retail computer system used mainly in shops and stores that debits a customer's ***credit card*** at the till, and simultaneously updates the retailer's stock records.

elephant Informal term for a large corporate entity that is slow but dominant and displays a tendency towards the creation of monopolies. *See* ***monopoly***.

eligible bank Bank that is entitled to discount acceptances at the Bank of England.

eligible reserves For a US bank, its cash held plus its reserves at the local Federal Reserve Bank.

Elves of Wall Street US banking and stockbroking community centred on ***Wall Street***. The term is an Americanization of Harold Wilson's description of the Swiss banking community as the ***gnomes*** of Zurich.

e-mail Abbreviation of ***electronic mail***.

emalangeni Standard currency unit of Swaziland, divided into 100 cents.

embargo Prohibition of the import or export of specified goods from or to a particular country or bloc, generally for political reasons.

embezzlement Theft by an employee of money belonging to his or her employer.

EMCF Abbreviation of ***European Monetary Cooperation Fund***.

EMI Abbreviation of ***European Monetary Institute***.

emolument *Salary*, particularly that paid to the holder of high office.

employee buy-out *Takeover* of a company by employees who have purchased a majority of its shares.

employee share ownership plan (ESOP) Way in which employees can purchase shares in the company for which they work. *See also* ***earn-out***.

employer Person or company that employs a workforce in exchange for *wages* and *salaries*.

employment The act of employing somebody, the provision of work, or the state of having a job.

employment bureau Business that acts as an intermediary between employers and employees, supplying labour in exchange for a *commission* payment by the employer.

emptor Purchaser.

EMS Abbreviation of ***European Monetary System***.

EMU Abbreviation of ***European Monetary Union***.

encashment Exchanging a cheque, money order or postal order for cash.

encoding Applying coded numbers (using ***magnetic ink character recognition***) to a cheque or other credit document so that it can be "read" and processed by a computer.

encryption *See* ***data security***.

endorse To sign one's name on a ***bill of exchange*** (e.g. a ***cheque***) to certify its validity.

endorsee Person who receives the value of a cheque through *endorsement*.

endorsement Term (which in banking may be spelled ***indorsement***) with two meanings:

1. It is a signature or explanatory statement on a document. ***Open cheques*** cashed at a bank or transferred by the payee to a third party must bear the payee's endorsement on the reverse.
2. It is a confirmatory statement.

endorser Person who signs an ***endorsement***.

enforcement order Court order dealing with default on a loan subject to the Consumer Credit Act (1974). *See also* ***default notice***.

enterprise Any undertaking, but particularly a bold or remarkable one, or the quality of boldness and imagination in an undertaking.

He showed great enterprise in developing an entirely new market.

Enterprise Allowance Scheme (EAS) UK government scheme set up to encourage the establishment of new businesses by the unemployed by offering, among other incentives, grants and tax concessions.

Enterprise Investment Scheme (EIS) UK government scheme of 1994 that allows relief when shares in a company (not quoted on the Stock Exchange) are issued on subscription. It replaced the former Business Expansion Scheme (BES).

EIS *See* ***Enterprise Investment Scheme***.

enterprise zone Geographical area in which economic activity is promoted by the government. Small businesses are encouraged, and the relocation of firms and industries to enterprise zones is helped by the provision of ***incentives***. *See also* ***Enterprise Allowance Scheme***.

entertainment allowance Amount an executive is allowed to spend on the entertainment of clients or prospective clients during the course of his or her business.

entertainment expenses The expense of entertaining business associates and potential clients, *e.g.* the cost of meals in restaurants.

entrepreneur Person who controls a commercial enterprise – the risk-taker and profit-maker – the person who assembles the factors of production and supervises their combination. The term also has the connotation of someone who has an idea and then finds the money to back it.

entrepreneurial veteran Entrepreneur with extensive experience of business. Often, it is someone who has taken many risks successfully in the past.

entrepreneurial virgin Entrepreneur with little experience.

entry Term with two meanings:

1. It is the appearance of a company on a certain market.
2. It is an item of information entered onto a record, *e.g.* in double-entry ***book-keeping***.

entry and exit Term that refers to the appearance of companies in an industry and the disappearance of other companies, as new companies are established and others diversify, go into ***liquidation***, or merely cease to trade.*See* ***barrier to entry***.

entry charge Cost of entry into a building, market, etc. Stock exchanges levy entry charges on firms applying for a listing.

EPOS Abbreviation of ***electronic point of sale***.

EPS Abbreviation of ***earnings per share (in pence)***.

equalization Return on ***capital*** invested in a ***unit trust***. All investors in a trust receive an equal sum per unit held, although some may only have invested in the period since the last ***distribution***. The distribution paid on the latter's stock therefore comprises the ***dividend*** and an equalization that brings the return up to par. *See* ***parity***.

equalization of estates Equal distribution of an ***estate*** among two or more parties. Equalization of estates normally results from a court case in which a beneficiary applies unsuccessfully for a greater share of the estate, the court ruling that all beneficiaries have equal rights.

equitable lien Lien that arises from a dispute over ***equity***.

equities Alternative term for ***ordinary shares***. Equities entitle their holder to share in the issuing company's profits. Ordinary shareholders bear the ultimate risk, and receive payment in liquidation only when all other claims have been satisfied.

equity Term with four meanings:

1. It refers to the ordinary share capital (risk capital) of a company. *See* ***equities***.
2. It is the residual value of the ***variation margins*** and ***initial margins*** of a liquidated ***future***.
3. It is the residual value of common ***stock*** over the debit balance of a margin account.

4. It is the difference between the market value of a property and the outstanding mortgage on it.
5. It is used to describe the concept of fairness, of central importance to a branch of law distinct from common law, and as such it has a significant effect on all kinds of contracts, dealings and trusts.

equity capital Capital of a company that belongs to the owners of the company (in many cases, holders of ordinary shares), rather than capital provided by owners of ***fixed-interest securities***. *See* ***equity***.

equity dilution Reduction in the unit value of ***ordinary shares*** effected by a ***bonus issue***.

equity gearing Ratio of a company's borrowing to its ***equity***.

equity play Any investment strategy operated on the stock market.

ergonomics Study of workers and the choices that confront them in ordinary working situations. Ergonomics has as its goal an increase in the efficiency of the workforce and therefore in productivity. *See also* ***time and motion***.

ERM Abbreviation of ***exchange rate mechanism***.

errors and omissions excepted (E & OE) Denial of responsibility for clerical errors and omissions, often included in invoices as a safeguard.

escalator clause Also known as an escalation clause, condition of a long-term contract that sets out the agreement concerning rising costs *e.g.* of raw materials and labour.

escape clause In a contract, clause that allows one or other party to withdraw from the contract should certain events take place. *E.g.* in a ***lease***, it is possible to have a clause that allows the ***lessee*** to withdraw should the ***lessor*** increase the ***rent***.

ESCB Abbreviation of ***European System of Central Banks***.

escheat Confiscation of a property. Escheat is a legal doctrine that states that property or titles revert to the crown in the event that the owner or holder dies intestate and without heirs. *See also* ***intestacy***.

escrow Document held in ***trust*** by a third party. *E.g.* deeds and titles may be held in escrow until a person reaches the age of majority, or until some specified condition has been met.

escrow account Bank account for holding foreign earnings from export sales, for use in making purchases abroad. The term is also used for an account whose accumulated funds are used for paying insurance premiums, taxes, etc.

escudo Standard currency unit of Cape Verde and Portugal, divided into 100 centavos.

establishment charge Also called establishment fee, the overheads of a department store or shopping centre which are divided up and paid by the individual departments or shops. Establishment charges include rent, rates, taxes, light, and heating.

estate Term with two meanings:

1. It is the residual possessions of someone who has died.
2. It is land, most especially a large area of land owned by one person.

estimate Approximate valuation of an uncertain quantity. It may be an approximate price quoted by a company before it undertakes work. In making such an estimate, the firm binds itself to complete the work at that price unless there is a change in the price of some key variable. An estimate therefore differs from a contractually-binding ***quotation***. *E.g.* a printer's estimate could be revised if an increase occurred in the cost of paper.

The term also refers to UK government documents setting out proposed ***expenditure*** that accompany requests to Parliament for funds (*e.g.* the naval estimates).

estoppel Legal restrictions on a person's actions. The law insists that a person must bear liability for previous actions. Estoppel is generally used to prevent a denial of responsibility. *E.g.* the parties to a ***contract*** cannot subsequently claim that they were unaware of its conditions.

ETF Abbreviation of ***electronic transfer of funds***.

ethical Describing an action that conforms to the moral constraints of an industry or society. "Professional ethics" restrict a number of undesirable practices that are not strictly illegal. *E.g.* it is unethical but not illegal for a ***stockbroker*** to advise his or her clients to buy a ***share*** when the stockbroker fully intends to sell his or her own holding.

EU Abbreviation of ***European Union***.

euro Standard currency unit of the European Monetary Union (*see **European Monetary System***).

euroaussie Popular term for an Australian government bond traded ***offshore***, but not necessarily in Europe.

Eurobank Bank that deals in ***eurocurrency***.

eurobond Medium- or long-term bearer bond denominated in a *eurocurrency*. Eurobonds are issued by governments or multinational companies. The eurobond market developed in the 1960s and is independent of the stock market. *See* ***bearer bond***.

Eurocard *Credit card* issued by *Mastercard*.

eurocheque *Cheque* issued by an administrative consortium of European Union banks that may be cashed (without additional charge) at EU banks outside the country of origin.

Euroclear Clearing house for *eurobonds*, set up in Brussels in 1968.

eurocredit Loan made in a *eurocurrency*.

eurocurrency Currency of any nation held *offshore* in a European country. The eurocurrency markets deal in very large-scale loans and deposits rather than the purchase or sale of *foreign exchange*.

eurocurrency deposit Bank account holding European currency deposited by a person or company that is not resident in the currency's country.

eurodollar deposit Bank account holding US dollars deposited by a person or company that is not resident in the USA.

eurodollars US dollars held outside the USA, particularly those circulating in Europe. The post-war economic ascendancy of the USA has made the eurodollar an international currency medium. *See also* ***eurocurrency***.

euromarket *Market* in which *eurocurrency* is traded.

European Bank for Reconstruction and Development (EBRD) Financial institution, established in London in 1990, which encourages open-market practices and private enterprise in Central and Eastern Europe.

European Banking Federation Organization of European bankers dedicated to pursuing the aims of the Treaty of Rome, as far as they affect their business.

European Central Bank (ECB) EU central bank, proposed in 1995 and due to be established in 1988 and functional by 1998, as formulated by the Maastricht Treaty. It will deal with the single European currency (euro) and lay down monetary policy throughout the EU.

European Commission (EC) Major institution of the EU, established in 1967, responsible for implementing the Treaty of Rome. It introduces EU legislation and reconciles disagreements between members.

European Community (EC) Short form of European Economic Community (EEC), now called the ***European Union*** (EU).

European Currency Unit (ECU) Unit of account in use by the European Economic Community (EEC) from 1979 and now by the ***European Union*** (EU). The value of the ECU is calculated by taking a weighted average of the current value of EU member-states' own currencies. It exists only on paper, but is used to settle intra-Union debts and in the calculation of Union budgets. Because it is an inherently stable currency, the ECU is increasingly favoured in the international money markets and as a medium for international trade.

European Economic Community (EEC) Association of some twelve European nations that were joined by a customs union and committed to the promotion of free trade within the boundaries of the community, now renamed the ***European Union*** (EU). It was often abbreviated to European Community (EC) and was originally known as the Common Market.

European Exchange Rate Mechanism *See* ***Exchange Rate Mechanism*** (ERM).

European Free Trade Association (EFTA) Trade association, established in 1960 between several west European countries, some of whom left when they joined the European Union.

European Investment Bank (EIB) Bank established in 1958 with headquarters in Brussels, administered by the Finance Ministers of its member countries. Its main business is making loans, financed mainly by public bond issues.

European Monetary Agreement (EMA) Agreement that allows currencies of European member states to be traded without restriction. It was made by the then Organization for European Economic Cooperation (now the OECD) in 1958.

European Monetary Cooperation Fund (EMCF) Fund established in 1973 and used mainly to intervene in foreign exchange markets to support currencies of member states (on request).

European Monetary Institute (EMI) Institute created in 1991 under the Maastricht Treat to manage currency reserves of EU central banks, with a view towards a single monetary policy and the use of the ECU.

European Monetary System (EMS) System established in 1979 for stabilizing exchange rates between EU member states (*see* ***Exchange***

E

Rate Mechanism). It can also be seen as a step towards the ***European Central Bank*** (ECB) and a single currency as part of European Monetary Union.

European Monetary Union (EMU) *See **European Monetary System**.*

European Settlements Office (ESO) Settlement system for ECU bills of exchange founded by the Bank of England in 1993. Its members have terminals ***on-line*** to the ESO, enabling same-day real-time settlements.

European snake Method that lasted for a year (1972-1973) by which the ***Inner Six*** EEC (now EU) countries agreed to limit to 2.25% (up or down) variations in exchange rates against the US dollar.

European System of Central Banks (ESCB) Projected EU banking system made up of the central banks of member states and the ***European Central Bank*** (ECB).

European Union (EU) Association of European nations formerly known as the European Economy Community (EEC) or European Community (EC), and before that the Common Market. It is intended that in the long run all the factors of production may be moved within the community at will, and remaining customs barriers are expected to be removed some time in the near future. The EU operates a protectionist policy by maintaining common tariffs on imports, and generates a substantial portion of its income from import duties and value-added tax. In finance, its committed aims include a ***European Monetary System***, and all that it entails.

euroyen Japanese currency held ***offshore***. *See also **eurocurrency**.*

eurosclerosis Popular term for a "seizure" (breakdown) in the ***euromarkets*** caused by ***illiquidity*** or some other financial panic.

event of default In a loan agreement, a clause that if breached requires repayment of the loan immediately.

ex ante Latin for "from before": what is expected to be the position after some future event. *See also **ex post**.*

exceptional items Below-the-line ***costs*** and ***revenues*** that arise outside the normal business activities of a quoted company. The sale or purchase of new buildings or plant are examples of exceptional items.

excess capacity Capacity to produce goods over and above the current rate. Excess capacity is more strictly used to denote the increase in production necessary to bring the average cost to a minimum.

excess profits tax Tax paid on a company's profit over and above a level that is thought to be normal. These profits are caused by economic conditions which favour the company but act against the interests of the majority.

exchange Term with two meanings:

1. It is to give one thing and take an equivalent in return.
2. It is any place where goods or stocks are traded.

exchange control Control of foreign exchange dealings by the government, either by means of restrictions on trade or by direct intervention in the market. Exchange controls help a government to exert some influence over the international value of its own currency. In the UK, exchange controls were abolished in 1979.

exchange dealings Trading of stocks, shares and other financial instruments on an exchange.

exchange equalization account Account held by the Bank of England since 1932 that holds the Treasury's gold reserves and foreign currency. It is used to buy foreign currencies to support sterling.

exchange exposure Extent of the risk that results from quoting assests or liabilities in a foreign currency, because variations in the ***exchange rate*** can affect the values.

exchanger Person who exchanges one currency for another.

exchange gain Profit made by a importer if there is a favourable change in the ***exchange rate***.

exchange loss Loss made by an importer if there is an unfavourable change in the ***exchange rate***.

exchange permit Document needed by an importer's government that allows the importer to exchange his or her own country's currency into another currency (to pay the seller abroad).

exchange rate The price at which one currency may be exchanged for another. Such transactions may be carried out on either the spot or forward markets, and are usually conducted either to permit investment abroad or to pay for imports. There is, in addition, considerable speculation on the exchange rates. *See* ***forward market; spot market***.

Exchange Rate Mechanism (ERM) EU regulation that limits variations in the exchange rates of its member states to within close defined limits. It is a vital feature of the ***European Monetary System*** (EMS). Britain (and Italy) left the ERM in 1992.

exchange rate spread Difference between the price paid for foreign currency and what it is sold for.

exchange restrictions *Exchange control* that enables a government to limit the sale or purchase of foreign or domestic currency, usually in order to maintain the *exchange rate* for its own currency at an artificial level.

Exchequer Broadly, the central depository of government funds. As the department charged with the supervision of the nation's economic affairs, the Treasury is responsible for ensuring that all monies due to the government are paid into the Exchequer, and all spending approved by parliament is paid for from Exchequer funds.

excise duty Duty levied on home-produced goods, either to control consumption and thus influence spending, or to raise revenue. Goods that currently attract excise duty in the UK are alcohol, petrol and tobacco.

exercise notice Notice issued when the holder of an *option* wishes to take up his or her right either to buy or to sell the security for which the option has been agreed.

exclusive agreement Agreement whereby an agent is authorized to act as sole agent in representing a particular company or product.

ex coupon Stock that does not give the purchaser the right to the next interest payment due to be paid on it.

ex dividend Stock that does not give the purchaser the right to the next *dividend* payment, or to any dividend payment due within a specified period, generally the next calendar month. However, he or she does have the right to receive subsequent dividends.

executive Person charged with decision-making, specifically a member of the management of a company.

executive director Also called a working director, a company director who is an employee of the company and therefore involved in the day-to-day management of the company.

executive share option Allocation of shares to a company's executives or rights to buy shares at less than market value, used as an incentive or reward for senior employees.

executor Person appointed to see that the terms of a will or bequest are carried out.

exemplary damages Punitive damages awarded in an attempt to compensate for damage to an intangible thing (such as feelings or reputation) or to deter others from repeating the action that resulted in the award.

exercise To make use of a right or option.

exercise notice Formal notification that a ***call option*** is to be taken up. The price paid is known as the exercise price or ***striking price***.

exercise price Alternative term for ***striking price***.

ex factory A near synonym for ***ex warehouse***, indicating that the goods concerned are collected from the manufacturer's factory rather than his warehouse. The manufacturer therefore pays no storage costs.

ex-gratia Describing a payment made in thanks, *e.g.* a tip, or ***golden handshake*** payment to a retiring worker.

ex-growth Euphemism for decline.

exhaustive events Set of possible events that collectively cover every possible occurrence in a given context. It is a useful concept in corporate planning.

exit To leave a ***market*** by selling all relevant stocks and shares, or to cease production.

ex new Alternative term for ***ex rights***.

ex officio By virtue of office. A person may gain an authority in one area because he or she holds an office in another.

expansion Development or growth of a business, either by ***takeover*** or ***merger***, or by an increase in sales, production or investment by a firm.

expectations Prospects; that which is anticipated. Expectations of future business activity are one of the most significant influences on ***investment*** and thus have a significant effect on the level of unemployment.

expenditure Money spent on attaining some object.

expense account Sum of money that an employee can spend on personal expenses (such as travel and entertainment) in order to do his or her job.

expenses Costs incurred by a business or individual in the course of normal activities.

expiry date Date on which an agreement lapses.

exploding warrant Warrant introduced in order to dilute the shareholding of a company ***raider*** during a ***takeover bid***. It is also known as a springing warrant.

export To sell goods and services outside the country of origin, or a term that refers to the goods or services themselves. *See also* ***import***.

Export Credits Guarantee Department UK government department, established in 1991 and partly privatized, that makes available export credit insurance and guarantees to repay banks that give credit (over two years or more) to exporters. *See also* ***buyer credit***.

export declaration Statement provided to the Customs and Excise detailing the cost, price, destination and nature of goods leaving the country. *See* ***excise***.

export duty Tax levied on exports. Because export duties tend to discourage export and adversely affect the ***balance of payments***, they are seldom raised.

export house Company that assists other companies involved in the export trade, either by providing short- or medium-term credit (*e.g.* an export finance house) or by acting as an overseas agent for companies that do not maintain their own representatives in the countries to which they export.

export incentive Government incentives to promote exports. They include direct-tax incentives, subsidies, favourable terms for insurance and the provision of cheap credit.

export leasing Practice of selling goods for export to a leasing company in the country of origin. The leasing company ships them overseas and leases them to a foreign customer.

export restitution EU term for subsidies paid to member food exporters.

ex post Describing the position that arises after a certain event has taken place. *See also* ***ex ante***.

exposure Extent of ***risk***.

expropriation Dispossession; the confiscation of, *e.g.*, an ***estate*** or ***property***.

ex quay Describing goods that are sold for collection after they have been unloaded from a ship. The seller therefore pays freightage and the charge of unloading.

ex rights Also known as ex new, a stock exchange term for shares that are sold minus the right to take up ***bonus issues***.

ex ship Describing goods sold to a purchaser who must pay the cost of unloading. The seller therefore pays only the cost of freightage.

extended Prolonged or offered.

extended credit Credit that is to be repaid over a very long period of time. *See also* ***long credit***.

external Something that is outside, such as external trade.

external account Account held with a UK bank by a non-resident.

external trade Trade with countries other than one's own.

extractive industry Companies and people involved in primary production, *e.g.* fishing, farming and mining. *See also* ***primary production***.

extraordinary Describing additional items, expenditure, etc., acquired or incurred in addition to normal business.

extraordinary items Non-recurrent material items listed below the line on a ***balance sheet***, such as the sale or purchase of premises.

extrinsic value Constituent part of the value of a traded ***option*** not calculated by difference in ***market price*** to ***exercise price***. Extrinsic value is governed by such factors as time to run and the volatility of the market concerned.

ex warehouse Price exclusive of all delivery costs. The purchaser must arrange for the collection, loading and delivery of the goods concerned from the seller's warehouse.

ex works Price exclusive of all delivery costs except those of loading. The purchaser must arrange for the collection and delivery of the goods concerned.

F

face value Alternative term for ***nominal value***.

facility Loan made available by a bank to a company or individual. *See also* ***agency fee***.

facsimile transmission *See* ***fax***.

facsimile signature Signature applied using a rubber stamp, a practice unliked by banks because of possible misuse.

factor Company that undertakes ***factoring*** or, in Scotland, the manager of an estate of land.

factoring Activity of managing the ***trade debts*** of another firm. Commonly, a company sells due debts to a factor at a discount. The factor then makes a profit by recovering the debts at a price nearer the face value. Factoring relieves companies of the burden of administering debts and gives them access to ready cash before payment is due. *See also* ***nominal value***.

factor of production Collective term for those things necessary for production to take place. Factors of production are most usually divided into the following categories: capital, labour and land.

facultative endorsement Special endorsement to a ***bill of exchange*** that waives a duty toward the endorser. *See* ***waive***.

failure investment Practice of buying shares in companies that are doing badly, in the hope that their performance will improve.

fair copy Copy of a document, including any alterations and revisions. Also known as final copy.

fair price provisions (US **fair price amendments)** Clause in a corporate charter whereby a buyer of the company's shares must pay the same amount or make the same consideration for all shares purchased. It is used as a defensive tactic against bootstrapping (*see* ***bootstrap***). Fair-price provisions are also price controls, generally instituted by a government, that guarantee fair prices to the consumer by ensuring that the manufacturer and retailer make reasonable rather than excessive profits.

fallen angel Company, or shares in a company, whose ***rating*** has recently fallen significantly.

family company Company founded by and owned almost exclusively by members of one family.

fan club Group of investors in the same shares, but who do not co-operate as a *concert party*.

Fannie Mae Name referring to the Federal National Mortgage Association.

FAPA Abbreviation of Fellow of the Association of Authorized Public Accountants.

FAS Abbreviation of *free alongside ship*.

FASB Abbreviation of *Financial Accounting Standards Board*.

fate Decision whether or not to pay a cheque or other negotiable instrument when it is presented for payment. *See also* ***advise fate***.

fax Short for facsimile transmission, a document transmitted via telephone lines to a computer or fax machine.

FCA Abbreviation of Fellow of the Institute of Chartered Accountants. *See* ***chartered accountant***.

FCCA Abbreviation of Fellow of the Chartered Association of Certified Accountants. *See* ***certified accountant***.

Fed, or FED Abbreviation of *Federal Reserve System*.

Federal Agency Securities The federal agency securities market can be divided into the federally sponsored agency securities market and the federally related institution securities market. Federally sponsored agencies or government-sponsored entities are privately owned, publicly chartered entities created by Congress to reduce the cost of capital for certain borrowing sectors of the economy deemed worthy of assistance, including homeowners, farmers, and students.

Federal Credit Unions A credit union is a financial cooperative that aids its members by encouraging thrift and by providing members with a source of credit for provident purposes at reasonable rates of interest. Federal *credit unions* serve occupational, associational, and residential groups.

Federal Deposit Insurance Corporation An independent executive agency, originally established by the *Banking Act of 1933*, to insure the deposits of all banks entitled to federal deposit insurance.

federal funds Deposits held by US federal reserve banks that bear no interest. *See* ***central bank.***

federal funding rate US ***interest rate*** at which one ***federal reserve bank*** borrows funds from another. It is regulated by the federal reserve.

federal home loan banks Banks in the USA that provide secured loans to their ***savings and loan*** customers, who must hold stock in the regional bank.

federal reserve banks Central banks of the USA, each of which is controlled by a state government. *See* ***central bank.***

Federal Reserve Board Board that controls the growth of US bank reserves and the ***money supply***. *See* ***Federal Reserve System*** (Fed).

Federal Reserve System (Fed, or FED) US central bank system, under which 12 regional ***federal reserve banks*** are governed by the Federal Reserve Board in Washington, appointed by the President. Like the Bank of England in the UK, it sets banking policy and controls the ***money supply***.

Fed funds Usually short-term funds immediately available at a ***federal reserve bank.***

Fed window Colloquial term for the Federal Discount Window, by means of which US banks can borrow from the ***Federal Reserve System*** (Fed).

Fedwire Electronic funds transfer system that links the US federal reserve banks with branches and depositors.

fee Amount charged for a service performed. *E.g.*, a stockbroker charges a fee for buying and selling shares for clients, and accountants charge fees for carrying out company audits. *See also* ***commission.***

fee simple Property held in fee simple may be bequeathed and inherited without limitation. It is effectively the highest form of land ownership for any citizen, ending only if the owner dies ***intestate***, without heirs, in which case the property passes to the crown.

feemail Popular term describing the exorbitant fees charged by lawyers who handle ***greenmail*** cases.

fiat money Paper money that a government decrees is legal tender.

fictitious assets Assets that do not exist but are entered onto a company's ***balance sheet*** to balance the books. *E.g.* a ***trading loss*** may be one example of a fictitious asset for tax purposes.

fictitious payee Non-existent person named as the payee on a ***bill of exchange***; the bill is treated as if it were made ***payable to bearer***.

fidelity guarantee Guarantee of the trustworthiness of a person for employment purposes.

fiduciary Person or body acting in trust. Anyone holding, say, cash in trust for another is said to be acting in a fiduciary capacity.

fiduciary issue Money issued by the Bank of England backed by securities, mainly in the form of the government's debt to the Bank. It is termed fiduciary because of the public's trust that the government will repay the debts backing the issue.

FIFO Abbreviation of ***first in first out***.

fight the tape Practice of selling when prices are rising and buying when prices are falling. The tape is the ticker tape that once relayed prices to brokers.

fill or kill On a ***futures*** market, an order to trade that must be either fulfilled immediately or cancelled.

FIMBRA Abbreviation of ***Financial Intermediaries and Brokers Regulatory Authority***, a former ***self-regulating organization*** (SRO).

final accounts Normally, the ***annual accounts***. However, the term may also refer to the final report submitted by a liquidator at the end of ***liquidation***.

final dividend Last share ***dividend*** paid by a company during a trading year.

finance Term with two meanings:

1. It is a noun, meaning resources of money and their management.

He is trying to raise the finance to float another company.

2. It is a verb, meaning to supply money for a certain purpose.

He finally found a backer who would finance the whole operation.

Finance Act Annual legislation enforcing the measures set out in the UK government's ***budget***.

finance house Also known as a finance company or an industrial bank, a company that provides finance (credit), *e.g.* to operate ***hire purchase*** transactions on behalf of retailers of consumer goods such as cars and electronic and electrical equipment.

finance house base rate Interest rate (based on the London Bank Inter Offer Rate, LIBOR) charged by a ***finance house*** for hire purchase and other forms of borrowing.

financial Of or to do with ***finance***.

financial accountant Accountant who is concerned with the movement of cash, rather than with money that is involved in production (*see* ***cost accountant***). The financial accountant is responsible for overseeing the level of cash available for paying debts and for investment, and for managing and recording all financial transactions.

Financial Accounting Standards Board (FASB) Private regulatory body that sets the accounting standards for US public companies. *See also* ***Securities and Exchange Commission*** (SEC).

financial adviser Person (or institution) who gives advice on raising, lending or managing money, or on particular transactions, usually for a fee.

Financial Analysts Federation An international non-profit professional organization whose members are financial analyst societies located in major cities of the USA and Canada; organized in 1947. The total membership of these societies consists of financial analysts engaged in the profession of security analysis and investment management.

The federation is administered by an 18-member board of directors elected by and responsible to the constituent societies through appointed delegates.

financial futures Contracts for the delivery of financial instruments (*i.e.* a currency) on a future date. Financial futures are used to ***hedge*** against the rise and fall of interest and exchange rates.

financial institution Bank, building society, finance house or other institution that collects, invests and lends funds.

financial instrument ***Bond***, ***certificate of deposit***, ***treasury bill*** or any other method of financing.

Financial Intermediaries, Managers and Brokers Regulatory Association (FIMBRA) Former organization (a ***self-regulating organization***, or SRO) that regulated financial advisers and firms selling and managing securities and unit trusts. In 1994 its functions were taken over by the ***Personal Investment Authority*** (PIA). *See also* ***financial intermediary***.

financial intermediary Bank, building society, finance house, insurance company or other business that collects funds (from depositors, or members) to use for making loans (to borrowers). Any person or organization that sells insurance (but is not an employee of an insurance company) is also regarded as a financial intermediary.

Financial Services Act (FSA) Act of Parliament in the UK of 1988, introduced to prevent abuse of the de-regulated stock exchange system, principally by placing all people or institutions involved in financial services under the authority of a ***self-regulating organization*** (SRO).

financial statement Document summarizing a company's activities, assests and liabilities, including the ***balance sheet*** and ***profit and loss account***.

financial supermarket Financial institution that provides more than one type of financial service. A significant number sprang up after ***deregulation***. A financial supermarket may also be known as a ***boutique***. *See also* ***Big Bang; Chinese wall***.

financial institution *See* ***finance house***.

Financial Times Stock Exchange 100 Index (FTSE, or FOOTSIE) Index of shares of the 100 largest companies, a weighted average which is updated every minute during the working day. The index value of 1000 was set on the base date of 3 January 1984.

Financial Times 30 Index (FT Index, or FT-30 Index) Index of changes in prices of 30 major industrial and commercial ordinary shares on the London Stock Exchange, updated hourly during the working day. The index value of 100 was set on the base date of 1 July 1935.

financial year Period of twelve months, beginning anywhere in the calendar year, used for company accounting purposes. The financial year is the period of twelve months beginning on 1 April to which ***corporation tax*** rates apply. *See also* ***fiscal year***.

fine Money paid as a penalty, usually for an illegal act.

fine bank bill *Bill of exchange* accepted by or drawn on an eligible bank. It is also termed a prime bank bill.

fine bill *Bill of exchange* for which the backer is extremely creditworthy and so there is little or no risk.

fine price Price of a security on a market in which the difference between the buying and selling prices is very small.

fine rate Best rate of interest that can be obtained in a given situation.

firm Commonly, any company or business. Strictly, a firm is a partnership of professionally qualified people, such as lawyers, accountants, surveyors or civil engineers. In this case, firms are legally distinct from companies and so do not, for instance, issue shares. Also, the ***liability*** of individual partners is not (and legally cannot be) limited. *See also* ***incorporation***.

firm bid (or **offer)** Bid (or offer) that has no conditions. *See* ***subject bid (***or ***offer)***.

firm commitment Bank undertaking to lend up to a certain sum at a specific interest rate over a period. The potential borrower pays a ***commitment fee***, which is non-returnable if the loan is not taken out.

firm market Market in which prices are steady.

firm price Guaranteed price, usually offered only if the cost of providing goods or services can be assessed accurately.

first class paper ***Bills*** issued by financial institutions of high standing, *e.g.* the ***Treasury***.

first in first out (FIFO) Accountancy principle whereby ***stock-in-trade*** is assumed to be issued to customers in the order that it is received. Thus, stock currently held may be valued at current prices. *See also* ***last in first out***.

first mortgage debenture ***Debenture*** giving the holder first charge over a company's property.

fiscal year Period of twelve months for the purposes of tax calculation. In the UK the fiscal year runs from 6 April to the following 5 April.

fishing expedition Two or more requests made to a bank to discover the financial status of a person or company.

fixed Unchanging, not subject to movement. The term is commonly found in phrases such as ***fixed assets***, ***fixed charge***, ***fixed costs***, ***fixed deposit***, ***fixed exchange rate***, ***fixed interest securities***, ***fixed trust***.

fixed assets Sometimes also known as ***capital assets***, assets used in the furtherance of a company's business, *e.g.* machinery or property.

fixed capital Alternative term for ***fixed assets***.

fixed charge Legal ***mortgage***. It is also used as an alternative term for ***fixed costs***.

fixed costs Costs that do not vary with short-term changes in the level of output (such as heating costs or rates).

fixed deposit Money placed in a ***deposit account***, *i.e.* an account from which it cannot be withdrawn without suitable notice being given. The US equivalent is time deposit.

fixed exchange rate ***Exchange rate*** that the government attempts to control and fix in the short term by instructing the Bank of England to buy or sell foreign exchange reserves, or by introducing ***tariffs***.

fixed expenses Expenses that are incurred regardless of the level of other activities. *See* ***overheads***.

fixed-interest securities Securities for which the income is fixed and does not vary. They include ***bonds***, ***debentures*** and ***gilt-edged securities***.

fixed rate Describing a charge or interest that does not change. *See also* ***floating rate***.

fixed-rate loan Loan with an interest rate fixed at the beginning of the loan period (irrespective of subsequent changes in the cost of borrowing). *See also* ***floating-rate loan***.

fixed-rate mortgage Mortgage with an interest rate determined at the beginning of the loan period and fixed for at least the first few years.

fixed trust Unit trust in which investors' money is invested in a set portfolio.

fixed yield Return that remains the same.

fixing Setting the price for gold on the London Gold Market, which is done twice a day.

fixture Any ***chattel*** attached or annexed to land, in which case it becomes part of the property.

flashpack Product package that carries a printed special offer (*i.e.*, discounted) price.

flat yield Yield on a fixed interest security shown by relating the income from the security to the present market price. It is also known as the running yield.

flexible trust Unit trust in which investors' money is not invested in a set portfolio, but moved from one investment to another in order to increase earnings.

flight capital Capital that is removed from a country that seems to be politically (or economically) unstable, and taken to a more stable environment. *See also* ***funk money***.

flip Practice of buying then selling shares (usually in the manner of a ***stag***) at high speed in order to make a fast profit.

float Term with two broad meanings:

1. It is cash or funds used either to give change to customers or to pay for expenses.
2. To float is to sell shares in order to raise share ***capital*** and obtain listing on the stock exchange. It is also now more frequently used to mean to start a new company.

floater Security owned by the bearer, the person who holds it. More formally it is termed a bearer security.

floating asset Alternative term for ***current asset***.

floating debt Short-term government borrowing, *e.g.* ***Treasury bills***.

floating exchange rate Also known as a free exchange rate, an exchange rate that is not in any way manipulated by a central bank, but which moves according to ***supply and demand***.

floating money Money for which no profitable investment can be found quickly, usually at a time of high liquidity.

floating pound Pound sterling left to the laws of supply and demand to find its own level on foreign money exchanges.

floating rate Charge or rate of interest for a loan (such as a mortgage) that may change during the period of the loan.

floating-rate loan Loan that does not have a ***fixed rate*** during the period of the loan.

floating-rate note Security issued by a borrower on the ***Eurobonds*** market that has a variable rate of interest.

floating warranty Guarantee given by one party that induces a second to enter into a contract with a third party.

Before using the mortgage broker, the home buyer sought a floating warranty from the estate agent.

floor Usually refers to the trading area of an exchange. *See also* ***floor trader***.

florin Standard currency unit in Aruba and the Netherlands Antilles, divided into 100 cents. It is also an unofficial name for the Dutch guilden (guilder).

florint Standard currency unit in Hungary, divided into 100 filler.

flotation Act of selling shares in a company to raise capital and be listed on the stock exchange.

floor trader Someone who is authorized to trade on the floor of a stock or commodities exchange.

flotation Act of selling shares in a company to raise capital and be listed on the stock exchange.

Flow of Funds Accounts A national statistical system developed by the Federal Reserve Board and published regularly since 1947. The Flow of Funds Accounts is constructed to show the financial activities of the US economy in a manner that enables financial activities to be related to the non-financial activities of the US economic functions that turn out income, savings, and goods and services.

fluctuation Movement of prices up or down on a market. Downward fluctuation is also known as slippage.

FOB Abbreviation of *free on board.*

FOOTSIE *See Financial Times Stock Exchange 100 Index.*

foreclosure If a property has been mortgaged, *i.e.* stands as security against a loan, the lender may take possession and ownership of the property if the borrower fails to pay off the loan. Such an act of possession is known as foreclosure and requires a foreclosure order issued by the court.

foreclosure order *See foreclosure.*

foreign aid Aid, most often in the form of loans or investment, to developing and Third World countries.

foreign bank Bank with headquarters abroad that is authorized to open offices in the UK.

foreign bill *Bill of exchange* that is drawn in a foreign country. *See also inland bill.*

foreign currency Money of any non-UK country.

foreign currency account Also called a nostro account, an account held by a UK bank in a foreign country. The term also describes a UK bank account whose funds are in a foreign currency.

foreign currency swap Exchange of currency for a foreign currency on the understanding that the trade will at a later date be reversed.

foreign currency translation Accounting procedure in which sums stated in a foreign currency are converted into sterling, either at the current exchange rate or at the rate that prevailed at the time of the entry.

foreign draft *Bill of exchange* that is payable abroad, or a bank draft drawn on a foreign branch, usually in the foreign currency.

foreign exchange (FOREX, or FX) Currency of a foreign country, and the buying and selling of such currencies.

foreign-exchange broker *Broker* who deals in foreign currencies on the *foreign exchange market*, usually on behalf of commercial banks.

foreign-exchange dealer Bank employee who deals in foreign exchange on the *foreign exchange market* on behalf of the bank's customers, who pay a commission for such services.

foreign exchange market Market where foreign currencies are traded by foreign-exchange brokers (intermediaries) and foreign-exchange dealers (bank employees). *Options* and *futures* on forward exchange rates are also traded.

foreign exchange risk Risk taken in buying or selling foreign currency (because the exchange rate could change unfavourably between buying and selling).

foreign investment Acquisition of another country's *assets* through any form of investment. It serves to stimulate economic growth in the investing nation and helps to maintain a favourable *balance of payments*.

FOREX Abbreviation of *foreign exchange*.

forfaiting Specialist banking service by which the bank buys foreign debts at a discount *without recourse*, thus removing the risk to the seller of non-payment.

forged share transfer If a bank accepts a share certificate with a forged stock transfer form, the bank is liable to the company that issued the shares.

forged signature Any cheque or other bill of exchange carrying a forged signature is invalid and inoperative.

Form 10K The *Securities and Exchange Commission*'s (SEC) annual report form, Form 10-K must be filed with the SEC within ninety days of a company's fiscal year-end.

forward To send something on to someone (*e.g.* to a new address) or something (*e.g.* a ***futures*** contract) to be completed some time in the future, or an adjective describing something (such as a transaction) in the future.

forward contract A cash contract by which two parties agree to the exchange of an asset (for example, foreign exchange) to be delivered by the seller to the buyer at some specified future date.

forward dating Practice of dating documents in advance. *E.g.* an invoice or a cheque may be dated some time in the future. It is also known as postdating.

forwardation Situation in which spot goods are bought by a dealer (usually on a *commodities* market) and carried forward to deliver against a forward contract (because the spot goods are cheaper than goods for forward delivery). *See also* ***backwardation***.

forward dealing Accepting or awarding a contract (most usually on a *commodities* market) for settlement or delivery by a prearranged future date. *See also* ***futures***.

forward exchange contract Agreement to buy foreign exchange at some future date at an agreed rate of exchange.

forward integration Taking on by a company of activities at a subsequent stage of production or distribution (which are carried out by another company). *E.g.* an oil production company undertakes forward integration when it invests in refineries, tankers and petrol stations.

forward market Market in (contracts or options for) goods that are to be delivered at a future date. *See also* ***buy forward; futures; spot market***.

forward price Price quoted for goods not immediately available or not yet manufactured. The forward price is usually lower than the eventual retail price because it takes into account only the estimated costs of manufacture at some future date. More specifically, it is the price quoted in a ***futures*** deal.

forward purchase Buying of *securities* or *commodities* in advance of delivery. *See* ***futures***.

forward rate Exchange rate quoted on a ***forward exchange contract***.

founder's shares Alternative term for ***deferred ordinary shares.***

fractional banking Practice in which a government requires its banks to keep a fixed fraction between deposits (cash reserves) and liabilities.

franchise Licence bought by a retailer or supplier of services that entitles him or her to sell the goods of a particular manufacturer under a particular trading name. This system enables the manufacturer to have direct control over who sells the goods, and often gives the seller exclusive rights to sell those goods in his or her area.

franc Standard currency unit of Belgium, Benin, Burkina-Faso, Burundi, Cameroon, Central African Republic, Chad, Comoros, Congo, Cote d'Ivoire, Djibouti, Equatorial Guinea, France and its dependencies, Gabon, Guinea, Liechtenstein, Luxembourg, Madagascar, Mali, Monaco, Niger, Senegal, Switzerland, Togo and Rwanda. In all cases it is divided into 100 centimes. The franc in the countries of the French African Community (CFA) all use the CFA franc, which is pegged to the French franc; teritories and ex-territories in the Pacific area use to CFP franc. Others are distinguished by their country, such as Belgian franc and Swiss franc.

franco Alternative term for ***rendu.***

fraud Illegal practice of obtaining money from people under false pretences. *E.g.* fraud is committed if facts pertaining to a contract are purposefully misrepresented. Fraudulently diverting one's company's or employer's money for one's own use is ***embezzlement.***

free alongside ship (FAS) An exporter who sells goods FAS pays for their carriage up to the point when they are standing on the dockside waiting to be loaded. *See also* ***free on board.***

free capital ***Working capital*** of a bank or other financial institution.

free competition Situation in which rival companies are allowed to compete freely with each other for a share of the market. In a free competition or free market economy, the laws of ***supply and demand*** regulate prices. *See also* ***perfect competition.***

free contract Alternative term for ***rendu.***

free depreciation In accounting, depreciation of an ***asset*** over any time period the company thinks fit.

free enterprise Economic system under which individuals or groups may own the factors of production and exploit them for their own benefit within the limits of the law.

freehold Land or buildings that are owned freehold are owned absolutely by the freeholder. *See also* ***leasehold***.

free lunch Non-existent benefit ("There's no such thing as a free lunch"; one way or another the eater pays).

free market Term with two meanings:

1. It is a market that operated essentially by the laws of ***supply and demand***.
2. On the stock market, it is a situation in which a particular **security** is freely available and in reasonably large quantities.

free market economy Economy in which the allocation of resources is determined by the level of ***supply and demand*** without intervention by the state. No pure free-market economy exists.

free on board (FOB) An exporter who sells goods FOB pays for the carriage up to the point where they are loaded aboard ship. *See also* ***free alongside ship***.

free reserve Term with two meanings:

1. It is the excess of reserves held by a bank or insurance company over the minimum laid down by the regulator.
2. It is the total reserves held by a building society less its fixed assets.

free trade Concept of international trading in which there are no tariff barriers between countries.

freeze Broadly, act of stopping something (*e.g.* wages or prices) from moving.

The Government has decided to freeze wage levels of certain public-sector employees for the next twelve months.

freeze-out Situation in which a company successfully out-competes its competitors, causing a new ice-age for them and thus freezing them out of the market.

frictional unemployment Unemployment caused by the movement of people between jobs. Thus, there may be enough jobs to go round, but some people may experience periods of unemployment between the finish date of one job and the start date of the next.

friendly Used more and more frequently to mean something that is sympathetic to the needs of a particular person or group.

friendly society Society (first coming into existence in the 17th century, to help provide working people with some form of security) that provides mutual benefits to its members, such as life assurance and pensions in return for a yearly subscription. There are various kinds of friendly society, including:

accumulative society, which operates by keeping a float to cover claims.

affiliated society, which has centralized administration.

collecting society, so-called after the method of collecting subscriptions house-to-house.

deposit society, which adds part of the funds remaining after claims have been met to members' accounts, thus providing them not only with a form of insurance cover but also a method of saving.

dividing society, which periodically divides the funds remaining after all claims have been met between its members.

friendly takeover Purchase of control of a company that is welcomed by the ***target*** company's board and shareholders.

fringe benefit Items that are given to employees as part of their payment but apart from their wages or salary, *e.g.* a company car, health insurance, or goods at a discount.

fringes Popular US abbreviation of ***fringe benefits***.

front company Company established to conceal its true ownership or the true activities of its owners.

front door Popular term for the Bank of England's practice of lending money to discount houses in order to inject cash into the money market. *See also* ***back door***.

front-end The marketing (rather than the manufacturing) side of a company.

front-end finance UK bank loan to a foreign buyer for paying the UK exporter, usually covered by the ***Exports Credits Guarantee Department***.

front-end load In a transaction covering a period of time, to distribute the benefits towards the early part of the period. Bootstrapping is a form of front-end loading (*see* **bootstrap**).

front loading Administration charge (usually 5%) added to a loan which is paid off first, before actual loan repayments begin.

F

front money Alternative term for ***seed money***.

frozen account Account that is affected by a court order, with the consequence that no money may be deposited or withdrawn.

frozen assets In contrast to ***liquid assets***, frozen assets are those that may not be converted into ready money without incurring a loss of some kind, or which may not be converted because someone has a claim on them or there is an order that they may not be transferred. The latter is also called a frozen fund.

frozen fund *See **frozen assets**.*

FSA Abbreviation of ***Financial Services Act***.

FT Index *See **Financial Times 30 Index**.*

full-time employment Long-term employment that entails an employee putting in a full working week.

fully-paid shares Shares that have been fully paid for by the shareholder. A company may not ***call*** upon holders of such shares to make any further contribution to ***share capital***. Most shares are traded in this fully-paid form. The major exception is that of large new issues, in which trading sometimes begins while they are still partly-paid. *See **partly-paid shares**.*

functional currency For a company that does business in several countries, the currency of the country in which most business is done (which it is required to use).

fund As a verb, to make finance available.

He was unable to raise sufficient capital to fund the project.

As a noun, money set aside for a specific purpose (e.g. from which to pay pensions or insurance claims), or lent to an institution or government. More specifically, it is the money the UK government borrows from institutions and the public by issuing various forms of ***government bonds***.

fundamental analysis Analysis of the ***value*** of a company's ***stock***, in order to predict movements in its share prices.

fundamentalist *See **fundamental market analyst**.*

fundamental market analyst In contrast to the modus operandi of the technical market analyst, the fundamental market analyst (fundamentalist) takes the performance of the company in question as the basis for prediction of share-price movements.

funded debts Broadly, any short-term debt that has been converted into a long-term debt.

funding Practice of providing money for a specific purpose. *See **fund; tranche funding**.*

fund manager Person who manages the investment fund of an institution such as an insurance company or pension scheme. He or she is also sometimes called an investment manager.

fund of funds ***Unit trust***, organized and managed by an institution to invest in other of its own unit trusts.

funds broker Broker who negotiates short-term loans between US banks.

fungible Stock market term for ***securities*** that are in hand, *i.e.* that have not yet been settled.

funk money Funds that are speedily (and often secretly) moved abroad when the political situation changes for the worst. *See also **flight capital**.*

futures Contracts that are made for delivery of *e.g.* currencies or ***commodities*** on a future date. Futures markets provide an opportunity for ***speculation***, in that contracts may be bought and sold (with no intention on the part of the traders to take delivery of the goods) before the delivery date arrives and their prices may rise and fall in that time.

Following reports that bad weather in Brazil had seriously damaged the coffee crop, coffee futures rose sharply today.

FX Abbreviation of ***foreign exchange***.

FY Abbreviation of ***fiscal year***.

G

G5 *See* ***Group of Five.***

G7 *See* ***Group of Seven.***

G10 *See* ***Group of Ten.***

GAAP Abbreviation of generally accepted accounting principles, a code of practice set out by the US ***Financial Accounting Standards Board*** (FASB).

gadfly Shareholder who appears at shareholders' meetings and asks awkward questions.

gain Alternative term for ***profit***.

gainsharing Alternative term for ***profit-sharing.***

gain to redemption Difference between the amount realized by selling stock now and keeping it until ***maturity***.

galloping inflation *See* ***hyperinflation.***

gambling Applied figuratively to the commitment of money on any highly ***risky*** venture. Gambling on a stock market is similar to ***speculation*** in that it is shorter-term, riskier and less serious-minded than ***investment***. *See also* ***bet the ranch.***

gamma share Share that is traded infrequently and in small quantities.

G & A Abbreviation of ***general and administrative expenses.***

garnishee Person to whom a ***garnishee order*** is addressed.

garnishee order A remedy available to any judgement creditor, this order may be made by the court to holders of funds (third parties such as banks etc.) that no payments are to made until the court authorizes them. The third party is known as the garnishee and the court order is known as a garnishee order (an order from a County Court is called a garnishee summons). The purpose of the order is to protect the interests of creditors.

garnishee summons *See* ***garnishee order.***

GATT Abbreviation of ***General Agreement on Tariffs and Trade.***

gazetted Refers to items published in the *London Gazette* (in Scotland, the *Edinburgh Gazette*), a weekly publication that includes the details of appointments, bankruptcy orders, notices of winding-up, changes in company constitutions, etc. If information is gazetted, it is assumed that everybody in the nation has been notified, even if they have never seen or heard of the publication.

gazump To raise the asking price of a property after an offer has been agreed verbally or in writing and before the exchange of contracts, in order to take advantage of rising prices.

gazunder To reduce the price offered for a property after an offer price has been agreed verbally or in writing and before exchange of contracts, in order to take advantage of falling prices.

GDP Abbreviation of ***gross domestic product***.

gearing The proportion of long-term debt to equity finance on the balance sheet of a company. More specifically, it is the ratio of borrowed capital against total capital employed, expressed as a percentage. It is sometimes known as leverage.

general agent Agent with authority to represent the principal in all matters concerning a particular activity.

The sales representative acted as general agent for the company.

General Agreement on Tariffs and Trade (GATT) An international organization with more than eighty members countries, whose object is to negotiate on matters of trade policy, notably the reduction of ***tariffs*** and other barriers to free trade. *See also* ***most-favoured-nation clause; trade barrier***.

general and administrative expenses (G & A) Administrative expenses plus ***operating costs***.

general clearing Clearing of cheques outside London. General clearing takes place in one daily stage.

general expenses Non-specific expenses incurred in the day-to-day running of a company or business.

general lien The right to take possession of ***assets*** at will after default.

generally accepted accounting principles (GAAP) The conventions, rules, and procedures necessary to define accepted accounting practice at a particular time.

general offer Offer made to the general public. *E.g.* a person may offer to pay a certain amount for a piece of information, and members of the public accept the offer by sending the information.

general partner *Partner* whose liability for the debts of the partnership is unlimited.

general partnership Formal *partnership* in which each partner shares equally in the running of the firm.

general reserves Sometimes also known as revenue reserves, profits not distributed to a company's shareholders.

gentleman's agreement Verbal agreement between two parties who trust each other and have a strong sense of honour.

geographical diversification Diversification into new geographical areas. E.g. a company that owns a chain of stores in Scotland may diversify by acquiring similar shops in Wales and England.

Gesellschaft German equivalent of ***limited company*** (Ltd). *See also* ***Aktiengesellschaft*** *(AG);* ***Gesellschaft mit beschrankter Haftun*** *(GmbH).*

Gesellschaft mit beschrankter Haftun *(GmbH)* German equivalent of a UK ***private limited company*** (plc). *See also* **Aktiengesellschaft** *(AG).*

ghost worker Person who appears on the payroll of a company but does not work.

GIGO Acronym for garbage in, garbage out, a precept in the world of computing, meaning that the data delivered by a computer is only as good as the data supplied to it.

Giffen good Good that violates the law of demand. When the price of a Giffen good increases (such as a cosmetic), demand increases, instead of falling off as would normally be expected.

gift cheque Cheque printed with additional decoration (e.g. a picture), supplied by banks to customers who are willing to pay for their aesthetic value.

gilt Common term for ***gilt-edged security***.

gilt-edged security *Security* that carries little or no ***risk***, in particular, government-issued stocks, known as a gilt for short. In the USA, however, gilt-edged refers to bonds issued by companies with a good reputation for ***dividend*** payment and with a good profit record. *See also* ***Consol***.

gilt switching Process of selling one ***gilt-edged security*** and investing the entire proceeds in another. One reason for gilt switching may be to take advantage of changes in ***interest rates***, when a long-dated gilt may be switched for a short-dated gilt, or vice versa.

giro Banking system by means of which money may be transferred from one bank account to another without a cheque being written; also known as bank giro.

Giro also refers in the UK to the Post Office banking service ***Girobank***, and is slang for a cheque received as a social security payment.

Please transfer this money to his account by giro.

He has just gone to cash his giro.

Girobank Banking system set up by the UK Post Office in 1968 (until 1978 known as National Giro). It operates a ***giro*** system through 20,000 Post Offices throughout the UK.

Glass-Steagall Act Act of Congress in the USA of 1933 that separated the activities of commercial and investment bankers.

global custody Service, usually for ***fund managers***, for settling cross-border transactions, offered by major investment banks.

global equities market Worldwide market in ***equities***, involving principally the stock exchanges in London, New York and Tokyo.

Global equities have been hailed for several years now as the new era in securities markets.

globalization Increasing internationalization of all markets, industries and commerce.

global village Term coined by Marshall McLuhan to describe a world closely inter-connected by modern telecommunications, especially television, which greatly reduces the intellectual, cultural and trading isolation formerly caused by geographical separation.

GM Abbreviation of ***gross margin***.

GmbH Abbreviation of ***Gesellschaft mit beschrankter Haftu***.

GMP Abbreviation of ***guaranteed minimum pension***.

gnome Rhetorical term for a remote and detached financial operator, as in the "Gnomes of Zurich" blamed by UK Prime Minister Harold Wilson for the fall in the international value of the pound sterling during the Labour Government of 1966 to 1971.

Gnomes of Zurich *See* ***gnome***.

GNP Abbreviation of ***gross national product.***

godfather offer An offer that cannot be refused. In a ***takeover*** situation, a godfather offer for the company's shares is made at such a good price that the management of the target company can only accept it.

godown Far East term for a ***warehouse.***

gogo (fund) Investment fund that is being actively traded, producing high capital gains and high market prices.

going private Removing a company from stock exchange listing, a process achieved by the company purchasing its own shares. Going private is usually the result of a decision by the principal shareholders that they require more direct control of the company. Its primary purpose is to reduce interference by outside investors and to render the company considerably less vulnerable to takeover bids.

going public To offer shares in a company to financial institutions and the general public, and thereby receive a listing on the stock exchange.

gold Precious metal, widely and historically used as a primary medium of exchange independent of the value of national currencies. *See* ***gold bullion; gold coins.***

gold and dollar reserves Stock of ***gold*** and US national currency held by the US government or central bank.

gold and foreign exchange reserves As ***gold and dollar reserves,*** with national currencies other than the US dollar included in the stock.

gold bug Investor who uses gold ***reserves*** as a cushion against ***inflation.***

gold bullion Gold in the form of 400-ounce (11.3-kilogram) bars. Banks, central banks and gold dealers normally hold gold in the form of bullion.

gold coins Modern coins made from gold are usually held only by collectors and investors. They can be bought and sold, at prices that rise and fall with the market price of gold. *See* ***krugerrand.***

golden credit card ***Credit card*** with special privileges such as a high credit limit and facility for unsecured bank loans. Such cards are usually issued only to high-income groups and senior company employees.

golden handcuffs Contractual arrangement between a company and its employee whereby the employee has a very strong financial incentive (other than loss of normal salary) to remain with the company, such as a low-interest mortgage or share options which expire if the employee resigns.

golden handshake Gratuitous payment made by a company to an employee who is leaving, or has recently left. Such a payment may be made out of goodwill, or to maintain good relations with the employee, or to induce the employee to resign where there are no grounds, or dubious grounds, for statutory dismissal or redundancy.

golden hello Payment other than normal salary paid to an employee on joining a company in order to induce him or her to do so.

golden parachute Term in a contract of employment whereby the employer is bound to pay the employee a substantial sum of money in the event of dismissal or redundancy.

gold fixing Activity that occurs twice a day when the five dealers of gold bullion on the London exchange meet to determine the price of gold.

gold reserves Funds held by a nation in the form of gold. They fluctuate with the ***balance of payments*** if they are used for international transactions.

gold (or **golden) share** Single share in a company that has special voting rights such that it can outvote all other shares in certain circumstances.

gold standard Historical arrangement whereby the comparative values of national currencies such as the pound sterling or US dollar were determined by a fixed price for gold.

good faith *See* ***bona fide***.

good money Federal funds in the USA that are available immediately.

goods Physical items manufactured, sold or exchanged; contrasted with ***services*** where no physical items are transferred.

goods on approval Goods delivered to a customer for which payment is not required unless the customer is satisfied. If the customer is not satisfied in a stated period of time the goods are returned to the vendor. A retailer may hold goods on approval, and return them if they are not sold.

goods on assignment Method of trading in goods whereby they are sent to an agent on consignment. Although the agent has no title to the goods he may sell them on to a buyer. If the goods are not sold, they are returned to the owner.

good-till-cancelled (GTC) Describing an order that remains in force unless it is expressly cancelled. Cancellation is usually dependent upon a satisfactory profit level being reached. It is also known as a resting order or an open order.

goodwill Value of a business over and above the book value of its identifiable or physical assets. Or it is the amount paid on acquisition of a business over its current stock market valuation. It can refer *e.g.* to the literal good will of the established customers of a retail business (shop or restaurant) whose benevolent habit (or custom) of using it cannot be shown in the accounts.

goodwill account *See* ***dangling debit.***

gourde Standard currency unit of Haiti, divided into 100 centimes.

government bond Fixed-interest security issued by a government agent such as the Treasury. It is also known as a ***Treasury bond.***

government broker Firm of brokers used by the UK government to transact its business in ***gilt-edged securities*** and to provide the Treasury with advice.

government securities Alternative term for ***gilt-edged securities.***

graft Informal term for money made in in illegal dealings undertaken while in public office.

Graham-Rudman Amendment Legislation, introduced in stages in the USA, aimed at amending the Constitution to make it unconstitutional to run a budget deficit.

granny bond Colloquial name for a ***National Savings Pensioners Guaranteed Income Bond***, an index-linked savings bond issued by the ***National Savings Bank*** (originally available only to people over the age of retirement).

grant Funds provided by a government, government body or other institution (*e.g.* the Leverhulme Trust or the Nuffield Foundation).

The theatre company received a smaller grant from the Arts Council this year than last.

grant price In instances where US employees have a preferential option on their company's stock, the grant price is the price at which they may exercise that option.

gratuity Payment made voluntarily in excess of statutory or contractual obligation, *e.g.* a tip in a restaurant or a bonus payment on retirement.

Great Yellow Father Popular US name for the Kodak Corporation.

greenback Informal name for the US dollar.

The central bank has no plans to cut its support of falling currency despite a stronger greenback.

green baize door Alternative term for ***Chinese Wall***.

green book Informal name for the *Unlisted Securities Market,* published by the London Stock Exchange, setting out requirements for entry into the ***Unlisted Securities Market*** (USM) and associated regulations.

green currency Currency of an EU country (based on the European Currency Unit, ECU) that uses an artificial rate of exchange to protect farm prices from fluctuations in the real rates of exchange. *See* ***Common Agricultural Policy*** (CAP).

green grass project Project for the construction of a new factory or processing plant where none existed before (by contrast with the extension or replacement of an existing facility). It is also known as a green field project.

greenmail Procedure whereby a person with a sufficient shareholding in a company seeks a sum of money, or the repurchase by the company of his shares at an unreasonably high price, in order to induce him or her to refrain from making a ***takeover bid***.

green pound Notional unit of currency used in the administration of the ***Common Agricultural Policy*** of the European Union to determine the relative prices (and hence subsidies) of farm produce from the different countries of the EU.

green shoe When a company goes public it may grant its underwriting firm an option on extra quantities of shares. This prevents the underwriter making a loss should the issue be undersubscribed and the underwriter have to buy shares on the open market to cover a short position.

Gresham's Law A monetary principle named after Sir Thomas Gresham, Master of the English Mint under Queen Elizabeth who, while not the first to recognize it, was the first clearly to enunciate it and give it official standing. This principle is that an overvalued money of equal legal tender power tends to displace an undervalued money; that bad money (mutilated or debased money) drives good money out of circulation; or that cheaper money supplants dearer money.

grey (US **gray)** Normally describing something that is ambiguous, shady or too far off to identify.

grey knight In a ***takeover*** situation, a third party, acting as a counterbidder, whose intentions towards the target company are not at all clear. Grey knights are normally unwelcome to both the ***target*** and the original ***raider***. *See also* ***white knight.***

grey market Any semi-legal market; one that keeps within the letter but not the spirit of the law. The term is most usually applied to the market dealing in any stock or share whose issue has been announced but which has not yet taken place. Traders therefore gamble on the eventual selling price of the issue when it comes onto the market.

grey wave Normally used in venture capital circles to describe a company or new industry that shows potential but whose realization is, however, a long way in the future. *See also* ***venture capital.***

gross Term with two meanings:

1. It is twelve dozen (144) units.
2. It is an amount calculated before the deduction of certain items, the items being conventionally specified according to context. *E.g.* a salary or interest paid "gross of tax" is paid before deduction of tax, in contrast to "net of tax", where the tax is deducted before payment.

gross domestic product (GDP) Measure of the value of goods and services produced within a country, normally in one year. GDP does not take into account the value of goods and services generated overseas. It is sometimes also known as gross value added. *See also* ***gross national product.***

gross earnings Earnings before ***tax*** has been deducted.

grossing up Calculation of a gross amount from the net amount by adding back the amount deducted.

gross interest Interest on a deposit or investment before deduction of income tax. After tax deduction it is termed net interest.

gross mark-up Amount by which a ***trader*** increases the purchase price of an item in order to sell it at a ***profit***, usually expressed as a percentage of its purchase price.

gross margin (GM) Similar to ***gross mark-up***, but expressed as a percentage of the trader's selling price. It is also sometimes used instead of ***gross profit.***

gross profit *Profit* on a transaction or series of transactions before deduction of ***indirect expenses***, interest or taxation. *I.e.* the sales revenue or fees minus only those costs directly incurred in the purchase, manufacture and delivery of the goods concerned.

gross margin Difference between the selling price of an article and the direct cost of the materials and components used in its manufacture.

gross national product. (GNP) Measure of the value of all goods and services produced by a country, including those produced overseas, usually in one year. *See also* ***gross domestic product.***

gross yield Return on an investment calculated before tax is deducted.

ground rent Payment made, normally annually, by the occupier of a building to the owner of the land on which the building stands (the freeholder). Ground rent is paid only if the building is occupied ***leasehold.*** If it is not paid, the property owner has the right to terminate the lease.

ground rent receipt Proof that ***ground rent*** has been paid, required by a bank that makes a loan secured by a ***leasehold*** property.

group Another name for a ***conglomerate.***

The A & G Group plc now has ten subsidiary companies.

group accounts Alternative term for ***consolidated accounts.***

Group of Five Five leading industrial nations (France, Japan, Germany, the UK and the USA), which meet from time to time to discuss common economic problems.

Group of Seven Seven leading non-communist industrial nations consisting of the ***Group of Five*** countires, Canada and Italy.

The G-7 countries managed to keep exchange rates close to the targets set out in the Louvre Accord.

Group of Ten Also known as the Paris Club, the ten countires Belgium, Canada, France, Germany, Italy, Japan, the Netherlands, Sweden, the UK, and the USA. These countries signed an agreement in 1962 to increase the funds available to the ***International Monetary Fund*** (IMF) and to aid those member countries with ***balance of payments*** difficulties.

growth Process of increase in an entity, activity or quantity.

Strong demand from our customers has led to growth in sales.

Growth may also be the speed or rate of increase in any entity, activity or quantity.

The growth in GDP forecast for the current year is 2%.

growth funds Long-term investments that concentrate on capital growth.

growth stocks ***Stocks*** or ***shares*** that are expected to provide the investor with a larger proportion of capital growth (*i.e.* growth in the value of the stock or share) to income (in the form of dividends) than other shares.

growth recession Situation in which the ***gross national product*** and unemployment are both increasing slowly.

GTC Abbreviation of ***good-till-cancelled.***

guarantee Term with two meanings:

1. It is a document stating that goods or services are of good (merchandizable) quality.

The washing machine came with a five-year guarantee.

2. It is a promise to pay the debt of someone else in the event that the debtor defaults. A guarantee is not to be confused with ***indemnity***.

guaranteed equity bond Performance-related lump-sum investment that guarantees the capital and a minimum return, as well as retaining potential for income from the stock market.

guarantor Person who guarantees, if necessary, to pay someone else's debt.

Her father agreed to act as guarantor for her bank loan.

guaranty bond Type of surety that protects against loss resulting from the failure of someone (specified) to do something (also specified).

guinea Former unit of British currency valued at 1 pound and 1 shilling (£1.05 sterling), occasionally still referred to in transactions with a marked ceremonial or traditional aspect.

guilden Also called guilder, the standard currency unit in the Netherlands, the Netherlands Antilles and Surinam, divided into 100 cents.

gyration Fluctuation on the financial markets.

The deregulation of the London Stock Exchange has helped to cushion the London market against the recent wild gyration in trading.

H

hack Writer-to-order or journalist. The term has gained a new meaning in the field of computing. To hack is to enter a computer database illegally by breaking the security codes, *e.g.* in order either to steal computer time, steal data or "amend" files.

hacker Someone who is enthusiastically knowledgeable in the field of computers or one who spends his or her time breaking into other people's computer systems.

haggle To persistently discuss a price or the terms of an agreement in an attempt to reduce or improve them.

haircut Normally, a ***discount*** on the market value of a ***bond***. It may also be any discount or deduction from the normal value, or a cutting of the budget for a particular project or operation without harming the budget itself.

half a bar Half a million pounds sterling.

half a crown Defunct UK coin that was worth 2 shillings and 6 pence (12½ new pence), half the value of the crown coin.

half-commission man Person whose business is to introduce new clients to a ***stockbroking*** firm, receiving in return a share of the ***commission*** received from those clients.

half sovereign UK gold coin worth half of 1 pound sterling (£0.5). It is still minted (if only rarely) and bought by collectors or as a hedge against inflation. *See* ***gold coins***.

hallmark Mark imprinted onto precious metals and their alloys (*e.g.* platinum, gold or silver) to show that the metal is of a certain quality. The term has also come to mean any sign of high quality. *See also* ***assay***.

hammering Stock Exchange term that refers to the announcement of the inability of a member to pay his or her debts.

hammer out To enter into extended negotiations and to discuss the details of an agreement at length.

We managed to hammer out an agreement, but it took us several months of negotiations.

Hang Seng Index Index of share prices on the Hong Kong Stock Exchange.

hard arbitrage Borrowing of a (considerable) sum of money from a bank and re-lending it profitably on a secondary market, a device disliked by central banks.

hard copy Text typed or printed on paper of a document that has been written or stored on a computer disk or on microfilm.

hard currency Currency, used in international trade, from a country with a stable and prosperous economy. It is thus in high demand and preferred to less stable or legally restricted currencies.

hard dollars Dollars traded on the foreign exchange markets, for which demand is persistently high because of a US trade surplus. The value of hard dollars tends to rise.

See also ***dollar gap***.

hard goods Consumer durables, *e.g.* furniture and household appliances.

hard numbers Financial projection that can be relied upon.

haulage Charge made for transporting goods by road. It does not normally include a charge for loading and unloading.

headage Per capita payment for livestock.

headhunter Person or agency that finds suitable (usually high-grade) staff for posts that companies have vacant, taking a commission from the company involved in relation to the "head's" salary.

heavy shares Shares that command a relatively high price on the stock market.

hedging Method of protecting oneself from price fluctuations. Hedging happens commonly on the commodities ***futures*** market.

hell or high water contract Informal US term for a guarantee that a ***municipal bond*** will be paid, "come hell or high water".

hereditament Piece of land, originally just large enough to support one family, but now used to mean any plot of land.

hidden Describing something that is not obvious, as in the following entries.

hidden price increase Decline in the real value of a good or service occasioned by a decrease in its quality or quantity rather than by a rise in its price. *See* ***real value***.

hidden reserves Reserves not declared on a company's balance sheet.

hidden tax Tax included in the price of goods so that it is not obvious to the consumer. Most forms of indirect taxation are hidden in this way, *e.g.* tax (duty) on tobacco and alcohol.

hidden unemployment Another term for ***disguised unemployment***.

high-beta Describing shares that are volatile.

higgledy-piggledy growth Term coined in the 1960s to describe shares or companies whose earnings are relatively unpredictable.

high-end Normally describing goods that are produced for the top of the market and are consequently very expensive.

high-interest bank account Bank account that pays higher than normal interest rates in return for conditions on minimum deposits and the size of transactions.

high seas Waters that are not part of the territorial waters of any particular country.

High Street bank *See* ***big four***.

hightech Describing any business that makes extensive use of modern technology, particularly electronic systems.

high-tech banking Banking that uses electronic methods, such as ***automated telling machines*** (ATMs) and ***electronic mail***, rather than personal or paper-based transactions.

high-technology stock Shares in a company involved in ***hightech*** activities.

hike Increase.

He took a large pay hike when he changed jobs.

hire To pay a sum of money (usually expressed as so much per hour, day, week, etc.) for services or the use of goods (*e.g.* equipment or transport).

hire purchase (HP) Form of ***credit***, normally extended on ***consumer goods***, whereby the customer takes and uses the goods and pays for them in instalments (with interest) over an agreed period of time. The seller can in theory repossess the goods at any time if the hirer defaults (unlike a ***credit sale***).

historical cost Cost of an asset at the time it was acquired, rather than the current cost of its replacement.

historical cost accounting Method of assigning value to *e.g.* assets for accounting purposes. In historical cost accounting, the original cost of an asset is taken into account, rather than its replacement cost. *See* ***current cost accounting***.

historic dividend Total ***dividend*** paid on a company's shares in the last financial year.

hit bid Bargain in which a dealer sells immediately at a price a buyer is willing to pay, instead of waiting for a possibly better price.

hive off Splitting off of an operating arm of a company to make it into a ***subsidiary company***. It is said to hive off that part of its operation.

holder Someone who owns something or owns rights in something, such as shares, bills, bonds or credit cards.

holder for value Person who holds a ***bill of exchange*** for which a value has at one time been given.

holder in due course Person who has taken up a bill for value before payment is due, and who has no good reason to suspect the title of the previous holder. *See also* ***bearer***.

holding Investment in a company or in any ***security***.

holding company Company that exists to own shares in other companies, that are (depending on the level of shareholding) its subsidiaries. An immediate holding company is one that holds a controlling interest in another company, but in turn, the immediate holding company itself may be owned by a holding company.

hold over To defer settlement of a deal on the Stock Exchange until the next settlement day.

hollowization What happens when a country suffers a relatively sudden loss of skilled workers, ***capital*** and technology; similar to a ***brain-drain***.

home banking Method of banking from home using a computer and ***modem*** connected to the bank's computer.

home savings account Account, usually with a building society, in which a saver deposits funds for a future purchase of property.

honorarium Money paid to a professional such as an ***accountant*** or a ***solicitor***, when the professional does not request a ***fee***.

honorary Describing a position or its holder who is not rewarded with payment; *e.g.* an honorary president.

honorary secretary Someone who takes on the running of a society or charity in the same way as a ***company secretary*** but without payment.

horizontal diversification Diversification into industries or businesses at the same stage of production as the diversifying company. *E.g.* a suit manufacturer might diversify into leisurewear, and a yacht builder into the construction of motor boats.

See also ***horizontal integration; vertical diversification.***

horizontal integration Amalgamation of companies in the same stage of production, and which are therefore likely to possess similar skills.

horse trading Hard negotiations, normally ending in both parties making concessions to each other. *See also* ***tradeoff.***

hostile takeover Attempt to purchase control of a company that is unwelcome to some of the target's shareholders and directors. Unwelcome takeovers may be resisted by a gamut of ***defensive tactics.*** *See* ***crown jewel tactic; golden parachute; Jonestown defence; knight; poison pill; shark repellent; shark watcher; suicide pill.***

hot issue Issue of shares that are expected to sell extremely rapidly.

hot money Informal term for money obtained illegally (*e.g.*, by fraud or theft). In business, however, it is money that is moved rapidly and at short notice from one country to another to take advantage of changes in short-term interest rates or to avoid imminent devaluation of a currency. *See also* ***refugee money.***

house A business or ***company.*** The is also a popular nickname for the London Stock Exchange.

house cheque Cheque presented for payment at the bank (or a branch of the bank) on which it is drawn, thus not requiring clearing.

HP Abbreviation of ***hire purchase.***

human capital Value of a company's employees.

hustle To work hard to make sales and profits. The term has connotations of forwardness and aggression.

hyperinflation Inflation that is running extremely high; also known as galloping inflation.

After the World War I, Germany suffered a crippling period of hyperinflation.

hypothecation A firm of shippers may borrow money from a ***bank*** using cargo it is currently shipping as ***security***. In this case, the bank takes out a ***lien*** on the cargo and this is conveyed in a letter of hypothecation.

In the USA, hypothecation is putting up securities as collateral on a margin account.

I

IAS Abbreviation of ***internal audit*** system.

IBBR Abbreviation of Inter Bank Bid Rate (*see* ***London Inter Bank Bid Rate***).

IBMBR Abbreviation of Inter Bank Market Bid Rate (*see* ***London Inter Bank Bid Rate***).

IBOR Abbreviation of Inter Bank Offered Rate (*see* ***London Inter Bank Offerred Rate***).

IBRD Abbreviation of ***International Bank for Reconstruction and Development.***

ICC Abbreviation of International **Chamber of Commerce.**

ICON Abbreviation of ***indexed currency option note.***

IDB Abbreviation of ***Inter-American Development Bank*** and ***inter-dealer broker.***

idle money Bank account funds that are not invested, also termed idle balance.

ignorantia juris neminem excusat Latin for "ignorance of the law is no defence". It is a doctrine which warns that people who break the law will be punished, regardless of whether or not they are aware that they are committing a crime.

illiquidity Situation in which an ***asset*** is not easily converted into cash, or in which a person is unable to raise cash quickly and/or easily. *See also* ***liquidity.***

illegal Something that is against the law. *See also* ***unlawful.***

IMF Abbreviation of ***International Monetary Fund.***

impact day Day on which a company is scheduled to publish details of a new issue.

imperfect Broadly, actual rather than pure theoretical structures and transactions; more precisely, any economic state that is not perfectly efficient.

imperfect competition Situation of competition in which the goods are not homogenous, *i.e.* they are not perfect substitutes for each other. This dissimilarity gives the producer a small amount of control over price. It is also known as monopolistic competition. *See also* ***perfect competition***.

imperfect market Any market that does not enjoy free competition, good communications, regular demand and uniform goods.

imperfect oligopoly *Oligopoly* in which the goods produced are slightly different from each other. This difference may allow the seller to alter the price in relation to other sellers without a significant effect on sales.

impersonal account On a ***book-keeping*** ledger, an account that deals with ***capital*** and ***assets*** (the ***real accounts***) or income and expenditure (the ***nominal accounts***) or a combination of the two. The only element of the ledger the impersonal accounts do not cover is the record of debtors and creditors (the ***personal accounts***).

implied terms Terms of a ***contract*** that are not expressly stated, but that the law considers necessary to the sense of the contract and therefore implicit.

import Goods and services brought into a country for sale, from abroad.

importation The act of importing.

import ban Ban of specified imports, often for political rather than economic reasons.

importers' entry of goods The customs regulations in force in the country to which exports are being despatched, and which the exporter must note and observe.

import specie point Point in the variation of exchange rates at which it becomes cheaper for a nation on the ***gold standard*** to import gold than buy foreign currency.

imprest Sum of money made available for petty expenses. *See* ***petty cash***.

imputation system UK ***taxation*** system, established in 1973, which partly governs the payment of ***corporation tax***. Under this system, a shareholder's ***dividends*** are taxed at source, and he or she is issued with a ***credit*** for the tax imputed.

inactive Describing something that is not working or moving. *See also* ***active***.

inactive account Another term for ***dormant account***.

inactive market Alternative term for ***dull market***.

in-and-out trader Stock-market trader who buys and rapidly sells a security on the same day.

in arrears Describing a payment that is late, behind an agreed schedule.

Inc Abbreviation of incorporated. *See* ***incorporation***.

incentive Positive motive (sometimes artificially generated) for performing some task.

incentive bonus Also known as a productivity bonus, extra money paid to an employee to encourage him or her to work harder (and therefore more productively).

incestuous share dealing Dealing in the shares of associated firms in order to win tax concessions. Incestuous share dealing is often illegal, but need not necessarily be so.

incidental expenses Minor expenses not directly relevant to the running of a business.

incidentals Non-material items, particularly those referred to in a company's ***accounts***.

income Money, goods or services received from any activity. Income may be either a return on one of the factors of production – a ***salary***, ***rent***, ***interest*** or ***profit*** - or a transfer payment made for some other reason, such as ***unemployment benefit***. The definition includes non-monetary income such as the benefit derived from the possession of ***assets***.

income and expenditure account Similar in form to a ***profit and loss account***, an income and expenditure account records all cash transactions over a given period.

income bond Investment in a unit trust that produces a good annual income as opposed to capital growth realizable at the end of a certain period of time.

income bracket Range of income (wages, salaries), normally rated from a specific minimum to a specific maximum. The term is also applied to people in that range.

She is in the middle income bracket.

income option Facility with many accounts in banks, building societies and National Savings that allows a depositor to collect interest monthly, quarterly, six-monthly or annually.

income statement Alternative term for ***profit and loss account***.

income tax Tax paid on income, such as fees, salaries or wages.

inconvertible Describing money that cannot be exchanged for gold of equal value. UK currency has been inconvertible since the country came off the ***gold standard*** in 1931.

incorporation The process of setting up a business as a legal entity.

increment Amount of increase.

incremental cost Extra cost incurred when a company agrees to take on a new project.

incremental increase Increase that occurs in stages or steps, or successive increases by one unit.

indebtedness State of owing money or services to someone else, or the amount of money owed.

indebtedness date Alternative term for ***indebtedness day***.

indebtedness day When a company issues a prospectus, it must make known the day on which its statement of debt (the extent of its indebtedness) was made. It is assumed that the indebtedness figure was correct at that time, called the indebtedness day.

indemnity Undertaking that gives protection against ***loss*** or damage. Indemnity may be in the form of replacement or repair of property lost or damaged, or provision of cash to the value of the property.

indent Order for goods from abroad, often placed with an ***agent***.

indenture ***Deed*** or ***instrument*** to which there is more than one party. It is so called because such deeds were formerly cut or torn (indented) into portions, one for each party, to prevent forgery and provide proof of each person's involvement in the transaction. Indentures were formerly widely used to bind an apprentice to his master for the period of his apprenticeship.

independent Describing a person or organization that is free to act unilaterally and is not dependent on any other person or organization.

independent company Company that operates entirely under its own authority, and is not owned or controlled (in part or in whole) by any other company.

index Form of measurement or comparison; a listing giving an indication of change.

index arbitrage Process of selling stocks at the same time as buying stock-index futures, or vice versa. It is a form of program trading.

indexation Form of ***index-linking*** that ties ***income*** to the ***retail price index*** and therefore prevents a fall in real wages during a period of ***inflation***.

indexed currency option note (ICON) Document that records a debt whose value depends on the effective exchange rate between the currencies concerned. A pre-arranged rate is set between defined limits for interest payments but changes if the limits are exceeded.

indexed portfolio Portfolio linked to a stock index, such as the ***Financial Times Stock Exchange 100 Index*** (FOOTSIE).

index fund Investment fund that is linked directly to a share index, in that it has investments in shares on that index.

index futures Futures contracts that are based on the figures provided by indices.

index-linked gilts ***Gilt-edged securities*** that have a variable rate of interest adjusted to take account of inflation (using ***index-linking*** to the ***retail price index***).

index-linking System of linking costs, prices or wages to the price fluctuations of an economy in order to allow for ***inflation*** and maintain value in real terms. Index-linking is most often used to relate ***income*** to the ***retail price index***. In a year of 4% inflation, therefore, it would be usual for an index-linked salary to rise by the same amount.

index number Weighted average that permits the comparison of prices or production over a number of years. The components selected for comparison are weighted according to their importance and then averaged. Figures are compared to those for a ***base year***, selected for its typicality and given the index number 100 or 1000.

indication-only price Price quoted by a ***market maker*** that indicates what he or she thinks a security is worth although he or she is not prepared to deal in it.

indicator Measurable variable used to suggest overall change among a group of linked variables too complex to yield to simple analysis. Thus a variety of economic indicators – such as ***price***, ***income***, ***imports***, ***exports***, ***money supply*** and so on – are studied in an attempt to estimate the state of a national economy.

indirect Describing something that is associated with, but not immediately connected to, something else; something at one remove. *E.g.* indirect ***taxation*** consists of taxes levied on ***expenditure*** rather than ***income***.

indirect costs Costs of items or activities, such as maintenance of buildings and machinery, that are not used in the production of goods, nor immediately necessary for their production.

indirect expenses Expenses incurred in production, but not directly attributable to any one factor of production.

indirect production Production of goods for sale by employing labour and machinery and using a system of divided labour in order to make a profit. *See also* ***direct production***.

indirect taxation Tax paid to one person or organization (often a retailer), who then pays it to the government. ***Value-added tax*** is a form of indirect taxation.

individual retirement account (IRA) The US Tax Reform Act of 1976 authorized a qualified retirement plan for individuals.

individual savings plan (ISA) Tax-free method of saving announced by the UK government in 1997 and planned for introduction in 1999, when ***personal equity plans*** (PEPs) and ***tax-exempt special savings accounts*** (TESSAs) are due to lose their tax-free staus. There will be no lower limit to the amount that can be invested but the planned maximum is £50,000.

indorsement *See* ***endorsement***.

industrial bank One of a group of smaller finance houses, which operate rather like a merchant bank, receiving investment from the general public. *See* ***finance house***.

industrial espionage Attempt by one company or group to gain access to confidential information about another, generally to acquire commercial advantage and improve efficiency by imitation.

industrial estate Area of land set aside for (usually light) industry.

industrial revenue bonds (US) A special classification of ***municipal bonds***, also called lease rental bonds, typically issued by a municipality to provide funds. For example, a plant is built to the specifications of a particular private company, that is then granted a long-term lease to the plant at a rental designed to be adequate for interest and principal payments on the bonds by the municipality.

industrials Shares in an industrial company, usually manufacturing. *See also* ***commercials***.

industrial sabotage Unfair competition between competitors. The term applies to any dubious tactics, not just physical sabotage.

industry Agglomeration of companies involved in the production of goods. The term is usually applied as a generic for a group of companies manufacturing very similar products, *e.g.* "the car industry".

inertia State of inactivity, or resistance to movement.

inertia selling Method of selling in which unsolicited goods are mailed to a "customer" and followed by an invoice.

infant industry Newly-established national industry in the early stages of growth.

infant's contract In general terms no contract is enforceable in the UK if it is made with a person under the age of 18.

inflation Persistent general increase in the level of prices. Strictly defined, inflation includes neither one-off increases in price (occasioned by *e.g.* a sudden scarcity of some product) nor any other increases caused by real factors. Its causes include an excess of demand over supply and increases in the money supply, perhaps brought about by increased government expenditure, which causes a decline in the real value of money.

inflation accounting Alternative term for ***current cost accounting*** or current purchasing power accounting.

inflation-adjusted Describing wages that have been modified to maintain real income by increasing pay in line with inflation. The term may also be applied to the economist's technique of discounting price changes to obtain a truer picture of quantitative changes in output.

inflation tax Extra revenue brought into the government because inflation has brought new tax payers on stream or pushed taxpayers or taxable items into higher brackets.

infopreneur Person who makes a living by collecting, assessing and selling information to interested parties.

information float Time it takes to relay information from one person or organization to another. *E.g.* the information float using the postal service is at least one day, whereas the float using computer link-up could be a matter of seconds.

information services Economic sector in which information is traded and sold. *E.g.* most financial services are information services, as are the City pages of newspapers.

information technology (IT) Area of micro-electronics that combines computing and telecommunications technologies in the organization, storing, retrieval and transfer of information.

informative advertising Advertising that concentrates on providing the target with information about the product, thereby helping consumers to choose between products.

infrastructure Public utilities of a country. Also known as social overhead capital, the infrastructure includes roads, railways, airports, communications systems, (*e.g.* telephones), housing, water and sewerage systems, and other public amenities.

ingot Bar of metal that has been cast in a mould, possibly for ***assay***. *See also* ***bullion***.

inheritance Possessions or titles passed to one or more persons on the death of another.

inheritance tax (IHT) Tax paid on inheritances by heirs, often calculated in relation to the closeness of the relationship between the heir and the deceased person. In the UK at the present time, ***capital gains tax*** covers income from inheritances.

initial allowance Amount deducted from a company's profits for the purposes of calculating tax in the first year after ***acquisition***.

initial margin ***Deposit*** that must be paid on selling or buying a ***contract*** on a ***futures*** market. *See also* ***equity***.

initial public offering (IPO) First share offer made by a company ***going public***.

initial public offering window (IPO window) Period of time between an announcement of an ***initial public offering*** and the start of dealing in the shares offered on a stock market. Grey market trading takes place in the IPO window (*see* ***grey market***).

initial yield ***Current yield*** of a ***unit trust*** or other collective investment expressed as a percentage of the ***offer price***.

injunction Restraining order issued by a court. An injunction instructs a named person to perform a certain duty or forbids him or her to commit a specific act. Failure to comply with an injunction is considered contempt of court.

inland bill ***Bill of exchange*** that is drawn and payable within the UK. *See also* ***foreign bill***.

Inland Revenue UK government department whose major responsibility is the collection of various taxes, such as ***income tax***, ***capital gains tax*** and ***corporation tax***.

Inland Revenue Service (IRS) US equivalent of the UK's ***Inland Revenue***.

Inner Six Six EU countries: Belgium, France, Germany, Italy, Luxembourg and the Netherlands. *See* ***European snake***.

innoventure ***Venture capital*** scheme based on an innovative product or service. Such schemes are regarded as being particularly risky.

in play Describing a ***quoted company*** for which a ***takeover*** bid is expected to be launched in the very near future.

input tax In the ***value-added tax*** system, the tax that is collected from the seller of goods by the ***Customs and Excise***. *See also* ***output tax***.

inscribed stock Now discontinued method of registering the name of a stockholder, by which the holder was issued with a slip indicating that the holder's name had been registered. This slip did not have the status of a certificate. It was also known as registered stock.

insider Person with special knowledge derived from holding a privileged position within a group or company.

insider dealing Also known as insider trading, illegal transactions made on the basis of privileged information. Most insider dealing concerns trading in stocks and shares whose value is likely to be affected by the release of news of which only a few people are aware.

insider trading Alternative term for ***insider dealing***.

insolvency State in which total liabilities (excluding ***equity capital***) exceed total ***assets***; therefore, it is the inability to pay ***debts*** when called upon to do so. If insolvency is chronic, ***bankruptcy*** or ***liquidation*** generally follow.

insolvency payment Payment funded by the ***deposit protection scheme*** to a depositor or investor in a bank or building society that fails. It is up to 90% of a deposit of up to £20,000 (i.e., a maximum of £18,000 per investor).

instalment Part payment of a ***debt***, such as one undertaken as part of a ***credit sale*** or ***hire purchase*** agreement. Instalment payments fall due at fixed and specified intervals and when totalled equal the original debt, usually with the addition of ***interest*** payments.

instant Often abbreviated to inst., a little-used term meaning "of this month". *E.g.* a letter written in November mentioning the "13th inst." refers to 13 November. *See also* ***ultimo***.

instant access account Interest-bearing account obtainable at a bank or building society from which money may be withdrawn without giving notice. It generally pays less interest than an account that requires notice of withdrawal. *See* ***sight deposit; time deposit***.

Institute of Bankers *See* ***Chartered Institute of Bankers, The***

Institute of Bankers in Ireland Professional organization for bankers in the Republic of Ireland. It co-ordinates the training of bank personnel and oversees the practice of banking in Ireland.

Institute of Bankers in Scotland *See* ***Chartered Institute of Bankers in Scotland, The***.

Institute of Certified Public Accountants Professional organization of certified accountants in the UK.

Institute of Chartered Accountants Professional organization of chartered accounts in the UK, divided into the Institute of Chartered Accountants in England and Wales, the Institute of Chartered Accountants in Ireland and the Institute of Chartered Accountants in Scotland. They set educational standards and co-ordinate training, set examinations and oversee the practice of accountancy.

institution Organization, particularly one concerned with the promotion of a specific subject or some public object (*e.g.* the Royal United Services Institution). The term "*The* Institution" is used to denote the collective of ***institutional investors***.

institutional investor Corporate rather than individual investor; a company which invests funds on behalf of clients, generally intending to reap profits only in the long term. Institutional investors include banks, insurance companies, pension funds and unit trusts. At the present time, institutional investors hold from 50% to 70% of all ***negotiable securities***.

in-store concession In order to diversify and maintain their own profits, some large stores allow smaller retail operations to set up and staff areas of the store for the sale of their own goods. The store then takes a percentage of the in-store concession's takings in payment.

instrument Broadly, any legally binding document.

integration Amalgamation of two or more companies to improve efficiency. Also, an industry is said to be integrated if products from different partaking companies are compatible.

intellectual property Expression of the theory that ideas as well as tangible inventions and innovations are unique to one person or group and should be patentable. Intellectual property currently has no clear standing in UK law, other than in ***copyright***.

intensive Term most commonly used to indicate something that is extremely important to something else.

intent Planned action or intention.

Inter-American Development Bank (IDB) Bank established in 1959 by the USA and other American countries for financing regional development in Latin America.

interbank Term with two possible meanings:

1. It is a ***market*** in which financial institutions lend each other (frequently large) sums of money for short periods. The ***interest*** rate offered is known as the ***London Inter Bank Offered Rate*** (LIBOR). Interbank loans developed as a way of averting short-term liquidity crises.
2. It is an association of some 3,000 US banks collectively responsible for the issuing and administration of the ***Mastercharge*** credit card.

Inter Bank Bid Rate (IBBR) *See* ***London Inter Bank Bid Rate.***

interbank market Term with two meanings:

1. It is the market in foreign currencies between banks.
2. It is the part of the money market where banks make loans to each other, charged at the ***London Inter Bank Offered Rate*** (LIBOR).

Inter Bank Market Bid Rate (IBMBR) *See* ***London Inter Bank Market Bid Rate.***

Inter Bank Offered Rate (IBOR) *See* ***London Inter Bank Offered Rate.***

interbank sterling market ***Money market*** involving all UK banks, allowing speedy informal trading to best use or obtain funds. Transactions are carried out through ***brokers***.

inter-dealer broker (IDB) Person who matches deals between anonymous buyers and sellers on behalf of two ***market makers***.

interest Term with three possible meanings:

1. It is a charge made by a lender to a borrower in exchange for the service of lending funds. It is usually expressed as a percentage of the sum borrowed, but may be paid in kind.

The bank made me a loan at 10% interest.

In 1997 Niger borrowed £11 million from neighbouring Libya, paying interest that included 1,500 camels per year.

2. It is a payment made by a bank or building society to customers on some forms of savings account.

My building society pays 7% interest.

3. It is money that is invested in a company, usually in return for ***equity*** or ***shares***, thus making the investor "interested" in the performance of the company. In this sense, an interest may be in anything that yields a return.

He has an interest in several small companies.

interest cover Ratio of earnings to the fixed-***interest*** payments necessary to service loan ***capital***.

interest-only mortgage Mortgage in which the motgagor pays back only interest during the mortgage period because he or she has a personal equity plan (PEP) or other asset to repay the capital at the end.

interest rate ***Interest*** charged to a borrower or paid to an investor, usually expressed as a percentage per annum.

interest rate futures Financial ***futures*** purchased as a hedge against an adverse change in ***interest rates***. If interest rate changes on the hedger's financial instruments produce a loss, the futures contract offsets it. *See also* ***hedging***.

interest warrant Government cheque issued by the Bank of England for paying interest due on a loan. A company may also issue an interest warrant.

interest yield On a fixed-interest security, the rate of interest expressed as a percentage of the price paid. It is also termed the running yield.

interim In the meantime. The term usually refers to the halfway point in a financial year.

interim accounts Short financial statement produced by a company (often unaudited) in the middle of the year, halfway between publication of the ***annual accounts***.

interim dividend Any dividend other than the final dividend declared at the conclusion of each trading year. Interim dividends may be made as a reward for a particularly good economic performance or simply as an effective advance on the final dividend, which will be correspondingly reduced in value. Most UK companies quoted on the stock market make interim dividend payment per annum; it is unusual for a firm to exceed this frequency of interim payments.

interim note Means of advising an investor that he/she has been allotted shares and will eventually receive a share certificate.

interim receiver Person appointed by a court to act as ***receiver***, until a receiver proper is appointed.

interim report Short statement published at the end of the first half of a public company's financial year, detailing results for the previous six months and declaring any ***interim dividend***.

intermediary Person who acts between and deals with two parties who themselves make no direct contact with each other.

internal audit Audit of a company's books that takes place virtually continuously and is undertaken by internal staff, rather than by an external auditor. Internal auditing is carried out in order to monitor company profitability and guard against fraud.

internal check System of ***accounting*** that ensures that each person's work and financial dealings are checked by an independent third party within the company. Together with an ***internal audit***, internal checks act to promote efficiency and prevent fraud.

internal control Combination of self-regulatory measures by which a company ensures that each employee is accountable, safeguards its ***assets*** and institutes an accurate system of ***accounting***, therefore enhancing its own efficiency.

internal rate of return (IRR) Term with two meanings:

1. It is a hypothetical ***interest rate***, equivalent to the marginal efficiency of ***capital***, which is used to assess the investor's ***yield*** and therefore determine the viability of an investment. If the internal rate of return is higher than the current rate of interest at which the investor could borrow, the investment is worthwhile.
2. It is the discount rate at which, applied to the expected pattern of cash expenditure and income of a capital project, would give a net

present value of zero. It may be compared with the return on alternative investments, or on some target rate of return.

Internal Revenue Service (IRS) US equivalent to the UK's ***Inland Revenue***.

International Bank for Economic Cooperation (IBEX) International institution that served as the central bank for the communist (some now ex-communist) countries of the Council of Mutual Economic Assistance (CMEA), later the Organization for Economic Cooperation (OIEC).

International Bank for Reconstruction and Development (IBRD) Part of the ***World Bank***, established in 1945 with headquarters in Washington D.C., to help economic reconstruction in countries after World War II. It makes loans to developing nations or guarantees loans from other sources. The bank's capital comes from the member nations of the ***International Monetary Fund*** (IMF).

International Monetary Fund (IMF) International organization set up in 1944 after the Bretton Woods conference, to organize and administer the international monetary system. It was designed to help countries in financial difficulties, especially with their ***balance of payments***. It makes loans and provides financial advisers.

international money order Method of transferring small sums between countries. An order (designated in US dollars or pounds sterling) may be bought, and encashed, at a bank.

intervention price Price slightly below the ***threshold price*** at which the ***European Commission*** intervenes to purchase agricultural surpluses, thus supporting home markets and helping to achieve the average or ***target price***.

intestacy Situation in which a person dies without making a valid will, leaving the estate without a designated heir. If a person dies intestate, the Crown divides the estate between surviving relatives, making provision first for the spouse, and then for any children. If neither spouse nor children are living, other relatives are entitled to share in the estate. If no relatives can be traced, the estate goes to the crown.

in the bank Describing a ***discount house*** that is forced to borrow from the Bank of England.

in-the-money option Term with two meanings:

1. It is an option to buy shares (***call option***) for which the price on the

open market has risen above the price fixed (called the option's *exercise price*).

2. It is an option to sell (***put option***) for which the market price has fallen in relation to the ***exercise price***. An in-the-money option is said to carry ***intrinsic value***.

in the window Describing anything obviously for sale. *E.g.*, a company may put an unquoted subsidiary in the window by discreetly inviting potential purchasers to make themselves known. The term is also a virtual synonym for ***in play***.

intracapital *Capital* placed at the disposal of an ***intrapreneur***.

intrapreneur Member of the staff of a company who is given relative autonomy in order that he or she may make use of entrepreneurial skills to the advantage of the company. *See also* ***entrepreneur***.

intrinsic value Value of the materials from which an object is made rather than its market or face value. *E.g.* a coin may be said to be worth so much and is exchanged on the basis of that stated value, but the metal used in minting it may be worth much less. Intrinsic value is also the value (if any) of a traded ***option*** that is in-the-money, brought about by a favourable difference between ***market price*** and ***exercise price***.

introduction Means of offering a new share issue to the public, through the medium of a stock exchange but without the publication of a ***prospectus*** and the provision of an application form. Introductions are possible only if there is a large number of potential shareholders and no large ***bargains*** have been struck to market the ***stock***.

inventory Term with two meanings:

1. It is the list of the stocks of raw materials, goods in production or finished goods owned and stored by a company, giving details of their ***cost***, ***value*** and ***price***.
2. It is an itemized account of the contents of a rented property, against which the contents are checked when the tenant leaves.

inventory control Stock control. Most efficient businesses are managed, using inventories, in such a way that minimum levels of ***stock-in-trade*** sufficient to meet any likely demand are always maintained.

investment Term defined in two different ways by two schools of thought:

1. It is expenditure on real or financial assets rather than the funding of consumption. In this sense, expenditure consists of the purchase of any asset which is expected to increase in value.

We have invested our money in short-term treasury bonds.

2. To an economist, it covers spending that results in economic growth. E.g. money spent on the purchase of machinery or the building of plant that will produce goods and services for sale. Investment extends to funds applied to the improvement of the infrastructure, and the term may also be applied to the expenditure on human resources.

In an effort to improve the nation's economy, the government is investing in a huge road-building programme as well as making an enormous investment in the re-education of its workforce.

investment adviser Person who advises individuals or institutions on financial matters related to investment in its widest sense.

investment allowance Alternative term for ***capital allowance***.

investment bank US bank that mainly acts as intermediary between investors and companies wanting to issue shares. It also carries out many of the functions performed by a ***merchant bank*** in the UK.

investment banking Practice of providing finance for businesses.

Investment Company Act of 1940 (US) An act designed to control many abuses associated with investment companies and investment advisers.

investment instrument Any medium of investment, including ***stocks***, ***shares*** and ***securities*** of all kinds, ***unit trusts*** and funds, grouped investment media, and so on.

investment manager *See **fund manager**.*

Investment Services Directive (ISD) ***Directive*** of the European Union (EU), issued in 1996, that deals with cross-border transactions by investment banks and dealers in securities.

investment trust Investment scheme, similar to a ***unit trust***, in which a small investor is able to invest in a range of shares through the agency of the scheme's managers.

invisible asset *See **tangible asset**.*

invisible earnings ***Income*** earned from payment for services rather than goods, on a national scale. Invisible earnings include profits from tourism, shipping, and the provision of insurance, banking and other financial services. They are also called invisibles.

investment grant Grant of money made available by the government to companies for certain purposes.

inward investment Alternative term for ***foreign investment***.

invisibles *See* ***invisible earnings***.

invisible exports Services (rather than goods) provided to foreign people, organizations and countries. Invisible exports include banking, shipping and insurance services.

invisible trade Trade in services rather than tangible goods. *See* ***invisible exports***.

invitation to treat Suggestion, made by one person to another, that he or she enter into negotiations which may result in a formal offer to trade. The difference between an invitation to treat and an ***offer*** proper is that an invitation does not bind the parties concerned to the conditions of the invitation, whereas the terms of an offer are legally binding.

invoice Document that summarizes a business transaction and often doubles as a request for payment. An invoice lists and describes the goods (or services) ordered and details their price, and usually records the dates and times of dispatch and delivery.

invoice discounting ***Discount*** offered on unpaid ***invoices*** sold to a ***factoring*** company, which will then try to claim the money owed on its own account. The size of the discount will reflect the likely difficulty of securing payment. *See also* ***discounting bank***.

IOU Abbreviation of "I owe you," a non-negotiable written note recording a ***debt***.

IPO Abbreviation of ***initial public offering***.

Irish Bank Federation Organization formed in 1973 with headquarters in Dublin. It advises authorities at home and abroad on matters related to banking in Ireland, representing its members and promoting their interests.

IRR Abbreviation of ***internal rate return***.

irrevocable Describing something (e.g. an order) that is unalterable and cannot be revoked.

irrevocable and confirmed credit Credit facilities that are confirmed by a bank in London on an account held by a non-UK resident.

irrevocable documentary acceptance credit Credit facilities arranged by an overseas customer with a bank in London, who is then presented with a letter of credit to facilitate foreign trade.

IRS Abbreviation of ***Inland Revenue Service***.

ISA Abbreviation of ***Individual Savings Account***.

ISD Abbreviation of ***Investment Services Directive***.

issuance Procedure of issuing ***securities***, carried out by a ***company*** or ***issuing house***.

issue Term with two meanings:

1. It is the quantity of a particular ***stock*** or ***share*** offered to the public.
2. It is the total number of banknotes in print at a given time.

issue by tender Stocks and shares may be issued by the process of inviting tenders above a stated minimum price and then selling to the highest bidder. *See also* ***application and allotment***.

issuing bank Financial institution that administrates a new issue of shares.

issuing house Connecting link between those who need ***capital*** and those willing to lend. Often, an issuing house also operates as a share issue ***underwriter*** or ***merchant bank***.

issued capital That part of a company's capital that comes from a share issue. It is also known as subscribed capital.

issued price The published price of a stock or share.

IT Abbreviation of ***information technology***.

J

jajo Abbreviation of January, April, July, October, the months in which some stock ***options*** expire.

jerry building Speculative construction of buildings (normally residential property at times of housing shortage) that leads to bad workmanship and use of poor-quality materials.

job Regular work for which a person is paid either a salary or wages, or a particular project or piece of work.

After two years unemployed he eventually found a job.

The price for the job was £500.

jobber Also known as a stockjobber, a member of the London Stock Exchange who deals in securities with stockbrokers and other jobbers, but not with the public. Before the ***Big Bang***, the London Stock Exchange was the only exchange in the world on which the activities of the stockbrokers and jobbers were kept separate. This practice has now been discontinued and jobbers have been replaced by ***market makers***. In the USA, a jobber is any middleman between a wholesaler and a retailer, or a person on a stock exchange who deals in securities that are worthless (*e.g.* junk bonds). The US synonym for jobber in the UK sense is ***dealer***.

jobber's book Before the ***Big Bang***, a book showing the ***position*** a ***jobber*** held in the market: whether he holds stock for which he has yet to find a buyer, or whether he is short on stock that he has already sold.

jobber's pitch On the London Stock Exchange, trading position on the floor of the exchange from which ***jobbers*** operated.

jobber's turn Profit made by a ***jobber*** on a deal.

jobbing backwards Looking back at past decisions, often – with hindsight – regretting them.

job card In costing a ***job***, a card on which is recorded the issue of parts or materials, hours of labour used, the cost of that labour and any associated overheads.

job description Formal document setting out the duties and responsibilities entailed in a particular job. Sometimes, the job description forms part of a contract of employment. *See also* ***job specification***.

job evaluation Evaluation of the skills and qualities necessary for a person to be able to perform a particular job, or of the ability of a person to do a job.

job lot Collection of ***stocks*** or ***goods*** sold together, perhaps to somebody who wants only some of them.

job-share Also known as a time-share, employment that is held by two people, each working part-time.

job specification Often shortened to job spec, a description (sometimes informal) of what a particular position or job entails. *See also* ***job description***.

joint Describing something that is a combination of two or more things, *e.g.* a joint company or a joint treasurer.

joint account Bank account in the names of two or more people.

joint and several Concept by which joint debtors (*e.g.* two or more partners in a company) are responsible for the debt, both jointly and as individuals. Joint and several liability gives the lender recourse to each of the partners in the debt in the event of default.

Joint Credit Card Company Company that runs ACCESS ***credit cards***, owned jointly by Lloyds Bank, Midland Bank, NatWest Bank and The Royal Bank of Scotland.

joint-stock bank Alternative term for a ***commercial bank*** that is constituted as a joint stock company.

joint-stock company Alternative term for limited company.

See ***limited liability company***.

joint tenancy Situation in which two or more people have equal rights to the tenancy of a property. If a joint tenant dies, the property reverts to the other tenants, and so on until one tenant remains, with sole tenancy rights. *See also* ***tenancy in common***.

Jonestown defence Any form of defensive tactics against a hostile takeover bid that is so extreme as to appear suicidal. *See also* ***poison pill***.

journal In accounting, a book in which daily transactions are recorded before being transferred to the books of account.

judgement Ruling made by a court in a particular case (also spelled judgment).

judgement debt Debt that has come before the courts and which is confirmed by the court as being repayable. The judgement creditor can then apply for repayment remedies through the court.

jumbo certificate of deposit Bank certificate confirming a customer's deposit of funds in excess of $100,000 for a fixed period.

jumpy Description of a market in which dealers are nervous and so likely to jump at the slightest movement.

junior capital Company shares that represent the company's ***equity***.

junior stock Shares offered to a company's executives at below the market price. Initially, junior stock has a low dividend rate, but may be converted to ordinary shares to provide a capital gain.

junk bond Bond, especially common in the USA, issued by a company with a low credit rating. It is often used to raise funds for ***leveraged buyouts***, secured against the assets of the target company.

K

K Thousand (1,000), often in finance expressed in units of currency.
She was earning 50K as a consultant.

kaffir Racist stock exchange nickname for shares in South African mining companies.

kamikaze pricing Granting of loans by a financial institution at very low interest rates to increase its share of the banking market.

kangaroo Stock exchange nickname for shares in Australian companies, especially those dealing in tobacco, property and mining.

Kaufmanized Markets in securities were said to be Kaufmanized when they reacted to information from the mouth of the US economist Henry Kaufman.

kerb On the London Metal Exchange, a period of time during which all metals are traded simultaneously. *See also* ***trading ring***.

kerb market Trading in securities that takes place outside an official exchange.

kerb trading Closing a deal on a financial futures market after hours. It is so called because originally traders would emerge from the exchange after official trading closed for the day and remain outside (on the kerb) to close any unfinished business.

key money Premium paid by a new tenant of a property to the previous leaseholder or landlord or in return for the granting of the lease, licence or tenancy.

Keynesianism School of economic thought, named after John Maynard Keynes (1883-1946), an economist greatly influential in the late 1930s. Keynesians believe that the best way to bring about economic change is by government intervention in the form of market controls and public investment. *See also* ***monetarism***.

kickback Form of bribery of a customer who is offered a discount price then charged the original price (for accounting purposes) and later reimbursed the difference.

kick-up Chance offered to holders of bonds to convert them into shares at a profit.

By offering an equity kick-up, the company was able to offer lower coupons on the issue.

kick upstairs To promote a senior executive to a position in which he or she has relatively little influence and can therefore do no (more) harm.

killer bees People who help a company to resist a ***takeover bid*** by making the target less attractive financially.

kina Standard currency unit of Papua New Guinea, divided into 100 toea.

kip Standard currency unit of Laos, divided into 100 at.

kite Another name for ***accommodation bill***. It is also slang for a cheque.

kite flying Raising money by way of an ***accommodation bill***.

kiting Fraudulent issuing of a cheque that is not backed by funds in the account.

knee-jerk Reflexive movement in a market that is sudden and largely artificial.

knight Third party who appears at the scene of a ***takeover*** battle. *See also* ***white knight; grey knight***.

knocking copy Advertising copy that relies on pointing out the faults of a competing product to sell its own.

knock-on effect Series of effects caused by a single action.

The failure of that one machine had a knock-on effect all the way down the production line.

know-how Saleable knowledge of techniques or processes.

A & G are the only company with the know-how to produce such state-of-the-art equipment.

know-how licence Licence in the USA to use knowledge about a particular process or technique for commercial purposes.

knowledge engineer Person who collects and files information on a sophisticated computer system, in order to produce knowledge rather than mere data.

koruna Standard currency unit of the Czech Republic and Slovakia, divided into 100 haleru.

króna Standard currency unit of Iceland (divided into 100 aurar) and Sweden (divided into 100 øre).

krone Standard currency unit of Denmark, the Faroe Islands, Greenland and Norway, divided into 100 øre.

kroon Standard currency unit of Estonia, divided into 100 cents.

krugerrand Gold coin of South Africa since 1967, containing 1 ounce of gold. Quarter-ounce and tenth-ounce coins are also minted. *See also* ***Britannia coins***.

kwacha Standard currency unit of Malawi (divided into 100 tambala) and Zambia (divided into 100 ngwee).

kwanza Standard currency unit of Angola, divided into 100 lwei.

kyat Standard currency unit of Myanmar (Burma), divided into 100 pyas.

L

labour People used in the production of goods or services.

labour costs Expenses incurred in providing labour in the production process. Labour costs can include not only wages and salaries, but also National Insurance contributions and contributions to pension schemes.

labour-intensive Describing an industry in which labour is the most important and costly factor of production. Thus, an industry in which the major cost is the payment of salaries, incentives and bonuses is labour-intensive.

laches Legal term for negligence in performing a duty, asserting a right or claiming a privilege.

lacklustre Uninspiring corporate performance, normally indicated by a poor stock market rating. *See also* ***price/earnings ratio***.

Lady Macbeth strategy During a hostile ***takeover***, a strategy undertaken by a party who seems at first to be acting as a ***white knight***, but subsequently joins the aggressor.

laesio enormis Latin for extraordinary injury. It is a doctrine (derived from Roman law) which states that a contract price must be fair and reasonable. An unfair or unreasonable price is grounds for terminating the contract.

Laffer Curve A diagram that illustrates a nonlinear relationship between tax rates and tax revenues for an economy. Such a relationship was popularized by Arthur Laffer and is commonly known as the Laffer curve.

laggard Share that does not keep up with the average price of comparable shares.

lame duck Weak individual or company; one ripe for ***takeover*** or unable to provide effective competition.

land bank Alternative term for ***agricultural bank***.

landlord's fixture Object, *e.g.* a fence, provided by the landlord of a property. Otherwise, a fixture provided by a tenant that may not be removed, either because an agreement has been made between the landlord and tenant or because the tenant has not removed it on vacating the property.

landmail Practice in the USA of buying the shareholding of an actual or potential corporate ***raider*** in return for land as opposed to cash. *See also* ***greenmail***.

land tax Tax on the ownership of land, normally paid in the form of ***rates***.

last in first out (LIFO) Term with two meanings:

1. It is an accounting term for a system of stock-keeping, whereby the latest items manufactured or bought are used or sold before old stock is cleared. In a period of deflation this has the effect of maximizing profit, because new goods or materials have cost less to manufacture or buy. *See also* ***base stock method; first in first out***.
2. It idescribes the method by which some companies make employees redundant, on the basis of length of service. Thus, the last people to be employed are the first to be laid off.

last trading day In trading in ***financial futures***, the last day on which trading may take place before delivery.

lats Standard currency unit of Latvia, divided into 100 santimi.

late-kerb Trading in metals that goes on after hours, usually over the telephone. *See* ***kerb trading***.

laundering Method of disguising the origin of funds by moving them rapidly from one account or country to another. It thus becomes a complicated business to trace their origins, movements and eventual destination. Counterfeit or stolen money may be laundered.

LAUTRO Former UK self-regulating organization (SRO) that governed the trading and operation of ***unit trusts***. *See also* ***Financial Services Act***.

lawyer Somebody licensed to practise law. The term may be applied to a solicitor, but is most usually (and loosely) used as a synonym for "attorney" or "barrister".

lay day Day on which a vessel may unload cargo without incurring port charges.

laying-off Making an employee redundant, either temporarily or permanently, usually because there are insufficient orders for the whole workforce to be employed.

LBO Abbreviation of ***leveraged buyout***.

LCE Abbreviation of ***London Commodities Exchange***. Now also known as

London FOX (***London Futures and Options Exchange***).

LCH Abbreviation of ***London Clearing House***.

leading indicator Measurable variable (such as factory construction) that moves in advance of the indicated item (such as the level of employment).

lead manager In a ***syndicate***, the company that does the administration. For this service, the lead manager usually receives a higher ***commission*** than the other members of the syndicate.

lease Contract giving temporary possession of a property, sometimes in areas where prices are appreciating so rapidly that it is not in the owner's best interests to sell. Buildings are the most common subjects of a lease, although it is possible to lease land and other possessions, such as vehicles and machinery. Long-term leases are often mortgaged, bought and sold. *See also* ***tenancy***.

lease-back Arrangement by which a property is sold on condition that it is immediately leased back to the original owner. ***Capital*** tied up in property is therefore freed for other uses.

lease financing Form of off-balance-sheet financing whereby goods (*e.g.* machinery) are leased rather than being purchased outright. Lease financing is therefore generally thought of as a type of disguised ***borrowing***.

leasehold Describing property held by ***lease***. On leasehold land, the lessee pays ***ground rent*** to the person who holds the ***freehold***.

Lebanese pound *See* ***livre***.

ledger Book in which trade transaction, credits and debits are recorded. The term is most accurately applied to the principal volume in a series of account books, which collates the details made in the ***books of original entry***.

leg One of the divisions of a corporation or company.

legal charge Another name for a ***mortgage***.

legal reserve Minimum sum that building societies and insurance companies have by law to hold as security for their customers.

legal tender Currency; coins or notes that may be offered as a medium of exchange. In the UK this means any number of banknotes, up to £10 in £1 and 50p coins, other "silver" (cupro-nickel) coins to the value of £5, and bronze coins up to 20p.

lek Standard currency unit of Albania, divided into 100 qindars.

lempira Standard currency unit of Honduras, divided into 100 centavos.

lender of the last resort ***Central bank*** that is prepared to lend to the banking system as a whole, including to commercial banks. In the UK the lender of the last resort is the ***Bank of England***. It must be prepared to advance money to discount houses which have insufficient funds to balance their books, preventing their bankruptcy. It therefore gives confidence to the markets and helps to prevent a damaging run on the banks. By acting as lender of the last resort, the Bank of England is able to influence the ***money supply*** and ***interest rates***. *See* ***discount house***.

lending Temporary grant of money, goods, equipment, people and so on, made on the understanding that the thing lent, or its equivalent, will be returned, often with additional (***interest***) payment.

leone Standard currency unit of Sierra Leone, divided into 100 cents.

lessee deposit Deposit that is paid by the lessee on rented property, intended to cover the lessor against damage or loss and returnable on termination of the lease.

letter Written document of agreement, often listing the terms and conditions of a business relationship.

letter of allotment Means by which shares are allotted. A letter of allotment may be used as proof of ownership and entitles the holder to a ***certificate*** for the number of shares stated in the letter. It should not be confused with ***allotment note***.

letter of comfort Letter from a parent company to a bank at which a subsidiary has applied for a loan which, while not offering to guarantee the loan, expresses an awareness of the situation an an intention of keeping the subsidiary in business.

letter of credit (L/C) Letter from a bank authorizing another bank to pay the sum specified to the person named in the letter. It is also referred to as documentary credit. *See also* ***letter of indication***.

letter of identification *See* ***letter of indication***.

letter of indication Letter from a bank to a depositor who has been issued with a ***letter of credit***. It is used with the latter as proof of the bearer's signature and identity. It is also called a letter of identification.

letter of intent Letter outlining some intended action sent to establish intent in the eyes of the law.

letter of regret Letter informing an applicant that he or she has been unsuccessful in applying for a new share issue.

letters of administration Court order that appoints someone to act as ***administrator*** in the winding-up of a deceased person's estate in the absence of an executor or if someone dies intestate, or to administer the winding-up of a company.

letters patent Document issued by the Patent Office attesting the holder's right to possession of a ***patent***.

lettuce Slang term for banknotes.

leu Standard currency unit of Moldavia and Romania, divided into 100 bani.

lev Standard currency unit of Bulgaria, divided into 100 stotinki.

leverage Alternative term for ***gearing***; the ratio of a company's debts to total ***capital*** or shareholders' funds. In a buoyant market, a high proportion of debt has a beneficial effect on share earnings, because it is usually possible for the company to earn more on its loan capital than it is paying in ***interest***. In such circumstances, high gearing is beneficial to shareholders. Conversely, a fall in demand or a rise in interest rates affects a highly-geared company adversely. A company's leverage or gearing often has a significant effect on its share price in an open market. *See also* ***leveraged buyout***.

leveraged buyout Buyout of a large company by a smaller one, the capital for which has been borrowed from a friendly source, secured on the assets of the company being bought. *See also* ***leverage***.

leveraged company Company that is seriously in debt.

liability A company's or person's debt. Long-term (or deferred) liabilities are usually distinguished from current liabilities, as are secured debts from unsecured debts.

liability management Management of a bank's funds by buying and selling on the ***interbank market*** or attracting ***institutional investors*** with such devices as certificates of deposit. The aim is to maintain a sufficient difference between the bank's liabilities (to pay out) and the maturity of its assets.

LIBID Abbreviation of ***London Inter Bank Bid Rate***.

LIBOR Abbreviation of ***London Inter Bank Offered Rate.***

licensed deposit taker Organization authorized by the Bank of England to accept deposits (but not allowed to call itself a bank).

lien The right to possession of property until such time that an outstanding ***liability*** has been repaid. A banker's lien gives a bank the right to retain or sell the property of a ***debtor*** in lieu of payment.

lien on shares The right to take possession of ***shares*** if a borrower defaults on payment.

life-belt Colloquial term for security for a bank loan.

LIFFE Abbreviation of ***London International Financial Futures and Options Exchange.***

LIFO Abbreviation of ***last in first out.***

LIMEAN Abbreviation of ***London Inter Bank Mean Rate.***

limit (order) On a stock or commodity exchange, an instruction given by a client to his or her ***stockbroker***, which specifies the maximum price the broker is authorized to pay to buy a shareholding, or the minimum he is to demand before selling. Limit order is also the US term for a ***stop loss order***.

limit (up/down) The maximum and minimum limits within which the price of some commodity futures and ***financial futures*** are permitted to fluctuate in one day's trading. *See* ***fluctuation***.

limited In a business context, something of restricted ***liability***, as in a ***limited company***.

limited company Also called a limited liability company, a company formed from a group of people, whose ***liability*** is limited to the extent of the investment they have made (usually to purchase shares in the company), although occasionally liability is limited by guarantee to a certain amount as specified in the memorandum.

limited liability Restriction of the owners' loss in a liquidated company to the amount of ***capital*** each has invested. The loss of the individual shareholder in such an eventuality is limited to the value of his or her holding. In the event of ***liquidation*** the company itself remains liable for its outstanding debts; creditors are generally paid by selling off or dividing up the bankrupt company's ***assets***. *See also* ***limited company***.

limited order Instruction to a ***broker*** containing conditions about price and timing.

L

limited partner Partner whose liability for the debts of the partnership is limited in law to the sum he or she invested in it. A limited partner does not generally share in the management of the firm. He or she may, however, offer advice and examine the books of account. *See* ***limited partnership***.

limited partnership Partnership in which one or more partners have only ***limited liability*** for the firm's debts. In each limited partnership there must be one general partner with unlimited liability. A limited partnership is therefore unpopular and a ***public limited company*** is preferred, because all shareholders in such a company have only limited liability. *See* ***general partnership***.

liquid Something that is readily accessible, such as ***assets*** that can be immediately realized in ***cash*** form. ***Money*** is by definition fully liquid, and cash kept in a bank is the most obvious liquid asset. Treasury bills, money at call and Post Office savings are similarly liquid.

liquid assets Assets that may be readily converted into money. *See* ***tangible asset***.

liquid assets ratio Ratio of the value of total assets held to the value of assets that may be converted into cash without loss.

liquidated damages Damages of an amount already specified in a ***contract***.

The terms of the contract provide for liquidated damages to be paid.

See also ***unliquidated damages***.

liquidation The ***winding-up*** of a company, so-called because the company's ***assets*** are liquidated – converted into cash money – in order that outstanding ***creditors*** may be paid (in whole or in part).

liquidity The ease with which an ***asset*** can be converted into money. Cash deposits in current bank accounts may be quickly withdrawn and are said to be highly liquid; money in most deposit accounts is slightly less so because notice must usually be given before withdrawal.

liquidity ratio For any business, current assets divided by current liabilities. It is also termed the current asset ratio.

lira Standard currency unit of Italy, San Marino and the Vatican City (divided into 100 centesimi), Cyprus and Turkey (divided into 100 kurus) and Malta (divided into 100 cents).

listed company Company whose shares are listed on a stock exchange.

listing ***Flotation*** of a company on a stock exchange; the sum of the actions that permits ***securities*** to be traded on a stock market. The issued shares are then listed in the exchange records and their price fluctuations recorded and published.

listing agreement Agreement to abide by the rules of the London Stock Exchange when applying for ***listing***.

litas Standard currency unit of Lithuania, divided into 100 centai.

Little Bang First stage of deregulation of the UK stock market, which applied only to overseas trading. *See* ***Big Bang***.

living debt Part of the ***National Debt*** used to pay for the infrastructure, hospital building, schools and other national assets.

livre Standard currency unit of Lebanon, also called the Lebanese pound, divided into 100 piastres.

LME Abbreviation of ***London Metals Exchange***.

loading Term with two meanings:

1. It is an additional charge to a bank account or an extra percentage added to the interest on a loan to pay for administration charges or a higher risk than usual.
2. It is the difference between the price of a ***unit trust*** and its actual value. Loading on unit trusts is generally charged only on purchase. It is levied to meet expenses and the cost of administration.

loading broker Someone who acts for a ship's owner, obtaining cargoes for the vessel to transport.

loan Sum of money borrowed by one person or organization from another on condition that it is repaid, generally for a specified time and often at an agreed rate of ***interest***. *See also* ***back-to-back loan; bank loan; personal loan***.

loan application form Bank document filled in by somebody wishing to borrow money, containing the nescessary information to satisfy the requirements of the ***Consumer Credit Act***.

loanback Method of borrowing from the funds of a personal pension scheme. It is also an alternative term for ***lease-back***.

loan creditor Person or organization (such as a bank) from which a business has borrowed money.

loan capital That part of a company's capital that is lent over a fixed period of time.

loan drawdown See *drawdown*.

loan guarantee scheme (LGS) UK government scheme introduced in 1981 to promote the establishment and development of small businesses. The government agrees to underwrite 70% of approved loans made to such firms in exchange for a 2.5% annual ***premium*** on this portion, and on condition that the lending institution underwrites the balance of 30%.

loan-loss provisions Reserves held by a bank or other lending institution against loans that are not repaid by the borrower.

loan rate ***Rate of interest*** charged for a ***loan***, often expressed as a certain percentage above ***base rate***.

loan selling Selling of a loan by one bank or financial institution to another. The borrower is not necessarily informed.

loan shark *Moneylender* who (quite legally) charges excessive rates of interest, usually for only short-term loans.

loan stock Security issued by a company in respect of loan funds made available by investors. It is smilar to a ***debenture***, although loan stock is often unsecured.

lobby banking Service offered to bank customers, who can (without going to the bank's counter or even when the counters are closed) withdraw and deposit money and request statements and cheque books.

local authority bond Bond issued by a local government authority. It is also known as a municipal bond.

local currency Currency of a foreign country with which an exporter or trader is dealing.

lock box Security chest or safe for personal use. The term also includes safe-deposit boxes provided by some banks.

lock-up On financial markets, an investment expected to yield profit only in the long term, and in which capital will therefore be "locked-up" for some time.

lock-up option In a situation in which a company is being threatened with an unwanted ***takeover***, a defensive tactic whereby the target company promises to sell its most attractive ***assets*** to a ***white knight***. See also ***crown jewel tactic***.

locus poenitentiae Latin for "opportunity to repent". It is an option open to the parties of an illegal ***contract***, who may save it by deciding not to carry out that part which is against the law.

lollipop Corporate incentive or reward.

Lombard rate Borrowing rate of interest charged to financial institutions by the German Bundesbank.

Lombard Street Street in London whose name, because it is the location of the head offices of many UK banks and discount houses, stands for the London ***money market***. The US equivalent is ***Wall Street***.

London Bankers' Clearing House Organization established in the 1770s that clears cheques drawn against UK ***clearing banks***.

London Clearing House (LCH) Organization established in 1888 that clears futures, options and other forward contracts.

London Commodities Exchange (LCE) Market that deals in cocoa, coffee, rubber, spices, tea and other commodities. In 1996 it merged with the ***London International Financial Futures and Options Exchange***.

London Foreign Exchange Market Market that deals in sterling and various foreign currencies, using contracts that are made verbally (using telephone lines or other electronic means) and later confirmed in writing.

London Futures and Options Exchange (London FOX) ***Commodity market*** that deals in ***futures*** and ***options***.

London Inter Bank Bid Rate (LIBBR) Rate of interest that banks use to buy from and sell funds to each other. *See also* ***London Inter Bank Offered Rate***

London Inter Bank Mean Rate (LIMEAN) Average of the ***London Inter Bank Bid Rate*** (LIBBR) and the ***London Inter Bank Offered Rate*** (LIBOR) .

London Inter Bank Offered Rate (LIBOR) Rate of interest that commercial banks offer to lend money for on the London interbank market. Along with the ***minimum lending rate***, LIBOR has a significant effect on bank ***interest rates***.

London International Financial Futures and Options Exchange (LIFFE) Financial futures market established in 1982 for dealing in options and futures contracts within the European time zone. Originally the

London International Financial Futures Exchange, its name changed in 1992 when it merged with the London Traded Options Market. (LTOM). A further merger in 1996 with the London Commodity Exchange (LCE) gave it unique status in the financial world.

London Money Market *See* ***money market.***

London Metal Exchange (LME) Market established in 1877 to deal in non-ferrous metals, including aluminium, copper, lead, nickel, tin and zinc.

London Traded Options Market *See* ***London International Financial Futures and Options Market.***

long Term with two meanings:

1. In the UK, it is the position taken by a ***bull*** speculator, who acquires quantities of a stock or commodity in excess of the amount contracted for, in expectation that the price will rise and permit the surplus to be sold at a profit.
2. In the USA, it is a ***security*** that someone has bought and actually owns.

long bill ***Bill of exchange*** with more than ten years to maturity.

long bond Bond with more than fifteen years to maturity. *See also* ***medium bond; short bond.***

long credit Loan that may be repaid over a long period of time. *See also* ***extended credit; short credit.***

long-dated gilt ***Gilt-edged security*** with a redemption term of more than fifteen years.

long hedge Hedge against a fall in the interest rate on the futures market. *See also* ***short hedge.***

long liquidation Long-term ***self-liquidating*** company.

longs Fixed-interest securities with redemption dates more than fifteen years in the future. *See* ***fixed-interest security.***

long tap Long-term government securities issued in unlimited numbers. *See* ***tap.***

long-term Period exceeding fifteen years, but more loosely applied to ***stocks*** issued for an indefinite period of time or in perpetuity. In the City, the phrase “long-term” is loosely applied to any period over one year.

long-term liability Debt that need not be repaid in the next three years. In ***accounting***, the term is sometimes applied to loans that are not due to be repaid in the current accounting period.

loop Circular chain of ***shareholdings***., e.g. A owns 20% of the stock of B; B owns 20% of the stock of C; C owns 20% of the stock of D; and D owns 20% of the stock of A.

loophole Any circumstance that permits the evasion of a custom or rule, but especially a legal inexactitude that offers an escape from a ***contract***.

loss Disadvantage, forfeiture of money or goods, or negative profit.

loss leader Product or service offered for sale at a substantial loss in order to attract customers. The hope is that shoppers who come to buy the loss leader will also purchase other goods in the same store.

lot Method of deciding by chance which ***stocks*** will be redeemed in a given year.

loti Standard currency unit of Lesotho, divided into 100 lisente. (The plural of loti is maloti.)

low-beta Describing shares that are relatively stable.

Some analysts expect the current trend to continue and so believe that low-betas are good buys.

low-load fund Mutual fund that charges a low initial fee.

Luddite Person belonging to a group of disaffected early 19th century workers who smashed industrial machinery in the belief that mechanization would lead to unemployment. Hence, it is now a contemptuous term applied to anyone who stubbornly opposes necessary change.

lump sum Sum of money paid to someone all at once, as opposed to being paid as a series of separate sums.

lump system System of payment under which workers receive a ***lump sum*** for each day's work or for the fulfilment of a daily quota. The lump system is common in the building industry, but frowned upon because it can enable employees to avoid ***taxation***.

luncheon voucher (LV) Voucher issued to a company's employees which can be used in payment for food at participating outlets. Luncheon vouchers are regarded as a tax-free ***perk***.

M

M0 *See* ***money supply***.

M1 *See* ***money supply***.

M2 *See* ***money supply***.

M3 *See* ***money supply***.

£M3 *See* ***money supply***.

macroeconomics Study of broad or ***aggregate*** economics. Macroeconomics concerns itself with the relationship between such major aggregates as prices, incomes, total consumption and total production, together with interest and exchange rates, savings and investment. *See also* ***microeconomics***.

made bills ***Bills of exchange*** traded in the UK but drawn and payable overseas.

magnetic ink character recognition (MICR) Printed characters on cheques and other credits that (because they are magnetic) can be "read" by a computer. A normal personal cheque includes MICR characters giving the cheque number, sort code and account number.

mail order System for buying and selling by post; the customer purchases goods direct from the manufacturer or distributor without the intervention of a ***middleman*** or retailer.

mail transfer (MT) Method of using banks to transfer funds between countries, often using the ***Society for Worldwide Interbank Financial Telecommunications*** (SWIFT) system.

mainstream corporation tax Company's overall corporation tax liability payable on gross profits. Tax actually paid is mainstream corporation tax minus any ***advance corporation tax*** (ACT) payments.

maintenance Broadly, the financial provision made by a husband for his ex-wife and any children after a divorce.

In law, also used to describe a contribution towards the cost of a legal action made by a person who has no legal or moral interest in the case.

major US equivalent of a ***blue chip*** company; a very large company within its market sector.

majority interest Shareholding that gives the holder control of a company, *i.e.* one of over 50%. *See also* ***minority interest***.

making a price Action of a stockbroker or market-maker when he or she quotes a ***bid price*** or ***offer price*** for a stock or share.

making up day Alternative term for ***settlement day***.

mala fide Latin for in bad faith; fraudulent. *See also* ***bona fide***.

maloti Plural of ***loti***.

managed account Investment account managed for a depositor by a bank's investment department.

managed currency Currency whose exchange rate is controlled (via a ***central bank***) by the government. The intervention is also called managed floating.

managed float *See* ***dirty float***.

managed floating *See* ***managed currency***.

managed fund Fund that is set up by an intermediary, and invested (using a ***stockbroker***) on behalf of an investor.

management Control and supervision of a company, asset or operation; the group of people who control and administer a company, as distinct from the workforce. The effectiveness of a firm's management is often of vital importance to its ***performance***, and management is therefore sometimes taken as a ***factor of production***.

management accountant Accountant who is involved in the day-to-day running of a business, providing management information upon which managers are able to make decisions. The distinction between cost and management accountancy is now becoming increasingly blurred.

management buy-out Purchase of a company by its managers, one of the most common forms of buyout.

management company Company that practises management consultancy.

manager's discretionary limits (MDLs) Limit on lending set by a bank on its branch managers (taking into account whether the requested loan is secured or unsecured).

managing director Senior executive director of a company, junior only to the ***chairman***, and charged with implementing the decisions made by the ***board***.

manat Standard currency unit of Azerbaijan (divided into 100 gopik) and Turkmenistan (divided into 100 tenesi).

M & A Abbreviation of ***mergers and acquisitions***.

mandate Written authority empowering one person to act on behalf of another. Mandates are cancelled when the mandator dies, is declared bankrupt, or certified insane. They are generally used to give access to the mandator's accounts (*e.g.* a ***standing order*** is a mandate).

mandatory grant Grant that must be paid to all people or organizations that fall into the qualifying categories. *See also* ***discretionary grant***.

mandatory liquid assests Non-interest earning reserves that ***clearing banks*** have to deposit with the Bank of England. Its cost, called the reserve asset cost, is usually passed on to the clearing bank's customers.

manufacturer's agent Agent who agrees to market a company's products, usually in a specific geographical area, on a ***commission*** basis. Such agents are often employed overseas to enhance a manufacturer's ***export*** trade.

manufacturing costs All expenses incurred by the manufacturer in the production of goods and services. They are also known as production costs.

manufacturing industry The aggregate of companies that produce goods rather than providing services.

manuscript signature Hand-written signature, as opposed to a ***facsimile signature***.

Mareva injunction Injunction that prevents the transfer of funds until a case concerning them has been heard in the UK courts.

margin Term with three meanings:

1. It is the proportion of the total cost of a product or service that represents the producer's profits.
2. When trading commodities or financial futures, it is the proportion of the contract that is put up.
3. Legally, a payment on account of a purchase, conferring ownership with its attendant risks and privileges upon the buyer, but subjecting him to a ***lien*** on the purchase to the extent that credit is advanced to finance the full purchase price secured by the purchase. The practice is more common in the USA than in the UK, where most dealing is done on account.

marginal In economics, the difference between two figures. *E.g.* a marginal unit is the last unit produced, or the first unit supplied, and is defined as the smallest additional amount that is economically viable to produce or buy.

marginal analysis Method used in ***microeconomics*** to study the effect of successive small changes in demand, output, prices and costs.

marginal cost Cost incurred in raising the level of output beyond the original target. Marginal cost calculations are used to justify going beyond that target (or, indeed, not doing so).

marginal relief Tax relief granted to a taxpayer whose ***income*** only marginally exceeds a specified level or tax ***bracket***. He or she receives a portion of the relief available to those in the lower bracket.

margin call In futures trading, if an adverse price movement more than eradicates a party's ***margin***, the balance of the deficit is called upon, often cancelling the ***bargain***. *See also* ***call option***.

margin dealing Term with three meanings:

1. It is the method of dealing commodities or financial futures in which only a proportion of the value of the contract is put up. *See* ***margin cover***.
2. It refers to high-gear dealing on the edge of a security's price; *i.e.* betting for low stakes on a high-risk change of price.
3. It describes transactions conducted on the margin of a loan from a broker or a speculator. The speculator deposits stock as collateral, but may still trade with any surplus accumulated as the result of a rise in market price.

margin loan Loan commonly made on limited ***security***. *E.g.* a group of several lenders may advance money secured on property to 75% of its value. A margin loan would then be secured on the remaining 25%. This would carry a higher risk and therefore attract a slightly higher rate of interest. It is also known as a top-up loan.

margin of solvency Amount by which a company's total assets are greater than its total liabilities (excluding share capital).

mark Abbreviation of ***Deutschmark*** (DM).

marked cheque Cheque that the bank has marked "good for payment", also called a certified cheque. Marked cheques are increasingly being replaced by ***banker's drafts***.

market Term with three meanings:

1. It is a place where goods and services are bought and sold.
2. It is the actual or potential demand for those goods and services.
3. It is an abstract expression denoting any area or condition in which buyers and sellers are in contact and able to do business together.

market capitalization Value of all the securities of a company at current market prices.

market forces Forces of ***supply and demand***, which together determine the price of goods and services on the open market.

market if touched (MIT) Instruction to a broker to sell shares as soon as the price reaches a designated level.

market leader Company that has the largest share of a particular market. Individual products that have the largest share of a market are known as ***brand leaders***.

market maker Market principal who encourages dealing by varying the price of his stock to promote its sale or purchase. The term is used especially with reference to the stock market.

market order Order to buy or sell securities on the stock market or a financial futures exchange at the best obtainable market price.

market research Survey that is conducted to assess consumer demand. Companies carry out market research in order to maximize the efficiency of their output and to determine potential markets which may be exploited in the future. In addition, market research often suggests ways in which goods and services may be more attractively presented to the public.

market risk Part of the total risk inherent in buying a stock, which depends on market movements as a whole rather than on the particular characteristics of the stock itself. *E.g.* during a market ***crash***, the share prices of many sound companies whose earning prospects remain unchanged may fall in line with less sound stock. This illustrates the market risk, rather than the specific risk inherent in stock market dealings.

market saturation Situation in which a ***market*** has as much of a product as it can sell.

market tending Control of a market's stock index, by intervention buying and selling.

market timer US investment manager who operates by moving his or her investment from one instrument to another depending on market prices.

marketing Distribution, promotion and presentation of a product.

marketing research Alternative term for ***market research***.

market value Price at which something is traded on the open market.

marking up Adjustment of price (say, by a retailer) to allow for a profit ***margin***. The retailer's mark up is equal to ***gross profit***.

markka Standard currency unit of Finland, divided into 100 pennia.

mark to market On a financial futures exchange, the adjustment of a customer's account to allow for profits or losses on his or her ***open contracts*** during the previous day's trading.

mark-up *See* ***marking up***.

marriage personal allowance Amount a married couple in the UK may earn before they are obliged to pay ***income tax***.

marzipan layer Broadly, middle management; the group of managers who are perceived, somewhat cynically, as unnecessary and indeed potentially harmful to a company's interests. The supposition is that the marzipan layer tends to develop into an overfed bureaucracy. They are alternatively known as the marzipan men or marzipan set.

Mastercard International organization that runs a major ***credit card***.

matched bargain Deals made by finding clients who wish to sell particular stocks and ones who wish to buy those same stocks.

matching Action of a bank in striking a balance between its assets and liabilities.

material adverse change In a bank loan agreement, a vague clause that requires the borrower to repay the loan if there is a material change in his or her financial circumstances.

maturity date Date, specified in advance, on which a financial instrument may be exchanged for its cash value.

maturity transformation Practice of using a short-term bank deposit to fund a long-term loan.

maximum fluctuation Also known as maximum slippage, the upper limit to which a price may change on any exchange in one day's trading. It is fixed in advance as a percentage of the current price, and trading in a contract is halted for the rest of the day if the maximum fluctuation price is reached.

maximum slippage *See* ***maximum fluctuation***.

May Day 1 May 1975, the day on which the minimum commission system was abolished; the New York Stock Exchange's equivalent of the ***Big Bang***.

MBA Abbreviation of Master of Business Administration. Associates of the Chartered Institute of Bankers can gain this Master's degree through the Institute's Lombard Scheme.

medium bond Bond with between five and fifteen years to maturity.

See also ***long bond; short bond***.

medium-dated gilt ***Gilt-edged security*** with a redemption term of between five and fifteen years.

medium-dated stock Stock with a redemption term of between five and fifteen years.

medium-term capital Loan capital lent in the medium-term, *i.e.* for between five and fifteen years.

member bank Bank that is part of a formal group or is a subsidiary of another bank, or in the USA is affiliated to the ***Federal Reserve System***.

meltdown Sizeable financial crisis; a severe crash. The term is taken from the nuclear power industry, where a "meltdown" in a reactor would trigger a major disaster.

memorandum Broadly, a reminder, very often a document that records the terms of an agreement or sets out an argument. It is often abbreviated to memo.

memorandum of association Document that has to be registered and filed at Companies House in the UK, giving details of a company's particulars and aims. It is accompanied by the ***articles of association***, which sets up the internal regulations of the company's operations, and states, among other things, the powers of the directors.

memorandum of satisfaction Document issued to certify that a ***mortgage*** has been paid in full.

mercantile agent Person or company that takes part in ***factoring***.

merchantable quality The quality possessed by goods deemed fit for sale; also termed merchandizable quality.

merchant bank Institution that specializes on raising capital, particularly for use in business or industry. *See also* ***venture capital***.

merger Fusion of two or more companies, as distinct from the ***takeover*** of one company by another. Mergers may be undertaken for various reasons, notably to improve the efficiency of two complementary companies by rationalizing output and taking advantage of ***economies of scale***, and to fight off unwelcome takeover bids from other large companies. The companies involved form one new company and their respective shareholders exchange their holding for shares in the new concern at an agreed rate.

mergers and acquisitions (M & A) Field of arranging ***mergers*** between companies or ***takeovers*** of companies, or the department within a large company that is formed to carry out this function.

megamerger Merger of two major companies to form one gigantic corporation, *e.g.* the 1986 merger between British Petroleum and Standard Oil of Ohio.

mergermania Fever that is believed to grip sectors of the business world from time to time. Mergermania occurs after a well-publicized merger or series of mergers; other companies become concerned that they will become adversely affected by the creation of larger and more powerful rivals and seek to merge themselves with other concerns as a protective measure.

method of advice Method used by a ***collecting bank*** to send documents to another bank that has issued a ***collection order***.

mezzanine finance Money lent to a small and growing, but financially viable, company. It is so called because the risk of making the loan falls between that of advancing ***venture capital*** and the safer course of putting the finance into established debt markets.

MICR *See* ***magnetic ink character recognition***.

microeconomics Study of the individual components of an economy in isolation. Microeconomics examines the choices open to specific people, companies and industries and has been developed to enable the study of subjects such as utility, price mechanisms, ***competition*** and ***margins***. *See also* ***macroeconomics***.

middleman Intermediary, usually a wholesaler, retailer or broker who acts as an agent between a buyer and a seller. Middlemen tend to push up prices by adding their own profit margin to the difference between buying and selling prices, and it may therefore be in the interests of the buyer and seller to "cut out the middleman" (as in ***mail order***).

middle-market price Price mid-way between the ***bid price*** and ***offer price*** on the open market. It is the price the Inland Revenue takes into account when calculating ***capital gains tax*** on share dealings.

middle price Alternative term for ***middle-market price***.

milker Person who steals travellers' cheques by removing a few cheques from the middle of someone's book of cheques. The loss is seldom reported immediately because the owner is not aware that they have been stolen.

minimerger ***Merger*** between two small companies.

minimum fluctuation Also known as the basis point, the lower limit to which a price may fall in one day's trading on an exchange. As with the ***maximum fluctuation***, it is fixed in advance and trading is halted for the day if the minimum fluctuation is reached.

minimum lending rate (MLR) Minimum rate at which the Bank of England, acting in its capacity of ***lender of the last resort***, is willing to discount ***bills of exchange*** and at which it offers short-term loans. The MLR has a direct effect on bank interest rates.

minimum offering period Minimum period of time for which an offer to the public to purchase shares may be left open. In the UK this period is usually 14 days.

minimum wage Lowest amount a company may pay a worker, often fixed by legislation or trade union agreements.

mining concession Land that is conceded to a mining concern for a certain period of time, so that the company is able to mine it.

minor In British law, a person under the age of 18; one who cannot legally conduct certain transactions or purchase certain goods.

minority Term with two meanings:

1. It is the status of a person under the age of 18; the state of being a minor.
2. It is the smaller portion of something, *i.e.* less than half the whole.

minority interest Shareholding that does not give the holder control of a company, *i.e.* a holding of less than 50%.

minority shareholder Person who holds a ***minority interest*** in a company.

mint Institution licensed to make coins or tokens. In the UK, the Royal Mint at Llantrisant is charged with the manufacture of British ***legal tender***, but there are several private mints that produce tokens, for example for gaming machines, coins aimed at collectors, and coinage for other countries.

In the United States coins are manufactured by the Bureau of the Mint.

mintage Process of minting coins or the charge a ***mint*** makes for manufacturing coins.

mint par of exchange Level of exchange for the coins of two countries that use the same metal (*e.g.*, gold or silver) for their coinage, taking into account the purity of the metal and the weight of the coins.

mint price Value of the number of coins that can be made from a single ***ingot*** of coinage metal.

mint ratio Ratio of the values of the two metals in the coins of a bimetallic currency (*see* ***bimetallism***).

MIRAS Acronym for ***mortgage interest relief at source***.

misfeance summons Application requesting that a court investigate the actions and conduct of a director of a company in ***liquidation***. The summons may be issued by any interested party, such as the official receiver, a creditor or a shareholder, and it requests the court to force the director concerned to compensate them for money misapplied or misappropriated.

misery index Index that estimates the relative ill-health of the economy by incorporating variables such as the level of inflation, unemployment and economic growth.

misrepresentation Any false statement that encourages a person or company to enter into a ***contract***. Misrepresentation may be either fraudulent, *i.e.* a deliberate intention to deceive, or innocent, *i.e.* the result of a genuine mistake. Under UK law the injured party may have the contract dissolved and claim suitable damages. *See also* ***mistake***.

mistake In legal parlance, any error, short of ***misrepresentation***, that induces a person or company to enter into a ***contract***. Mistakes may be mutual, *i.e.* common to both parties, or unilateral. Mutual mistakes include the innocent purchase or exchange of goods that are not in fact for sale; unilateral mistakes include more deliberate deceptions. Both mutual and unilateral mistakes may invalidate a contract, but they do not necessarily do so.

MIT Abbreviation of ***market if touched.***

mitigation Reduction in the severity of something.

mitigation of damage Minimization of a ***loss***. Mitigation of damage is the responsibility of the sufferer, and must be attempted if he or she is to win full ***compensation*** in court. Mitigation of damage, therefore, acts as a check against such acts as insurance fraud.

mixed economy Economy in which elements of free-market economies and planned economies co-exist.

MLR Abbreviation of ***minimum lending rate***.

MMC Abbreviation of ***Monopolies and Mergers Commission.***

mobile bank Small self-contained branch bank in a motor van, used for providing occasional banking facilities at remote locations and at events such as agricultural shows.

mock auction Auction that is in some way illegal. This may occur in several ways: when goods are sold for a price lower than the highest bid; when some goods are given away in order to attract bidders; when those who have not already bought lots are excluded from bidding; when part or all of the agreed price is privately returned to the bidder.

model code Stock Exchange code of conduct that sets out guidelines for share dealings by company directors. It specifies, broadly, that directors should not engage in questionable dealings with company stock, and in particular forbids share dealings in the two months preceding a company announcement of profit, loss, dividend, a proposed merger, takeover, sale of assets, and so on.

modem Short for modulator-demodulator, an electronic device that allows computer data to be transmitted (to another computer, possibly over a network) using telephone lines.

modern portfolio theory Theory of stock valuation developed in the early 1980s. It values stocks by estimating their future earnings discounted back to the present.

momentum In finance, the rate at which a ***price*** increases or decreases.

monetarism Group of economic theories which state in general that the level of prices and wages in an economy is ultimately determined by the amount of money in circulation (the ***money supply***); that variations in the amount of money (monetary growth) have no long-term effect on the level of real activity (*e.g.* output and hence unemployment); and that monetary growth can be controlled by government in order to control price inflation.

monetary base All money in circulation and at banks, including money on deposit at clearing banks and the Bank of England. It thus equals M0 of the ***money supply***.

monetary control Method used by a government to control the ***money supply*** through its ***central bank*** (in the UK the Bank of England).

monetary inflation Inflation that is caused by an increase in the ***money supply***.

monetary system System that controls the exchange rates of a group of countries, or a system that a single country uses to control its own currency exchange while ensuring there is enough money in circulation for internal use.

monetary union Agreement between countries in an economic union to have a common currency, fixed exchange rates and free movement of capital between countries It is a short-term aim of the European Union (EU).

monetary unit Country's standard currency unit.

money Medium of exchange; any generally accepted token that may be exchanged for goods or services. *See* ***legal tender***.

money at call Loans that may be called in at short notice, and which therefore attract only low rates of ***interest***.

money broker ***Money market*** dealer in short-term loans and securities. On the London Stock Exchange, six firms act as money brokers, channelling borrowed ***stocks*** from institutions onto the market, thereby enhancing the ***liquidity*** of the ***gilt-edged securities*** and ***equity*** markets in particular.

money had and received In law, money in the possession of one person which belongs to another. The term is applied whether or not the possessor obtained the money in good faith.

money laundering *See* ***laundering***.

moneylender Person licensed by the government to lend funds to others. The term is, however, used informally to describe any person lending money independently of banks and other financial institutions, often at high rates of interest; and as such carries certain negative connotations.

money lent and lodged Bank's lending ratio, a comparison of the total advances made and the total funds deposited.

money market Market operated by banks and other financial institutions to facilitate the short-term borrowing and lending of money. In the UK, the Bank of England is the ***lender of last resort***. A wider money market includes also the markets in bullion and foreign exchange.

money-market fund ***Unit trust***, the income from which is invested in high-yield, short-term instruments of credit. Money market funds are particularly popular when interest rates are high.

money-market instruments Financial products traded on the ***money market***, including certificates of deposit and other short-term instruments.

money-market unit trust Risk-free unit trust that invests in short-term ***money-market instruments***.

money of account Denomination of money that, although no longer coined (such as the ***guinea***), is still used in keeping some accounts.

money order Method of transmitting money via the UK Post Office, which avoids the need to send cash or cheques through the post. *See also* ***international money order***.

money runner Informal US term for a person who invests in markets throughout the world, probably creating ***hot money*** in the process.

money supply Total amount of money available at short notice in a given country. There are several categories of money supply: M0, M1, M2 and M3.

M0 is defined as notes and coin in circulation and in bank tills, plus the operational balances that banks place with the ***Bank of England***. M0 is the narrowest category and is sometimes called narrow money.

M1 is defined as notes and coin in circulation and money deposited in bank current accounts. It is the best gauge of money immediately available for exchange.

M2 is an obsolete definition of the money supply. It includes notes and coin in circulation and in bank current accounts, together with the funds saved in deposit accounts maintained with the clearing banks, National Giro Bank, Bank of England banking department, and discount houses.

M3 is defined as M2 plus interest-bearing non-sterling deposit accounts held by British residents, and other certificates of deposit. M3 is the broadest definition of the money supply and may also be known as broad money. A subsidiary measure, £M3, excludes non-sterling deposit accounts.

Monopolies and Mergers Commission (MMC) Government organization that monitors ***takeovers*** and ***mergers*** (in the public and national interest) and acts as watchdog over ***monopolies*** and restrictive trade practices.

monopolistic competition Alternative term for ***imperfect competition***.

monopoly Strictly, an industry with only one supplier. The term is also applied more widely to an industry controlled ("monopolized") by one company, which produces a sufficient proportion of the total output of that industry to effectively control ***supply*** and therefore ***price***. In the UK, monopolies, and mergers or takeovers that might lead to the creation of a monopoly, are subject to the scrutiny of the ***Monopolies and Mergers Commission***.

monopsony Industry in which there are many manufacturers but only one customer for the goods produced. By controlling demand the consumer can, in theory, set the price. Monopsonies generally evolve to serve nation states; the market for warships, for example, is a virtual monopsony in that the vessels produced are purchased only by the government of the nation concerned, or by other governments that have its approval.

moonlighting Informal term for the practice of having two jobs, one of them generally involving work in the evening or at night.

mopping up Procedure by which the Bank of England uses ***Treasury bonds*** to buy spare funds from ***discount houses***.

moral obligation Obligation, usually to perform some service or complete some transaction, that cannot be enforced in law but which is nevertheless met out of honour.

moratorium Grant of an extended period in which to repay a loan, or a period during which the repayment schedule is suspended.

mortgage Transfer of the deeds to a property as ***security*** for the repayment of a ***debt***., e.g. building societies that provide a loan for the purchase of a house take legal possession of the property until the loan and interest have been repaid. It is also called a ***legal charge***.

mortgage bond Certificate stating that a mortgage has been taken out and that a property is security against default.

mortgage debenture Debenture secured by the mortgage of a property or other asset owned by the institution concerned.

mortgagee Person who lends money using a ***mortgage*** as security.

mortgagee in possession ***Mortgagee*** who has taken possession of a mortgaged property, usually because the ***mortgagor*** has defaulted on repayments.

mortgage interest relief at source (MIRAS) Method by means of which income tax relief is granted immediately on ***mortgage*** interest. It is being phased out.

mortgagor Person who takes out a ***mortgage*** in order to borrow money (usually to buy a property).

most-favoured-nation clause In bilateral international trade agreements, clause stating that each country agrees to look upon the other as its "most-favoured" trading partner, thus offering each other the best tariffs, first refusal, etc.

MT Abbreviation of ***mail transfer***.

multilateralism Broadly, international trade. Multilateralism is the use of the proceeds of a sale in one country to fund purchases in another. Thus, a nation selling arms to Iran and using the proceeds to purchase weapons in Nicaragua is practising multilateralism.

multifunctional card Plastic card that can be used as a ***cheque card***, ***cash card*** and/or ***credit card***. Such cards are made available by Barclaycard and Visa.

multinational Concerning more than one nation.

multinational corporation ***Corporation*** that has operations and offices in more than one country.

multiple Term with three meanings:

1. It is a chain store; a group of shops in numerous locations but selling the same stock and under one ***management*** group.
2. It is the factor by which one multiplies the cost of producing a unit of goods, to arrive at a satisfactory selling price.
3. It means manyfold.

It would contravene the terms of the issue of British Gas shares if one person made multiple applications for the shares.

multiple exchange rate Variable ***exchange rate*** that some countries quote, often giving a more favourable rate to importers of wanted goods and to tourists.

municipal bond Equivalent to a ***local authority bond***.

muster roll Register of the holders of a ***security***.

mutilated bills A mutilated or repaired bill or cheque should be endorsed by the payee with the words "mutilation confirmed" or "torn in error". Mutilated or soiled banknotes are acceptable to the Bank of England (through a major bank or the Post Office) as long as enough of the notes remain.

mutual Describing a company owned by its depositors or members but which does not issue stocks or shares. Many building societies and insurance companies in the UK have this status.

mutual fund Alternative US term for ***unit trust***.

mutual savings bank ***Savings bank*** that is owned by its depositers and run by an elected board.

N

Naamloze Venootschap(NV) Dutch equivalent of the British ***public limited company*** (plc).

naira Standard currency unit of Nigeria, divided into 100 kobo.

naked debenture Alternative term for ***unsecured debenture***.

naked option Option to buy shares in which the seller of the option (the option writer) does not already own the shares. In this instance, the option writer hopes to buy back the option before it is exercised and so avoid having to supply the shares. If the option is exercised and the market price of the shares has risen, then the option writer makes a loss. An option writer who sells naked options is known as a naked writer.

naked writer *See* ***naked option***.

name day On the Stock Exchange, the day before ***account day***, on which sellers of ***securities*** are supplied with the names of those who have bought from them during the last ***account***.

narrow money Alternative term for M0. *See* ***money supply***.

NASDAQ Abbreviation of National Association of Securities Dealers Automated Quotations, the US equivalent of ***over-the-counter market*** (OTC), now trading in the UK.

national Concerning or administered by a nation state.

National Debt Debts owed by the government, *i.e.* the sum of government borrowing, covering such things as National Savings, Treasury bills, and government bonds. The US equivalent is called the Federal Debt.

National Giro Banking service available through UK Post Offices. It is commonly used for paying bills over a Post Office counter (by direct charge to the Giro account). *See also* ***giro***.

nationalization Government policy whereby industries previously in private ownership are bought by the state and subsequently controlled by the government. *See also* ***privatization***.

nationalized industry Industry that is owned by the state and controlled by the government, which was previously in private ownership. *See also* ***privatization***.

National Savings Bank (NSB) UK government savings bank established as the Post Office Savings Bank in 1861. Its name changed in 1969 but it is still opperated through the Post Office, where savers may deposit and withdraw money and invest in ***National Savings Certificates***, etc.

National Savings Capital Bond Five-year £100 bond offered since 1989 by the ***National Savings Bank*** aimed at non-tax payers, who receive 7.75% compound interest if the bond is left for the fill term.

National Savings Certificate Tax-free five-year certificate issued by the ***National Savings Bank*** through Post Offices and banks. Investors receive 4.5% interest plus an index-linked bonus if the certificate is left for the full term.

National Savings Children's Bonus Bond Tax-free bond issued by the ***National Savings Bank*** for a child under 16 years old. It continues to earn interest at 7.85% until the child is 21 years old, during which time a bonus is added every five years. The bond is aimed at parents and grandparents as a means of investing on behalf of the child.

National Savings First Option Bond Fixed interest rate savings tax-paid (= FIRST) bond issued by the ***National Savings Bank***. For a minimum investment of £1,000, an investor receives a guaranteed interest of 4.8% for the first year, increasing by 0.3% each year. The "option" is to cash in the bond after any 12-month period.

National Savings Income Bond Bond issued by the ***National Savings Bank***, aimed at non-tax payers because the interest (6.5% or 6.75% variable for over £25,000 worth) is paid gross every month and can therefore constitute a regular income.

National Savings Pensioners Guaranteed Income Bond Bond similar to the ***National Savings Income Bond*** issued by the ***National Savings Bank*** to pensioners aged 65 and over. For a minimum investment of £500 the bonds pay an interest of 7.75% gross, fixed for five years and paid monthly. They are known colloquially as granny bonds.

National Savings Premium Bond Stake in a form of lottery run by the UK government through the ***National Savings Bank*** since 1956. The bonds cost £1 each and carry no interest, but each week and month tax-free prizes (equivalent to 5.2% of the money paid in) are awarded to the holders of bonds selected by a random number generator out of the interest accumulated on all premium bonds. They are not transferable, but may be redeemed at any time at their face value.

National Savings Stock Register Organization run for the Department of National Savings which enables people to buy ***gilt-edged securities*** by post without having to employ a stockbroker. Interest is paid before tax, although it remains taxable.

natural economy Economy in which barter is the most common form of *exchange*.

natural increase Increase in population over a specified time, calculated by subtracting the number of deaths in that period from the number of births. A falling population is therefore subject to natural decrease.

natural justice Rules to be observed by an arbitrator when adjudicating a dispute. Broadly, he or she must act in good faith and demonstrate a lack of bias or personal involvement. All the documents pertaining to the case must be made available to both parties, and no evidence may be presented without each being present. Each party must have an equal opportunity to state its case.

natural rate of growth Used in theoretical economics to describe a rate of growth in an economy that is in equilibrium, *i.e.* an economy with no ***inflation*** and with unemployment at its natural level.

natural rate of interest Rate of interest at which the demand for and supply of loans is equal.

natural wastage Method of reducing the workforce of a firm without resorting to enforced redundancies. As far as possible, the employer does not replace employees who die, retire or resign.

NAV Abbreviation of ***net asset value***.

nearby futures Futures contracts that are closest to maturity. *See also* ***deferred futures***.

near money Liquid asset that can be transferred immediately (such as a ***bill of exchange*** or ***cheque***), although not as liquid as cash. It is also known as quasi-money.

near-term Short term; in the near future. US securities markets have been criticized for near-termism, the practice of examining price performance over a period of days rather than years.

negative cash flow ***Cash flow*** in which outgoings are greater than income.

negative easement Right of a landowner to prevent a neighbour from exploiting or affecting his or her land.

negative equity Asset that is currently worth less than the money borrowed to pay for it. An all-too-common example is a house whose current market price is less than the remaining value of the mortgage taken out to buy it.

negative income tax (NIT) System of taxation by which those earning less than a specified income receive tax credits to bring their income in line with a guaranteed minimum income.

negative interest Charge made by a bank for holding funds for a certain time.

negative pledge Contractural undertaking by a borrower not to use the same assets to obtain another bank loan elsewhere (without the lending bank's permission).

negligence Breach of a duty to take reasonable care. Negligence may be displayed by a doctor failing to make an accurate diagnosis, by a lawyer who fails to advise his or her client of the law, by a company chairman who fails to consider the interests of his shareholders, etc. Professional people frequently guard against actions brought for negligence by taking out professional indemnity insurance.

negotiable Concept of transfer of an asset that gives the transferee complete and undeniable ownership and free from equities or defences that could be raised against the transferor.

The company made a preliminary bid for the contract, but indicated that their terms were negotiable.

negotiable instrument Document that may be freely exchanged, usually by ***endorsement***, and which entitles the ***bearer*** to a sum of money. Negotiable instruments include ***cheques***, ***bills of exchange***, ***certificates of deposit*** and ***promissory notes***. *See also* ***negotiable***.

negotiable security Security that is easily passed from one owner to another by delivery. In the UK, very few instruments are negotiable in this way. *See also* ***negotiable***.

negotiation fee Charge made by a bank for arranging a loan.

net That which remains after all deductions and charges have been made. *See also* ***gross***.

net asset value (NAV) Value of a company's assets after the company's *liabilities* have been deducted.

net current assets Difference between current assets and current liabilities, equal to the ***working capital***.

net domestic product Value of ***gross domestic product*** after a figure for capital consumption has been deducted.

net interest Any ***interest*** after deduction of tax at source (such as interest paid into an account at a bank or building society).

net margin Difference between the selling price of an article and all the costs incurred in making and selling it.

net profit ratio Ratio of net ***profit*** to sales.

new cedi Standard currency unit of Ghana. *See* ***cedi***.

new dong Standard currency unit of Vietnam. *See* ***dong***.

new issue Stocks and shares that are about to be placed, or have recently been placed on the ***open market***. New issues may consist of stock in a recently-established ***limited company*** or supplementary issues made by established companies.

new issues market Alternative term for ***primary market***.

new time On the London Stock exchange, the last two days of an ***account***. Transactions conducted in new time are settled at the end of the next account; therefore, new time is effectively part of the next account period.

New York Metals Exchange (NYMEX) Organization that, with the Chicago Metals Exchange, conducts a significant part of the world's hard commodity trading. The two institutions are usually in fierce competition.

ngultrum Standard currency unit of Bhutan, divided into 100 chetrum.

NIC Acronym for newly industrializing country, a country which, although part of the Third World, has rapidly developed a substantial industrial base. In the 1980s this status was accorded to South Korea and Taiwan.

niche Market or section of a market controlled by an operator who is catering for a well-defined and usually small group of customers.

night safe Money safe at a bank that is accessible from the street into which traders can deposit takings after the bank has closed for the day. The money is credited to the trader's account the following day.

Nikkei Average Index of share prices on the Japanese Stock Exchange.

nil paid *New issue* of shares for which the issuing company has yet to be paid. The term is most commonly applied to rights issues.

NIT Abbreviation of ***negative income tax***.

NL Abbreviation of ***no liability***.

NMS Abbreviation of ***normal market size***.

no-brainer *Fund* that tracks the performance of a stock *index*. Its manager buys all the stocks listed on a major index, and hence no discretionary management is required. *See also* ***passive management***.

no liability (NL) Australian equivalent of a ***public limited company*** (plc).

no-load share Share sold at net asset value with no ***commission*** charge.

no-loan fund Form of US ***unit trust*** that employs no salesman and therefore incurs no commission or distribution costs. An investor thus avoids paying a commission on shares purchased, the only expense remaining being a relatively modest management fee. *See* ***mutual fund***.

nominal Existing in name only.

nominal accounts One of the three parts into which a book-keeping *ledger* is divided. The nominal accounts are the records of ***income*** and ***expenditure***. *See also* ***impersonal accounts; personal accounts; real accounts***.

nominal damages Damages awarded by a court which is satisfied that the plaintiff is in the right, but has suffered no actual loss.

nominal interest rate Rate of interest without an allowance for inflation. *See also* ***real interest rate***.

nominal partner *Partner* who lends his or her name to a firm, but who has invested no capital and does not take an active part in the company. He or she remains liable for the partnership's debts.

nominal value Also known as face value, the nominal value of something is the value or price written on it, *e.g.*, the denomination of a banknote or the par value of a share.

nominee A person or institution into whose name assets are transferred but having no beneficial interest in the asset concerned. *See* ***nominee shareholder***.

nominee shareholder Usually an institution that acquires shares in a company on behalf of somebody else (the beneficial owner). This enables the true shareholder's identity to be concealed and is often used when a person wishes to build up his or her shareholding prior to a ***takeover*** bid.

non-amortizing mortgage *See* ***balloon mortgage***.

non-business days Sundays and bank holidays, when banks are closed for business. They are not included in ***days of grace***, and ***bills of exchange*** that fall due on a non-business day are postponed until the next day.

non-contract market Alternative term for ***spot market***.

non-cumulative preference share Type of ***preference share*** for which unpaid interest (dividend) is not carried over to the next year.

non-domiciled Describing a person regarded by the authorities as "offshore", or non-resident, principally for ***tax*** purposes.

non-equity investment Any investment in securities except shares in companies (***equity***).

non-executive director Member of the ***board of directors*** who plays no active part in the day-to-day running of the company. He or she may attend board meetings and offer advice. Non-executive (or outside) directors are often well-known public figures whose appointment lends cachet to a company, or whose presence on the board is valued for their expertise, impartiality or wide-ranging contacts.

non-marketable securities That part of a ***national debt*** not traded on the stock market. Non-marketable securities include ***National Savings*** Certificates, Premium Savings Bonds, certificates of deposit, official funds in perpetual or terminable annuities, and the whole of the external national debt. About one-third of the total national debt is currently in the form of non-marketable securities.

non-participating preference share Type of ***preference share*** in which holders are paid a dividend before ordinary shareholders but do not receive additional dividends in a very profitable year.

non-performing asset That part of a company's ***capital*** that is currently yielding no ***return***, and on which none is expected. ***Fixed assets*** are generally classified as non-performing.

non-profit making organization (NPO) Company or institution that has a legal obligation to make no profit. The term is most usually applied to registered charities.

non-qualified Employee share option plan in which the gain made by the employee (*i.e.* the difference between the grant price and the market price) is taxed as ***income*** and not as a capital gain. *See* ***capital gains tax***.

non-resident Person who does not live in an area or state, or who lives there but does not meet the legal requirements for residence.

non-recourse finance Bank loan for a project where the bank is repaid only from the borrower's profits from the project. The bank has no recourse to any other of the borrower's assets.

non-revolving bank facility Bank loan to a company which is given a long time in which to draw money when it requires it from the facility. Once drawn the money (plus interest) has to be repaid in a fixed term.

nontariff barrier Barrier to trade that takes a form other than a financial imposition or ***tax***, *e.g.*, quantity or quality controls imposed on imports.

non-taxable income Income which for one reason or another is not subject to normal ***income tax***. Non-taxable income includes ***dividends***, money received by charities and interest on bank deposit accounts.

non-transferrable Describing a cheque that has been crossed so that it is payable only into the account of the named payee. *See* ***crossed cheque***.

non-voting shares Shares that carry no voting rights. Non-voting shares are issued to raise additional capital for the company, while permitting existing shareholders to retain control of the company. Such shares are often known as A-shares and generally rank *pari passu* with voting shares in respect of other rights.

no par value (NPV) Describing shares that have no stated value, but are valued at the current stock exchange price.

normal market size (NMS) Method of classifying shares, introduced in 1991, equal to 2.5 times the average daily customer turnover last year divided by the price of the share. It has replaced the classification into alpha, beta, gamma and delta shares.

nostro account Account kept by a bank with an overseas bank, usually in the foreign currency. *See also* ***vostro account***.

notary public Official licensed to attest the validity of documents and of the signatures on them by signing and/or sealing them. Dishonoured or protested bills also require the seal of a public notary.

note Token or proof of a transaction.

note circulation Area velocity of money, a measure of the speed at which cash circulates around the economy.

note of hand Alternative term for ***promissory note***.

notes to the accounts Information that by law must accompany a company's accounts, such as details of assets, debentures, investments, reserves and paid-up share capital.

notice Advice of a forthcoming action issued in advance, *e.g.* a notice to quit or notice of dismissal. The term is generally applied to the period that elapses between the moment an employee is informed that his or her services are no longer required, or an employee hands in his or her resignation, and the day on which he or she actually leaves.

He had been considering handing in his notice for a long time.

notice in lieu of distringas Notice issued by a shareholder and supported by a statutory declaration, that formally advises the issuing company of his or her holding. Such notices prevent any attempt by the company to transfer the shares in question to a third party.

notice of assessment Document isuued by the ***Inland Revenue*** detailing a person's taxable income and the amount of ***income tax*** payable.

notice of coding Document isuued by the ***Inland Revenue*** detailing a person's tax code for ***income tax*** purposes. A copy is also sent to the person's employer if he or she pays income tax ***pay as you earn*** (PAYE).

notice of second charge *See* ***second mortgage***.

noting and protest First two stages in the dishonouring of a ***bill of exchange***. The bill is first "noted", or witnessed, by a ***notary public***, who thereby testifies to its existence but not necessarily to its validity. It is then presented again, and if refused for a second time it is protested by being returned to the notary, who then testifies to its refusal. Noting must be completed within one working day of the bill's first being dishonoured.

notional income Non-financial benefit that an owner receives from an ***asset***. The term is most usually applied to the benefit received by the owner-occupier of a property. In such a case, the notional income is equal to the amount that would otherwise have had to be spent on ***rent***.

notional rent ***Peppercorn rent*** or minimal rent paid to establish a landlord-tenant relationship.

not negotiable Description applied to a document to which a transferee has no better claim than any previous bearer. Cheques, postal orders and bills of exchange may be crossed (*see* ***crossing***) "not negotiable" as a safeguard against theft.

novation The making of a contract between the parties to an original contract and a third party in which it is agreed that the third party shall replace one of the original parties.

novo kwanza Standard currency unit of Angola. *See* ***kwanza.***

NPO Abbreviation of ***non-profit-making organization.***

NPV Abbreviation of ***no par value.***

NSB Abbreviation of ***National Savings Bank.***

nuevo peso Standard currency unit of Mexico and Uruguay. *See* ***peso.***

null and void Phrase used when a contract is invalidated.

The court ruled that the contract be made null and void.

numbered account Bank account that is identified by a number only, usually in order to keep the identity of the account holder confidential. Bank accounts administered by banks in Switzerland are most often numbered.

number fudging Informal term for creative accountancy; the creation of a favourable account sheet without resort to actual fraud. It is also known as window dressing.

nurse an account Give time to someone whose bank account is overdrawn, to find funds to bring the account into credit.

NV Abbreviation of ***Naamloze Venootschap.***

NYMEX Abbreviation of ***New York Metals Exchange.***

NYSE Abbreviation of New York Stock Exchange, the largest security market in the United States. *See* ***stock exchange.***

O

obsolescence Loss of the value of something when it becomes out of date. In accounting, obsolescence refers to an asset that has to be written off, not through deterioration, but when its continued use becomes uneconomic. *E.g.* a piece of machinery may be superseded by a new, faster version; it is therefore uneconomic for the company to continue to use it, and the asset becomes obsolete. *See also* ***wear and tear; write off***.

odd lot Collection of ***stocks*** and ***shares*** that is so small and varied that they inconvenience the ***broker*** who agrees to deal them, and which he or she will therefore buy only at a low price. In the USA, an odd lot of fewer than 100 shares are dealt at a higher commission rate than larger quantities. *See also* ***round lot***.

offer Statement that one party is willing to sell something, at a certain price and under certain conditions. If a particular buyer is unwilling to buy at the offer price or under the conditions of the offer, he or she may make a ***bid*** against the seller's offer.

offer by prospectus In contrast to an ***offer for sale***, an offer by a company to sell shares or ***debentures*** directly to the public by issuing a ***prospectus***, instead of selling the shares to an ***issuing house***.

offer document Document sent to a company's shareholders by the maker of a ***takeover bid***, setting out the bidder's point of view and plans for the company should the bid be successful.

offer for sale An offer by a company to sell shares to an ***issuing house***, which then publishes a ***prospectus*** and sells the shares to the public. *See also* ***offer for sale by tender***.

offer for sale by tender Similar to an ordinary ***offer for sale*** except that the prospective buyers state the price they are willing to pay for a certain number of shares (above a minimum price specified in the ***prospectus***).

offer period During a ***takeover***, the length of time an offer of shares must remain open (at least 21 days).

offer price Price at which a ***market maker*** is prepared to sell a security. *See also* ***bid-offer spread; bid price***.

offer to purchase Alternative term for ***takeover bid***.

offering circular Document that in the USA contains information regarding offers of shares exempt from ***Securities and Exchange Commission*** regulations and registration.

Official List Formally the Stock Exchange Daily Official List (SEDOL), the official publication of the London Stock Exchange which appears daily at 5.30pm detailing price movements and dividend information for almost all securities quoted on the Exchange.

official quotations Figure quoted daily for almost all securities on the Stock Exchange ***Official List***.

official receiver (OR) *See* ***receivership***

official reserves Gold and currency reserves kept by the government. *See* ***gold and foreign exchange reserves***.

offset Term with three meanings:

1. Right of a bank to seize the bank balances of a guarantor or debtor of a defaulted loan.
2. Cancellation of the requirement to deliver commodities sold on a ***futures*** contract by buying an equal amount of the same commodity for the same delivery period.
3. Information encoded in the magnetic strip on a ***plastic card*** that confirms the holder's right to use the card.

offshore Describing a business that operates from a ***tax haven***.

offshore banking Banking transactions that take place overseas.

offshore banking unit (OBU) Foreign bank that deals in ***eurocurrency*** and foreign exchange settlements, located in a tax-favourable offshore banking centre.

offshore financing Raising of capital in countries other than one's own.

offshore fund Investment scheme operated from a ***tax haven***, by which investors may benefit from the haven's taxation privileges without leaving their home country. *See* ***tax shelter***.

Old Lady Popular name for the ***Bank of England***. *See* ***Old Lady of Threadneedle Street***.

Old Lady of Threadneedle Street The Bank of England, situated in Threadneedle Street in the City of London. It is a popular term of endearment dating from the early 19th century.

oligopoly Industry in which there are many buyers but few sellers. Such conditions give the producer or seller a certain amount of control over price, but leave him or her especially vulnerable to the actions of competitors. *See also* ***monopoly***.

on call Describing a repayment that must be made whenever the lender requires it (without notice).

oncost Another name for ***overheads***.

on demand Describing a ***bill of exchange*** that is payable to the bearer immediately on presentation, such as a cheque.

one-man Describing a business, company or operation involving only one person,

one-month money Money placed on the ***money market*** that cannot be withdrawn without penalty for one month.

one-year money Money placed on the ***money market*** that cannot be withdrawn without penalty for one year.

on-floor Describing transactions that are conducted and concluded on the floor of an exchange in the usual manner.

on-line Describing an electronic facility that is connected directly to a computer.

on stream When an asset or investment begins to function, it is said to come on stream.

open Unrestricted or unlimited. Also, to open is to take out a futures option.

open account Trade between an exporter and an importer without any built-in guarantee of payment. The exporter submits an invoice and expects to be paid in due course as is the case with any normal domestic transaction.

open cheque Alternative term for ***uncrossed cheque***.

open credit Credit that is extended to the customers of a bank who are deemed to be extremely creditworthy, and thus requiring no ***security***.

open contract Contract that has been bought or sold on a financial futures market, but has not been closed by making an offsetting transaction or taking delivery of the financial instrument involved. *See also* ***open position***.

open-end fund Alternative term in the US for ***unit trust***.

open indent Order for goods that does not specify a particular supplier. The agent receiving the indent may purchase suitable goods from any manufacturer at his or her own discretion.

opening a crossing Countermanding a crossing on a cheque (*see* ***crossed cheque***) by the drawer writing and initialling "pay cash". It then becomes an open or ***uncrossed cheque***.

opening bank Bank that opens a letter of credit, instructed by an importer to pay a foreign exporter.

opening bid First bid at an auction.

opening price Price of a share at the beginning of a day's business on a stock exchange. This may differ from the previous evening's closing price, generally because the price has been adjusted to take into account events that occurred overnight and the performance of other exchanges.

opening range On a financial ***futures*** market, the highest and lowest prices recorded at the opening.

opening sale Sale of an ***option*** contract where the seller becomes in effect the writer of the option by assuming responsibility for its performance.

open market Market in which goods are available to be bought and sold by anyone who cares to. Prices on an open market are determined by the laws of ***supply and demand***.

open order Alternative term for an order ***good-till-cancelled***.

open position Exposed position of a speculator who has bought or sold without making any hedging transactions, and who therefore gambles that the market will rise or fall as he or she predicted.

operating Describing the day-to-day running of something, such as a business or a machine.

operating budget Alternative term for ***cash budget***.

operating costs Expenses incurred in the day-to-day running of a company.

operating margin ***Operating profit*** expressed as a proportion of price or operating costs.

operating profit Earnings from normal business transactions. It does not include interest on loans or return on other investments.

operation Another term for a business (such as a company, partneship or firm) or the activities it undertakes.

She was called in to mastermind the company's new printing operation.

operation of law If one party obtains a legal judgement on a contract under which the party's liabilities are discharged, the contract is said to be discharged by operation of law, in that the legal requirements of the contract become merged with the requirements of the judgement. In cessation of a contract, operation of law means the effect of death, lunacy, bankruptcy in the case of, say, an agency contract plus garnishee or injunction in the case of the operation of a bank account.

operational (or **operations) research** Mathematical technique that can be applied, *e.g.* to discover how the various activities within an industry may be regulated to coexist with maximum efficiency.

opinion poll Survey of opinion carried out by interviewing a sample number of people, in person or by telephone, and detailing their preferences and opinions, usually in statistical form. Opinion polls are most commonly associated with politics, but are also widely used by manufacturers and advertisers to assess public taste and preferences.

opportunity cost Cost involved in using an asset (*e.g.* machinery) for one purpose rather than another. *E.g.* a company owning a building which it uses as storage space could rent it to someone else for, say, £500 per week. That sum is the opportunity cost of the building.

option An investor may pay a ***premium*** in return for the option to buy (a ***call option***) or sell (a ***put option***) a certain number of securities at an agreed price (known as the ***exercise price***), on or before a particular date. The dealer may exercise his or her option at any time within the specified period and normally does so at an advantageous time depending on market prices. Otherwise the dealer may allow the option to lapse.

option dealing Buying and selling in ***options***, which usually involves buying or selling goods or shares at some future date and at a pre-arranged price.

option money Premium paid in return for an ***option***.

option writer Someone who sells ***call options***, thereby agreeing to supply shares, or someone who sells ***put options***, agreeing to buy shares.

OR Abbreviation of official receiver. *See* ***receivership***.

order Either a demand from someone in authority that a particular action be taken (or that a person refrains from a particular action), or a request made to a supplier for a particular quantity of a certain product or for his or her services.

order and disposition In ***bankruptcy***, a means whereby a bankrupt's creditors may seize property to which the bankrupt has no title. Order and disposition comes into effect only if title is not obviously someone else's and if the bankrupt has led a third party into believing the goods are his or hers in order to receive credit. *See also* ***bankrupt; reputed owner***.

order cheque Cheque payable to a named person or to his or her order (by means of an ***endorsement)***.

order driven Describing an economy, industry or trading on a stock market that reacts in relation to the flow of incoming orders. *See also* ***quote driven***.

ordinary shares Shares whose holders are the owners of a company. They are entitled to a dividend after other preferential payments have been made (although payment of the dividend is at the discretion of the directors). Ordinary shares are sometimes classed as voting or non-voting shares, and are sometimes also known as ***equities***.

organogram Chart that shows the organization of a company, its hierarchy, and the relationships between departments.

originating bank In international trade transactions involving a foreign branch of a bank (with a head office in, say, London), the originating bank is the foreign branch at which the transaction originated. *See also* ***correspondent bank***.

OTC Abbreviation of over-the counter. *See* ***over-the-counter market***.

ougiya Standard currency unit of Mauritania, divided into 5 khoums.

outcry market On commodity markets, trading is recorded from the outcries of traders on the floor, although deals are sealed by private contract. Markets on which trading is carried on in this noisy manner are known as outcry markets and the style of trading is known as open outcry.

outgoer Farmer who accepts financial inducements to turn his or her agricultural land to another function, *e.g.* for leisure pursuits or a caravan site.

outgoings Money paid for something; expenditure.

outlay Money paid for something; expenditure.

out-of-date cheque Also known as an antedated cheque or stale cheque, a cheque drawn more than six months before it is presented for payment. Normally it is returned unpaid.

out-of-the-money option Option to buy shares (***call option***) for which the market price has fallen since the price was fixed. Equally, it is an option to sell (***put option***) for which the price on the market has risen above the agreed exercise price. In either case, the dealer makes a loss if he or she decides to exercise the option. *See* ***exercise price***.

output Amount produced by a company, single person or machine.

output tax In a ***value-added tax*** system, the tax that is charged by a supplier to a customer. *See also* ***input tax***.

outright buy stock Stock that is recommended unreservedly by market analysts.

outside broker A stock and share dealer who is not a member of any exchange.

outside director Alternative term for ***non-executive director***.

outwork Work done by an outside worker, normally operating at home. It often pays a company to employ workers to work at home, normally producing goods at a low rate of pay.

overbought If there are many buyers on a market, prices (*e.g.* of shares) are pushed to artificially high levels and the market is said to be overbought. *See* ***oversold***.

over-capitalization Situation in which a company has more capital than it can employ to its profit. *See also* ***gearing***.

overdraft When a bank customer withdraws more money from a bank account than is actually deposited with the bank, the excess is known as a bank overdraft. An overdraft facility must normally be agreed with the bank in question and interest on the overdraft is charged on a day-to-day basis. It attracts high rates of interest and ideally is used only for short-term borrowing.

overdraft facility *See* ***overdraft***.

O

overdrawn Describing a bank account that is in the red, becuase the account holder's withdrawals have exceeded the amount originally in the account.

overexposure Overabundance of risk. *E.g.* if a ***stockbroker*** is paid a salary largely dependent on the performance of a company and maintains a substantial shareholding in the firm, he or she is overexposed to the possibility of a downturn in the broking business.

overhead expenses Term sometimes used for ***indirect expenses***, sometimes for ***fixed costs***, and sometimes for both. Its precise meaning varies from company to company. *See also* ***overheads***.

overheads (US **overhead)** Costs incurred in the everyday running of a business and not variable according to output. Also known as indirect costs, fixed costs or supplementary costs, overheads include heating, lighting and energy costs, administration, insurance, rent and rates.

overheating Describing an unhealthy economic situation in which bank borrowing, balance of payment deficit, prices and wages are all rising.

overnight loan Bank loan to a ***discount house***, secured by ***bills of exchange*** and repayable the next day.

over-riding commission Commission paid to a broker in return for finding ***underwriters*** to an issue of shares. *See* ***share issue***.

overshoot Describing price trends on a currency market that continue to rise above levels anticipated by analysts.

oversold Describing a market in which there are too many sellers, so the price falls to an artificially low point, too rapidly. *See also* ***overbought***.

oversubscribed A sale of shares by ***application and allotment*** is said to be oversubscribed if the number of shares applied for exceeds the number of shares available. The situation is often remedied by a ***ballot***. *See also* ***allotment***.

over the counter Something that is legal, above board. *See also* ***over-the-counter market***.

over-the-counter market (OTC) Market on which securities not listed on any stock exchange may be bought and sold. In practice, the OTC market is operated by a limited number of market makers, often on the basis of matched bargains. *See also* ***unlisted securities market***.

over-trading Describing a potentially dangerous situation in which a company tries to take on more business than its working capital will allow.

ownership Basic right to possess something. It should not be confused with possession, for whereas a person may own something, he or she may still lose possession of it, *e.g.* to a bailee or to a thief. *See* ***bailment***.

own funds For a bank, building society or other financial instirution, the sum of its retained earnings, subordinated debt and any provision for losses.

P

pa Abbreviation of ***per annum***.

PA Abbreviation of ***personal account*** or personal assistant.

pa'anga Standard currency unit of Tonga, divided into 100 seniti.

package deal Deal that is all-inclusive, *i.e.* one that provides for the settlement of most or all the outstanding issues between the parties concerned.

packing Adding, to the payments on a loan, charges for services such as insurance, etc. without the borrower requesting them, or indeed fully understanding what he or she is buying. This practice is illegal.

pacman defence Method of defending against a hostile ***takeover***, whereby the target company makes a tender ***offer*** for the shares of the aggressor.

paid cheque Cheque that has been honoured by the bank on which it is drawn.

paid up Used either as a verb or an adjective to mean that a person has paid the money he or she owes or, more specifically, that he or she has paid a subscription. It is also used to distinguish fully-paid from ***partly-paid*** shares.

After we chased them for two weeks, they finally paid up.

He is a paid-up member of the union.

paid-up capital Capital obtained by a share issue in which the shares are fully paid. *See also* ***called-up capital; uncalled capital.***

painting the tape Method of creating an impression of activity around a share, by reporting fictitious transactions. Painting the tape is illegal.

paper Describing any form of ***loan***, but particularly a short-term loan such as a ***Treasury bill***. It refers to the paper on which a pledge to repay money at a specified time is recorded. Most paper is negotiable and can be bought or sold like any other commodity.

paper company Company established, usually with little capital, merely for financial purposes. *See also* ***shell company***.

paper currency Another name for ***paper money***.

paper money Paper tokens issued by a bank, representing a sum of money, which it "promises to pay the bearer on demand". Usually applied to banknotes, the term is sometimes extended to ***cheques*** and ***bills of exchange***. *See also* ***legal tender***.

par Equal to the face value or current rate. *See* ***parity***

parcel Block of shares that changes hands during a ***bargain***.

parent company Company that owns or part-owns, but more importantly controls, one or more ***subsidiary companies***.

pari passu Latin for with equal step, indicating simultaneous effect, often applied to new share issues. In this context, it means that the designated share will rank equally for ***dividends*** with comparable existing shares.

Paris Club *See* ***Group of Ten***.

parity Equality (in value).

It is unlikely that the US dollar will reach parity with sterling.

Parkinson's Law Work expands to fill the time allotted, a principle originally propounded by Professor C. Northcote Parkinson in 1957.

par of exchange Rate of exchange between two currencies for which there an equal supply and demand.

parole contract Simple, unwritten (*i.e.* verbal) contract.

part load Portion of the part of the share capital of open-ended investment companies not covered by underlying ***assets***. *See* ***share capital***.

participating loan Syndicated loan, for which there are two or more lenders. The lead bank or manager arranges the loan and its terms using agreed contributions from other banks or lenders.

participating preference shares ***Preference shares*** that entitle the shareholder to additional dividends or bonuses from the remaining profits of a company if the dividend on ordinary shares exceeds a specified amount.

particular lien The right to take possession of specified ***assets*** in the event of default. A particular lien relates only to the debt arising from the asset over which the lien is held.

part-time employment Long-term employment that entails an employee putting in less than a full working week.

partly-paid Describing securities and shares for which the full ***nominal value*** has not been paid and on which the holder is liable to pay the balance either on demand or on specified dates. Formerly, it was common for a company to ***call up*** only a part of the nominal value of each share, retaining the right to demand the balance when it became necessary to increase its ***capital***. This gave the company access to capital without the need for new share issues. The term also applies to new issues in which the issue price is to be paid in instalments.

partly-paid shares Shares that have not yet been fully-paid for by the shareholder. Many large new issues are paid for in two stages, to avoid ***liquidity*** problems for investors. *See also* ***fully-paid shares***; ***partly-paid***.

partner Person engaged in a business enterprise jointly with, and generally with the same status and responsibility as, another or others. *See* ***partnership***.

partnership Business association, in the UK normally formed by between two to twenty partners. The partners are jointly liable to the debts of the partnership, so that if one partner dies or decamps, the remainder are responsible for any debts. *See* ***deceased partner***.

partnership at will Partners are normally bound by a formal agreement; if not, the partnership is called a partnership at will, and may be broken at any time by any partner.

pass book Book issued by a bank or building society which details transactions of a customer's account. The account holder presents it when making deposits or withdrawals (unless he or she has a ***plastic card*** for use in an ***automated teller machine*** (ATM)). The pass book is then brought up to date the next time the account holder visits the bank or society.

passing a name Provision to a seller of the name of a potential buyer. A broker often "passes a name" in this way, but rarely guarantees the buyer's solvency when so doing.

passive balance ***Balance of payments*** that shows a ***deficit***.

passive management Form of mutual fund management, increasingly popular in the USA, in which a fund's investments are selected automatically to match the exact performance of the stock index. *See* ***managed fund***.

pass-through security A security representing an interest in an underlying pool of mortgages. Payments received on the underlying pool are passed through to the security investor.

pataca Standard currency unit of Macao, divided into 100 avos.

patent Authorization that grants the addressee the sole right to make, use or sell an invention for a specified period of time. Applicants for a patent must establish the novelty of their invention.

pawn Term with two meanings:

1. On the stock market, to obtain a bank loan using stocks as security.
2. To use goods (a ***pledge***) as security for a loan. *See* ***pawnbroker***.

pawnbroker Person who lends money secured against goods, called a **pledge**, and issues a formal receipt for them. Loans are normally made for a period of six months and seven days and, if not repaid in that time (with interest), the pawnbroker is entitled to sell the pawned goods.

pawnee Person who accepts goods as security for a loan; a ***pawnbroker***.

pawner Person who pawns or pledges goods. *See* ***pawnbroker***.

pay day Term with two meanings:

1. It is the day on which employees receive their wages.
2. It is an alternative term for ***settlement day***.

payable Due to be paid.

payable to bearer ***Bill of exchange*** on which the ***payee*** or, if the bill has been endorsed, the ***endorsee*** is not named. The bill is payable to the bearer.

payable to order ***Bill of exchange*** payable to an existent ***payee*** or order and not endorsed in blank. Only a bill payable to a payee or "bearer", a fictitious payee or endorsed in blank will be payable to bearer and therefore transferable by delivery without endorsements.

payables Informal term for a company's short-term ***debts*** (debtors).

pay-as-you-earn (PAYE) System of ***income tax*** collection whereby tax is deducted from current earnings at source. The employer is responsible for collecting the tax, and the employee receives only ***net*** wages.

PAYE Abbreviation of ***pay-as-you-earn***.

payee Person or people to whom money is to be paid. On a cheque, it is the person to whom the cheque is made payable (also known as the drawee).

payer Person who authorizes payment. On a cheque, it is the person who, as an account holder, signs the cheque (also known as the drawer).

paying agent Bank or other organization that pays capital or interest to holders of bonds, for which the agent may charge a fee.

paying banker Bank on which a cheque is drawn, *i.e.* the banker being asked to honour the cheque.

paying-in book Book of forms used to record the transaction when paying money (cash or cheques) into a bank account.

paying-in slip Blank form like those in a ***paying-in book*** and used for the same purpose.

payment Remuneration in money or kind.

part payment Interim payment or instalment.

payment in kind Payment, generally of wages, made in goods or services rather than in money. Payment of total wages in kind was made illegal in the UK in the 19th century, but part payment in kind is still common. *E.g.*, workers who receive luncheon vouchers or the use of a company car are receiving payment in kind. *See also* **perk**.

payment on account Part payment of an outstanding debt, usually coupled with an agreement to repay the balance on a specified date.

payment service Any service for transmitting money, such as a banker's draft, bank giro credit, cheque, credit card, debit card and telebanking, offered by retail banks and building societies.

payroll List of people employed (usually full-time) by a company and of the amount that each is due to be paid.

After only two years from start-up, they had 100 employees on the payroll.

payroll tax Tax on business undertakings, levied in relation to the number of people employed, or as a percentage of the total wage bill. Payroll tax is often used to control the relative elasticities of the supply and demand for labour. Its imposition deters companies from employing more workers than they currently require.

peculation Embezzlement, particularly the appropriation of public money or goods by an official.

pegged exchange rate Form of floating ***exchange rate*** in which the value of the currency is pegged between a pre-determined maximum and minimum value.

pegging the exchanges Maintenance of a fixed currency ***exchange rate***, by government intervention in the markets. Pegging the exchanges is generally resorted to in order to prevent an unfavourable rise or fall in the value of a currency.

penalty clause Clause in a ***contract*** stating that if one party breaks the contract (*e.g.* by late delivery of goods) it will be liable to pay a penalty, usually in money.

penny One-hundredth of a pound sterling (also called a new penny) and the bronze coin of that value or, colloquially, a US cent. Before the introduction of decimal currency in Britain in 1971, a penny was a two hundred and fortieth of a pound sterling. *See also* ***legal tender***.

penny bank Old type of savings bank, so called because it would accept deposits as little as one pre-1971 penny (0.4p).

penny shares Shares in a company that are traded in low denominations (usually under 50p). Penny shares are often highly volatile.

pennyweight Measure of weight, equivalent to one two hundred and fortieth of a pound ***Troy***. The term is often now used to mean anything of small weight.

Pension Benefit Guaranty Corporation (PBGC) A federal government agency established to administer two mandatory insurance programmes covering most private defined benefit pension plans.

pension mortgage Type of mortgage in which the borrower pays back only interest while funding a pension plan that will (at full term) provide a lump sum to pay off the capital (as well as providing a pension).

peppercorn rent Very small ***ground rent*** on a property, which normally serves only to establish the fact that the property is ***leasehold*** and not ***freehold***.

P/E ratio Abbreviation of ***price earnings ratio***.

per capita Latin for "by the head". It usually indicates that a sum will be divided equally among a group. Thus per capita income is calculated by dividing the total income received by a group by the number of people in that group.

per capita gross national product Value of gross national product divided by the number of people in the nation's population. It gives an indication of the wealth of the nation and its people.

per contra Latin for "by the opposite side". In accounting, an entry on the opposite side of an account or balance sheet. It is therefore a self-balancing item.

per diem Latin for "by the day". It usually applies to an allowance, rental or charge made on a daily basis.

perfect competition Situation of competition in which the products are perfectly similar, so that the consumer has no preference. There are a large number of producers and consumers, so that any producer who tries to raise the price of a product above market price is undercut by competitors, and consumers buy only at the lowest price. This model is frequently used by economists.

perfecting the sight Supplying the full details demanded on a ***bill of sight***.

perfect oligopoly ***Oligopoly*** in which the goods being produced by each seller are of the same type.

performance Earnings or losses made on a security or by a company.

This year, the company's performance was poor – it made substantial losses in most areas.

performance bond Bond delivered by a contractor to a public authority for a sum in excess of the value of a contract, and which is to be paid in the event of breach of contract. It is therefore a form of ***guarantee***. It is also known as a contract bond.

performance ratios Financial ratios that are used to measure the performance of an entity, division, department or personnel. Performance ratios can provide insights into a bank's profitability, return on investment, capital adequacy and liquidity.

period bill Fixed-term ***bill of exchange*** payable on a specified date, and not on demand.

perishable goods Goods that are liable to deterioration over a relatively short period of time. The term is most frequently applied to foodstuffs.

perk Abbreviation of perquisite, a casual ***benefit***. In general terms it is a ***payment in kind***, but is more specifically applicable to informal rather than formally agreed benefits.

permission to deal Authorization issued by a stock exchange that permits dealings in the shares of a company. Permission to deal must be sought three days after the issue of a ***prospectus***.

perpetual Eternal; valid for an indefinite time.

perpetual debenture Debenture that may not be repaid on ***demand***.

perpetual inventory Running record of all materials, parts or items of stock. Most frequently it is used in retailing, where stock turnover is relatively fast.

perpetual succession Continuation of a company after the departure or death of its members. A company is an individual legal entity which exists irrespective of its personnel, and which ceases to exist in law only after its ***liquidation***.

personal Pertaining to an individual, or private as opposed to public.

personal account Term with three meanings:

1. It is a bank account in the name of a single person (or more than one person, if it is a ***joint account***), as opposed to a ***business account*** or ***company account***.
2. On the stock market, it is an account maintained by a dealer on his or her own behalf and at personal risk, independent of the company for which he or she works.
3. In ***book-keeping***, it is an account that lists ***creditors*** and ***debtors***.

personal allowance Amount a person may earn before he or she is obliged to pay ***income tax***. This amount may vary from year to year.

personal cheque Cheque drawn on a ***personal account*** (rather than on a business or company account), or a cheque issued by a building society on behalf of an investor whose account does not provide cheque-book facilities. The latter is also known as a building society cheque.

personal equity plan (PEP) Government scheme, dating from 1986, that encourages people to save using a bank, building society or insurance company to invest in ***equities***. There are variations on the scheme, and several different kinds of PEPs are available. In 1977 the government announced that PEPs would lose their tax-free status in 1999, apparently to persuade investors to transfer to the planned new ***Individual Savings Accounts*** (ISAs).

personal identification number (PIN) Confidential number issued to holders of ***cash cards*** and ***credit cards*** that provides a safeguard against their unauthorized use at an ***automated teller machine*** (ATM).

Personal Investment Authority (PIA) ***Self-Regulating Organization*** (SRO) established in 1993 that oversees businesses dealing with private investors. It took over responsibilities of the ***Financial Intermediaries, Managers and Brokers Regulatory Association*** (FIMBRA) and the ***Life***

Assurance and Unit Trust Regulatory Organization (Lautro).

personal loan Loan made (usually by a bank, but now increasingly by registered brokers) to a private individual. This form of loan is generally fairly modest and intended for some specific purpose, such as the purchase of a car.

persuasive advertising Advertising that concentrates on the characteristics of the product, often intimating that use of the product will enhance the consumer's personal status in some way.

peseta Standard currency unit of Andorra and Spain (including the Canary Islands), divided into 100 centimos.

peso Standard currency unit of Argentina, Chile, Colombia, Cuba, the Dominican Republic, Guinea-Bissau, Mexico and the Philippines (divided into 100 centavos) and of Uruguay (divided into 100 centesimos). The latter is also known as the peso Uruguayo.

PET Abbreviation of ***property enterprise trust*** and potentially exempt transfer.

petrocurrency Money (usually US dollars) paid to the exporters of petroleum in exchange for their product. After the OPEC countries quadrupled prices in 1973, the amount of petrocurrency in circulation rose sharply and exceeded the capacity of the oil-exporting countries' economies to absorb it. Much of it was therefore invested in the world's financial markets, where it helped to offset the trade deficits caused by the OPEC price rise.

petrodollar *Petrocurrency* denominated in dollars.

petties Abbreviation of ***petty cash***, used most commonly on an invoice to denote charges made for various small items not separately enumerated.

petty cash Money in notes and coins kept for payment of small bills and day-to-day expenses. *See also* ***float***.

petty cash book Book in which ***petty cash*** transactions are recorded.

phantom withdrawals Unaccountable withdrawals from a bank account via an ***automated teller machine*** (ATM) without the involvement or consent of the card holder. In theory, nobody who is not in possession of the card and the associated PIN number can make such a withdrawal.

piece rate Payment to a worker based on his or her level of output. *See also* ***piecework; time rate***.

piecework Work that is paid per unit of output (*i.e.* instead of per hour of time worked). By linking earnings to output, the worker is given an incentive to increase productivity. *See also* ***piece rate***.

piggy bank Money box in which children can save coins, or a bank or savings account that is used for a similar purpose.

PIN Abbreviation of ***personal identification number***.

pin money Personal allowance (usually from a parent or spouse) for buying small personal items. By extension it also refers to earned income (not needed for essential expenditure) that is spent merely on luxury or trivial items.

piso Standard currency unit of the Philippines, divided into 100 centavos. *See also* ***peso***.

pit On a commodity exchange, the equivalent of a stock exchange ***trading floor***. It derives from the local nickname for the floor of the Chicago Commodities Exchange. Now, a pit is the floor of any open outcry exchange.

pitch Area in which a trader operates.

placement Process of issuing shares through an intermediary, usually a stockbroker or ***syndicate***. The intermediary "places" the shares with clients, frequently institutional investors, or with members of the public. A certain proportion of any share issue quoted on the London Stock Exchange must be made available to the public through the Exchange.

placing Security issued to raise new capital in a placement. Stockbrokers acting on behalf of the company concerned "place" shares by selling them to financial institutions and to the public. The term is also used as a synonym for ***placement***.

planned economy Economy in which some or all economic activity is planned and undertaken by the state, directly or indirectly, irrespective of the market forces of ***supply and demand***, and without ***private enterprise***. *See also* ***controlled economy***.

plant Fixtures or machinery used in an industrial process, or a general term for a factory or industrial complex.

plant hire Hire of machinery, often so that a manufacturer or service provider can cope with a sudden increase in demand.

plant register Register that details the ***plant*** owned by a company. A record is kept of purchase cost, running costs, current worth and annual ***depreciation***.

plastic Nickname for a ***cash card*** or ***credit card***, which can be used with an ***automated teller machine*** (ATM). Money obtained by such means is sometimes known as plastic money.

plastic card Generic name for a ***cash card***, ***cheque card***, ***credit card***, or ***debit card***. *See also* ***plastic***.

plastic money *See* ***plastic***.

PLC Abbreviation of ***public limited company***, also expressed as plc.

pledge Transfer of personal property from a debtor to a creditor as security for a ***debt***. Legal ownership of the property concerned remains with the pledger. *See also* ***pawnbroker***.

point Unit of price in which stocks are traded. One point generally equals £1 or $1.

point-of-sale terminal Electronic machine at the counter or checkout of a retail outlet that permits ***electronic funds transfer at point of sale*** (EFTPOS).

poison pill Technique used by companies facing a hostile ***takeover*** bid to make their stock as unattractive or inaccessible as possible. Stock may be diluted by new issues and company articles changed to require the approval of a greater proportion of the shareholders for the takeover. Expensive subsidiaries may be purchased to reduce the attractiveness of the company's balance sheet, and provision is often made for ***greenmail*** payments and for ***golden parachutes***.

policy Term with two meanings:

1. It is an agreement that a group of people (*e.g.* a company) will, in certain circumstances, act in a certain way.

It was the store's policy not to give refunds on any goods.

2. In insurance, it is a document setting out exactly the terms of the insurance contract.

poll List of names.

ponzi scheme Scheme in which investors are paid off by using capital from the investments of later investors. A ponzi scheme is fraudulent.

popular capitalism Capitalism that has reached a large number of the country's population, through increased personal investment, growth in small businesses, proliferation of profit-sharing schemes, etc.

porcupine provision Provision written into a company's ***articles of association***, or into a corporate charter or bylaw, designed to act as a deterrent to hostile ***takeovers***. An example of a porcupine provision is the ***poison pill*** defence.

portfolio Selection of securities held by a person or institution. Portfolios generally include a wide variety of stocks and bonds to spread the ***risk*** of investment, and the contents of a portfolio are managed – that is, continually changed in order to maximize income or growth. *See* ***managed fund***.

portfolio analysis Technique of strategic analysis used to distinguish the characteristics of different business units in a multi-business corporation.

portfolio insurance A form of ***hedging*** that uses Stock Index Futures contracts and index options to limit the downside risk of holding a diversified portfolio of common stocks. PI programmes are offered by major banks, brokerage firms, insurance companies, and other financial institutions.

position In general terms, the place of an investor in a fluctuating market.

postal account Bank or building society savings account that can be operated only by post (or through an ***automated teller machine*** (ATM)).

postal giro Way of sending money through the postal system. *See* ***giro; Girobank***.

postal order Order for the payment of money up to the value of £20 that can be purchased at any UK Post Office and encashed at a Post Office or paid into a bank account. A ***commission*** called poundage (95p on a £20 postal order) is paid by the person who buys the order.

post-bang Events or developments on the UK Stock Exchange that occurred after the ***Big Bang*** (October 1986).

postdate To affix some future date to a document, most commonly a cheque, thereby preventing the occurrence of actions or transactions concerning that document before the specified date.

postdated cheque *See* ***postdate***.

post-entry Events or developments that occur after a company's entry into a stock market.

P

poste restante Postal service that enables items to be sent to a person uncertain of his or her future whereabouts. Letters and packages are addressed care of a specific post office (a poste restante address) and collected by the addressee.

Post Office Organization responsible for the UK postal services and, through its 20,000 post offices, the payments of pensions, social security benefits, etc. This aspect is run by Post Office Counters Ltd.

Post Office Savings Bank *See* ***National Savings Bank.***

pot is clean Term that indicates that all shares allocated during an issue for offer to institutional investors have been taken up.

pound Standard currency unit of Cyprus (divided into 100 cents); Egypt, Lebanon (*see* ***Lebanese pound***), Sudan and Syria (divided into 100 piastres); and the Falkland Islands, Gibraltar and the United Kingdom (divided into 100 pence). *See also* ***punt.***

poundage *See* ***postal order.***

pound sterling Standard currency unit of the United Kingdom, so called to distinguish it from other currencies called the pound (*see* ***pound***).

power of attorney Legal agreement giving one person the authority to act in legal matters on behalf of another.

power lunch Substantial lunch, over which large deals are often finalized.

pre-authorized payment US equivalent of a banker's order such as a ***direct debit*** or ***standing order.***

precautionary savings Savings that are invested in very "safe" media (such as bank deposit accounts, building societies and National Savings) for meeting unforeseen needs.

pre-emption Right to purchase shares before they become generally available, usually offered in the case of new issues to existing shareholders. Rights of pre-emption are often proportional to the value of an existing holding.

preference Prior right; the superiority of one person or thing over another.

preference shares Also known as preferred stock, preference shares offer the shareholder preferential claims to dividends, usually at a fixed rate, and a prior claim to ordinary shareholders on the company's assets in the event of ***liquidation.*** The market price for preference shares tends to be more stable than that of ordinary shares. Preference shareholders may not vote at meetings of ordinary shareholders. Preference shares fall into five categories: cumulative, non-cumulative, redeemable, participating and convertible. *See also* ***participating preference share.***

preferential creditor Creditor entitled to repayment before the debts of other creditors are met. Secured creditors have preference over unsecured creditors, and in the case of the liquidation of a company, payment of outstanding tax and salaries have preference over the settlement of debts.

preferred ordinary shares Ordinary shares that carry additional rights, usually in respect of payment of dividend.

preferred stock Alternative term for ***preference shares***.

preliminary expenses Costs incurred during the formation of a company, including registration and promotion.

preliminary statement Announcement of a company's full year results a month or two before publication of its annual report.

premium Very broadly, a price, payment or bonus valued higher than the norm. The term has a number of specific meanings.

1. It is most often used to describe the payments, usually annual, made to an insurance company to maintain a policy.
2. It is the difference between the offer price of a new share issue and the price at which it begins trading, if the latter exceeds the former. The term is also used to describe the positive difference between the face value and redemption value of any stock or bond.
3. It is the amount by which a currency stands above its par value.

Premium Bond Common name for ***National Savings Premium Bond.***

premium brand Brand of a product that sells at a higher price than most others, usually because of some perceived quality.

Premium Savings Bond Common name for ***National Savings Premium Bond***.

prepayment Payment made in advance. When applied to a ***bill of exchange***, prepayment is the payment before the bill matures, and in the context of mortgages it is the repayment of the debt before its maturity.

pre-placement Activity that takes place before a share issue has been placed.

pre-refunding Practice of issuing shares to re-fund (*i.e.* pay for debts that are about to mature), not immediately before maturity of the old issue, but in advance of it, in order to take advantage of good ***interest rates***. *See also* ***refinancing***.

presenting bank Bank seeking payment of a financial document (such as a bill of exchange, cheque or banker's draft) from the drawer's bank.

present value Assessment of the current net ***cost*** or value of future expenditure or benefit. Most frequently it is used to measure return on ***capital*** investment.

president Chief executive of a US company, equivalent to a ***managing director*** in the UK.

prestige advertising Form of advertising in which the company sponsors prestigious sporting or cultural events.

pre-tax profit Profit calculated before allowance has been made for tax.

price Cost of purchasing a unit of goods or services. Very broadly, prices are generally set by the manufacturer and retailer, taking into account all ***fixed costs*** and ***variable costs*** and allowing for a ***profit*** margin.

price control Method of controlling ***inflation*** or allocation of resources in a centrally-planned economy by pegging prices within specified limits. Market forces make it difficult to control prices in this way in the long term, and the method is normally used only for short-term crisis management.

prices and incomes policy Government policy for controlling wages and prices as a means of checking ***inflation***. Five prices and income policies have been operated in the UK since World War II, all but one of them by Labour governments acting with the sometimes reluctant co-operation of the trade unions.

price/earnings ratio (P/E ratio) Way of measuring the demand for shares, equal to the market price of the ***ordinary shares*** of a company divided by the ***earnings per share***.

pricing Method used to set a ***price***, specifically by equating supply with demand.

primary capital Capital that is used in the start-up of a business. *See also* ***venture capital***.

primary commodity Commodity that is essential to a nation, *e.g.* food, fuel and raw materials for industry.

primary dealer Regulated dealer in US ***government securities.***

primary distribution Distribution of raw materials to manufacturers.

primary market Market in a new securities issues, also known as the new-issues market. *See also* ***secondary market; tertiary market.***

primary production Production of raw materials and foods. *See also* ***secondary production.***

prime Of high quality. In finance, the term is most often used to describe the debts incurred by a person or firm with a good credit rating.

prime bank bill *See* ***fine bank bill.***

prime entry In international trade, describing imported goods on which customs ***duty*** is levied as soon as they enter the country, and which are impounded until the duty is paid. *See also* **books of *prime entry*.**

prime rate Preferential interest rate charged in the USA for short-term loans made to people or organizations with a high credit rating. It is approximately equivalent to the ***minimum lending rate*** in the UK.

principal Term with two meanings:

1. It is a person who gives instructions to an ***agent.***
2. In finance, it is the original sum invested or lent, as distinct from any profits or interest it may earn.

private Describing a person or institution that is independent of the public or government sector.

private enterprise Undertaking by an individual or a private group working without significant support from the state.

private bank Commercial bank that is not owned by a joint-stock company. Such banks are now almost non-existent in the UK, but are still found in the USA. A private bank may also be a bank that is not a member of a ***clearing house***, but uses a member bank as an agent for this purpose.

private company Company whose shares are not available to the general public through the medium of a stock exchange, and whose members do not exceed 50 in number.

privately held Describing a company, capital or other possessions in the hands of a person or group of people.

private placing Sale of the whole of a new issue of shares to a financial institution.

private sector That part of the business activity of a country that is financed and controlled by individuals or private companies (*e.g.* shareholders or investment institutions). *See also* ***privatization.***

privatization Practice of offering shares in previously national industries, for sale to the general public. During the 1980s and 1990s Britain's Conservative government privatized several national industries including: British Aerospace, British Rail and British Telecom.

probate Acceptance of the validity of a will by a proper authority. A will that has not been probated has no legal force.

probate price In finance, a share price calculated for tax purposes by taking the lower of the bid and offer prices and adding to it one-quarter of the difference between the two. This process is known as quartering up.

produce As a noun, goods that are grown (agricultural produce); as a verb, to manufacture or grow goods.

produce exchange Alternative term for a ***commodity exchange.***

product That which is produced, either in terms of goods or services, or in terms of income.

product diversification Decision to begin the manufacture of new products, usually by horizontal or vertical diversification. The main purpose is to lessen the risk of commercial failure caused by a sudden fall in demand for a particular product. Diversification is also attractive to companies dependent upon seasonal or cyclical business.

production Broadly, practice of manufacturing goods for sale.

production costs Alternative term for ***manufacturing costs.***

productivity Output of any of the factors of production (land, labour and capital) per unit of input. Productivity may be enhanced by the improvement of any one of the three factors, most usually by the introduction of new technology or an incentive scheme. Productivity of land is generally measured in output per acre or hectare, that of labour in output per working hour, and that of capital as a percentage per annum.

productivity bargaining Bargaining process that results in a ***productivity deal.***

productivity bonus Alternative term for ***incentive bonus.***

productivity deal Agreement between management and labour, designed to enhance productivity, generally in return for bonuses in the form of increased wages or profit-sharing, or in return for changed working practices.

professional Originally, a member of one of the professions (*e.g.* medicine, law, accountancy). Increasingly the term is used to describe someone paid to do a job or perform a duty, particularly one requiring special skills or long training, or merely someone who takes his or her job seriously.

profit Surplus money, after all expenses have been met, generated by a firm or enterprise in the course of one accounting period.

profit-and-loss account Annual summary of a company's financial operations, required by law to be submitted by every trading company. The profit-and-loss account has three sections: the trading account, the profit-and-loss account and the appropriation account. The profit-and-loss section of the account takes the profit or loss figure from the trading account, and after accounting for income not concerned with trading and expenses such as those incurred in administration, deducts ***tax*** from the final profit or loss figure. *See also* ***account***.

profit a prendre The right to take something from another's land, e.g. fishing rights. *See also* ***easement***.

profit margin Gross ***profit***, usually expressed as a percentage of net ***sales***, or as simple ***net*** profit. Company policy generally specifies some profit margin below which it is hardly worthwhile producing goods.

profit-sharing Distribution of some or all of a firm's profits to its employees as a ***bonus***. The distribution may be in the form of cash or shares.

profits tax Tax levied on a company's profits.

profit-taking Selling stock and taking the profit on the transaction, instead of waiting for a better price. Profit-taking occurs when dealers believe that the market will not improve much more, at least in the short term.

pro forma invoice Form of invoice submitted before goods are despatched and used to confirm an order and to advise of despatch.

projection Estimate of future developments made on the basis of, or projected from, a knowledge of past and present events.

promissory note Document that states that a person promises to pay a certain sum of money on a certain date. It is also known as a note of hand.

promoter Entrepreneur, especially a person involved in the organization or launch of a business.

proof department Section of a bank that manages its commercial transactions.

property Legally, property is divided into real and personal property. Real property may be defined as land and buildings held freehold. Personal property consists of other personal possessions. More specifically, property is sometimes defined as something appreciating in value or yielding income.

property company Company that develops, invests in or trades property (buildings).

property enterprise trust (PET) Form of ***mutual fund*** which invests solely in ***enterprise zone*** properties in order to gain tax advantages for its investors.

pro rata Latin for "in proportion". *E.g.*, the total amount of dividend received by a shareholder is pro rata to his or her holding. *See also* ***pari passu***.

prospectus Document that describes a proposal, *e.g.* issued to prospective shareholders by a company intending to make a public issue of shares, giving details of past and present performance and of prospects. *See also* ***red herring***.

protected bear Alternative term for ***covered bear***.

protected transaction Transaction that occurs after a company goes into liquidation or a person is declared bankrupt. A protected transaction cannot be nullified by the liquidator.

protectionism Policy based on self-interest, *e.g.* one that shields an industry from overseas competition, usually by the imposition of selective or general ***quotas*** and tariffs. *See also* ***tariff barrier; dumping***.

protest Bank certificate confirming that a ***bill of exchange*** has been dishonoured (*see* ***dishonour***).

provision Allowance for some eventuality. In accounting, it is a sum written off to provide for depreciation of ***assets***.

proxy Authorization given by a voter to another person to allow that person to vote on his or her behalf, *e.g.* a shareholder may give someone proxy to vote at a company meeting which he or she is for some reason unable to attend.

prudence concept In accounting, the prudence concept calls for a cautious view, such as the exclusion on the ***balance sheet*** of money owed but not yet received, and the inclusion of all liabilities, whether or not they must be met immediately. It therefore postulates a ***worst-moment*** scenario. *See also* ***accounting principles***.

prudential ratio Bank's ***capital asset*** ratio that demonstrates caution and restraint on behalf of its investors.

PSBR Abbreviation of ***public sector borrowing requirement***.

PSL1 Abbreviation of ***public sector liquidity* 1**.

PSL2 Abbreviation of ***public sector liquidity* 2**.

psychographics Division of demographic groups for marketing purposes into categories related to psychology, *e.g.* lifestyle, usage-rate, sensitivity to quality or price, etc.

public Describing something that is the hands of the people and, as such, managed or controlled by the government; or that which is open to anyone.

public bank Alternative term for a ***commercial bank*** or joint-stock bank.

public deposits Government department credits on deposit at the Bank of England.

public limited company (PLC or plc) Company whose shares are available to the general public through a stock exchange.

public sector That part of the business activity of a country that is financed and controlled by the government. Public sector industries are often known as ***nationalized industries***.

Public Sector Borrowing Requirement (PSBR) Difference between the government's expenditures and receipts, generally financed mainly by issuing ***gilt-edged securities*** and other long-term loans.

public sector liquidity 1 Obsolete measure of the ***money supply***. It is equal to the private sector's holding of £M3, money-market instruments, and certificates of tax deposit.

public sector liquidity 2 Obsolete measure of the ***money supply***. It is equal to the private sector's holding of £M3, money-market instruments, and certificates of tax deposit excluding the holdings of building societies.

public trustee Person appointed by the state who undertakes to act as a trustee, executor, or investment adviser to any member of the general public.

puisne mortgage Mortgage not protected by the deposit of the title deeds. The lender may instead register the property with the Land Register or the Land Charges Register; this ensures that any transaction concerning the property must have the approval of the lender.

pula Standard currency unit of Botswana, divided into 100 thebe.

pull Colloquial for to withdraw, *e.g.* to cancel a deal just as it reaches the final stages of negotiation.

pullback After a period when market prices have been fluctuating erratically, the movement or return to more recognizable and predictable trends.

punt Standard currency unit of the Republic of Ireland, divided into 100 pence.

purchase To buy something, or the thing that has been bought.

pure competition Alternative term for ***perfect competition***.

pure demand Demand that may not be expressed by purchase for a variety of reasons.

put *See **put option**.*

put band Period for which a ***put option*** is valid.

put option Option to sell shares, commodities or financial futures at an agreed price on or before an agreed future date.

put-through Stock exchange dealing procedure used in cases of very large orders, where a stockbroker finds both a seller and a buyer and is therefore able to "put the shares through the market" in a single quick transaction.

pyramid selling Practice of selling distributorships, or the right to sell distributorships. The pyramid seller makes his or her profit from the sale of ***franchises*** and leaves the franchisee to dispose of the goods. In a typical system, each franchisee must guarantee to purchase a certain quantity of goods, which he or she then disposes of by recruiting distributors. Those at the bottom of the pyramid usually sell to family and friends.

Q

qualifying shares Fixed number (or percentage) of shares a person must hold before he or she is entitled to a position on the board of directors or a bonus issue.

quality control On a production line, the process of checking the quality of a product (or samples of it).

quango Abbreviation of quasi-autonomous non-governmental organization, which in the UK covers many semi-permanent public bodies set up to investigate certain cases or to deal with special problems. Examples of quangos are the Advisery Conciliation and Arbitration Service (ACAS) and the National Economic Development Council (NEDC).

quantity discount Discount offered to the purchaser of large numbers of goods.

quantity rebate Reduction in the price per unit of a product in return for bulk buying.

quantity surveyor Surveyor who specializes in calculating quantities of raw materials (and sometimes labour) needed for a construction project.

quantum meruit If a supplier only half-completes the work he or she has been contracted to do, the suppler may in some cases claim payment in proportion to the work completed, known as payment quantum meruit (as much as he has earned).

quarter day Four days that are generally taken to mark the quarters of the year. Traditionally these are the days on which payment such as rent are made. In England and Wales, the quarter days are Lady Day (25 March), Midsummer Day (24 June), Michaelmas (29 September) and Christmas Day (25 December).

quartering up *See **probate price**.*

quasi-autonomous non-governmental organisation *See **quango**.*

quasi-contract Contract that is either verbal or partly voidable, which a court decides is enforceable in part.

quasi-equity Loan stock or debt ***instrument*** that offers its holder rights and benefits similar to those offered to the holders of shares. *See* ***loan stock***.

quasi-money *See* ***near money***.

quetzal Standard currency unit of Guatamala, divided into 100 centavos.

queue (or **queueing) theory** Mathematical theory that can be used to analyse the problems involved in the physical provision of services, taking into account the arrival of customers, the time they have to wait to be served, how they queue, how long the service takes to be rendered and the length of time a service unit remains idle. It is especially useful in the design of such establishments as airports, banks, etc.

quick assets Another term for ***liquid assets***.

quick test *See* ***acid-test ratio***.

quid pro quo Literally, this for that. The principle of quid pro quo underlies all contracts in that a contract is an agreement to exchange something such as services for something else, such as cash.

quiet time Time between the registration of a new share issue and its being offered for sale.

quintal Term used in the US and sometimes in the north of England for 100lb ***avoirdupois***.

quorum Minimum number of people who have to be present at a meeting for it to go ahead and the decisions made by it to be valid. In the UK, the quorum for a members' meeting is noted in a company's ***articles of association***.

quota Amount of something (*e.g.* goods) allowed to one person, or company, normally fixed by a body in authority.

quotation (quote) Term with two meanings:

1. It is an **estimate** of how much something will cost.

I have asked our suppliers to quote on the job in hand.

2. It refers to the ***Official List*** of the stock exchange. Appearance of a company's shares on this list is known as a quotation.

quotation spread The difference between the ***offer price*** and the ***bid price*** on a security. It is also known as the bid-offer spread.

quoted company Company that has received listing on a stock exchange.

The shares of such a company may thus be traded on the open market. *See* ***Official List***.

quoted investment In accounting, an investment in shares or debentures that are quoted on an official exchange.

quoted price Price of a security as it is quoted on an exchange. The quoted price may fluctuate from day to day, or even minute to minute.

quote driven Stock market that reacts (in terms of prices) to the quotations of market makers rather than to the number and flow of incoming orders. *See also* ***order driven***.

quote machine Computer that allows a broker access to up-to-the-minute information on quoted prices.

QWL Abbreviation of quality of work-life, a concept that is at the basis of pushes towards improving working conditions.

R

rack rent Extremely high rent, which probably stretches a tenant to his or her financial limits.

R & D Abbreviation of ***research and development***.

raid To buy significant numbers of a company's shares sometimes as a prelude to a takeover bid.

raider Person or group initiating a hostile ***takeover*** by buying quantities of the ***target*** company's shares.

rally Rise in market prices after a period when prices have stagnated or consistently fallen, usually followed by a further fall. *See also* ***reaction***.

rand Standard currency unit of South Africa, divided into 100 cents. *See also* ***krugerrand***.

random walk theory Theory of stock movements developed in the 1950s and 1960s, which states that share prices move in a random way, and so their movements up or down cannot be predicted. *See also* ***higgledy-piggledy growth***.

rate Amount of money charged or paid, calculated according to a certain rule or ratio.

rateable value Value of a property for the purposes of calculating ***rates***, based on the estimated amount of ***rent*** the property would fetch (the ***annual value***) on the open market and with vacant possession.

rate of exchange (exchange rate) Rate at which the various currencies are exchanged for each other.

rate of interest (interest rate) Amount charged for loan services, normally expressed as a percentage of the loan.

rate of return Amount of money made on an investment (in the form of interest or a dividend), normally expressed as a percentage of the amount invested.

rates In the UK, a local government tax levied on householders and occupiers of commercial premises to pay for local works, expressed as a certain amount in the pound of the ***rateable value***. For private property, rates have been replaced by council tax, which is payable by the occupant.

rate support grant Payment made by the UK government to local authorities to support council services that are neither self-financing nor receive any other form of ***grant***.

ratification Official approval, giving something (*e.g.* a document) validity.

rating Grade assigned to *e.g.* bonds or preferred stocks by an official agency such as Standard & Poor's or Moody's, in order to guide investors. *See also* ***beta; triple-A rating***.

ratio Way of comparing quantities using proportions.

The ratio of men of marriageable age to women of marriageable age will shortly become two to one.

reaction Fall in market prices after a period of continuous price rises. *See also* ***rally***.

real Also called cruzeiro real, the standard currency unit of Brazil, divided into 100 centavos.

real accounts On a book-keeping ***ledger***, the record of ***assets*** and ***capital***. *See also* ***nominal accounts***.

real estate Any immovable property, particularly land with permanent buildings on it.

real interest rate Actual interest rate minus current inflation rate, a more accurate indicator of the likely yield of an investment.

realization account When a company is being wound up and its assets are being realized in order to pay creditors, or a partnership is being dissolved, a bank account may be opened in which to deposit receipts and upon which to draw payments to creditors. This is known as a realization account.

realize To put a plan into action, or sell assets for cash; the act of doing so is realization.

He had to realize his assets in order to pay his creditors.

real value Value of something when compared to fluctuations in price indexes, *i.e.* during times of ***inflation*** or ***deflation***., e.g. the real value of a 10% wage increase at a time of 5% inflation is only 5%, because the cash represented by the 10% increase will only buy 5% more goods. *See* ***retail price index***

rebate Sum of money returned to a payer because he or she has paid too much, or a discount on the price of something.

At the end of the year you will receive a tax rebate.

receipt Note stating that money has been paid or that goods have been received, such as a wharfinger receipt.

If you leave your watch with the jeweller to be repaired, make sure you get a receipt.

*See also **warrant**.*

receipts Payments received (as opposed to expediture).

receiver Official into whose hands a company with financial difficulties is placed, to ensure that, as far as possible, the creditors are paid.

receivership Company's state when a ***receiver*** is called in.

After several attempts at solving their financial problems, the company went into receivership.

receiving order Court order placing a company into the hands of a receiver.

recession Stage in a trade cycle during which the decline in economic activity accelerates, causing investment values to fall, companies to have to deal with adverse trading conditions, and unemployment to rise and so income and expenditure to fall. A recession may end in a ***depression*** unless there is a ***recovery***.

recognizance Contract between a court and a person by which the person is bound to perform a certain act, such as to appear in court on a certain date, to be of good behaviour so as not to cause a breach of the peace, or to stand bail for someone else.

recognized bank Any bank recognized by the Bank of England. For such recognition, the bank has to meet several strict criteria (including having capital and reserves in excess of a specified amount).

recognized investment exchange Market for securities recognized by the UK ***Securities and Exchange Commission*** (SEC).

recommendation Normally refers to financial advice, *e.g.* the recommendation of a market analyst to a broker or of a stockbroker to a client.

recommended retail price (RRP) Price at which a manufacturer suggests his goods should retail. The RRP is often specified on the ***packaging*** to indicate to the customer that the retailer is not overcharging him or her and to allow a comparison to be made between the prices of competing brands. *See also* ***retail***.

reconciliation Act of making two accounts, statements or people agree.

reconciliation statement Report that explains why two accounts do not agree.

recourse agreement In ***hire purchase*** transactions, agreement that enables the seller to repossess the goods in the event of the purchaser being unable to make the payments required.

recovery Upturn in the economy, the financial position of a company or in share prices. *See also* ***boom; depression; recession***.

recovery shares When a company's performance is improving after a period of difficulty, its share price is likely to go up. Shares in such a company are known as recovery shares.

recovery trust Type of trust invested in low-priced ***equities*** (on the supposition that the companies' fortunes will improve).

rectification of register If a court believes that an official list (*e.g.* a company's list of its shareholders) is incorrect it may make an order, known as a rectification of register, to have the list amended.

red To be in the red is to be in ***debt***; to have an ***overdrawn*** account.

At the end of last quarter, the company went into the red.

red-circle rate Rate of pay in the USA that is higher than usual for the job undertaken.

redemption Repayment of an outstanding loan or debenture stock by the borrower.

redemption date Date on which a ***loan*** or ***debenture*** is to be repaid. Redemption dates (plural) are those on which a ***stock*** is redeemable at par. In the case of Treasury stocks, the precise date of repayment is decided by the government. *See also* ***parity***.

redemption fee ***Premium*** paid to shareholders who surrender redeemable shares when asked to do so by a company.

redeemable preference shares ***Preference shares*** that the issuing company has the right to redeem, *i.e.* buy back under special circumstances.

redemption price Price at which forms of indebtedness (*e.g.* bills of exchange or bonds) are redeemed by the institution or government that issued them.

redemption yield Refers to ***bonds*** with a fixed ***redemption date***. Redemption yield takes into account capital gain upon redemption plus the dividend, and relates them to the market price of the bond.

red goods Goods, such as food, that are produced and consumed quickly.

red herring On Wall Street, an initial prospectus for a share issue, circulated before the price has been fixed and the issue has been ratified by the appropriate regulating authority.

red ink Appearing on a balance sheet, red ink shows that a company is making a loss, has debts or has greater liabilities than assets.

red-lining Practice among US lenders, illegal in some states, whereby declining neighbourhoods and Third World countries are blacklisted for mortgages and loans.

reducing balance depreciation Method of accounting for depreciation by calculating it in a period as a fixed proportion of the residual book value of an ***asset*** at the start of the period.

re-export To import goods from one country and to then export them to another.

reference bank Bank named in a variable-rate loan agreement that provides rates for fixing interest charges on the loan.

refer to drawer Instruction written on a cheque by the receiving bank, usually indicating that the account holder has insufficient funds in the account to honour the cheque.

refinancing Taking out a loan to pay back other borrowing. It is also known as refunding in the USA.

reflation Government action that attempts to boost a country's economy. This is done by increasing the money supply, usually by reducing interest rates and taxation. *See also* ***deflation; inflation***.

refugee capital Foreign funds invested in a country that is politically more stable. *See also* ***flight capital***

refunding Another term for ***refinancing***

register Official list, normally of names.

registered bond Bond that is registered in the name of the holder. It may be transferred to another holder only with the consent of the registered holder. *See also* ***bearer bond***

registered stock Alternative term for ***inscribed stock***.

register of charges List of charges payable by a company on its property, such as mortgages. A copy of this list must be filed by all UK companies at Companies House in London.

Register of Companies List of UK companies kept at Companies House in London, detailing registered addresses and names of directors.

register of debentures List drawn up by a company of those people who hold ***debentures***.

registered office Address of a company as listed on the Register of Companies at Companies House. This need not be the actual working address of the company.

regulated loan Loan of £15,000 or less, regulated by the 1974 Consumer Credit Act, that is not exempt under the 1974 Finance Act (which exempted loans for the alternation, improvement, purchase or repair of a private dwelling). *See also* ***cooling-off period***.

relative efficiency A company is relatively efficient if it combines, distributes, allocates or uses limited resources more effectively than a rival. Thus if two firms have the same input but different outputs, the firm producing the larger output is said to be the more efficient of the two.

relative strength Usually expressed as a ***ratio***, the relative strength of a share, commodity or anything else traded on the markets or elsewhere, is the performance of the particular investment compared to the performance of its market ***index***. *See also* ***beta***.

relief Help; normally refering to allowances made to certain taxpayers for various reasons. *See* ***tax relief***.

relocation Movement of a company's premises to another site.

remitting bank *See* ***collecting bank***.

rendu Form of contract by which an exporter pays to have goods delivered to a buyer's warehouse. It is also known as a franco or a free contract.

rent Money paid for the occupation or use of something for a period of time (*e.g.* a building, office, factory, car or television set). *See also* ***lease***.

rent back To sell one's property (offices, factory space, etc) on the understanding that the new owner will lease back the property to its original owner. It is a good way to raise capital by realizing property assets without having to vacate the premises.

rent roll List of rents payable to a particular estate.

renunciation Act of giving up ownership of shares.

repatriation Act of transferring capital from overseas to the home market.

repayment mortgage Mortgage in which repayments consist of interest payments and a contribution towards the repayment of the capital.

replevin In a case of ***distraint***, the return of goods to their owner while the court is deciding whether the distraint was lawful.

repo Abbreviation of repossession, or of ***repurchase agreement***.

report Verbal account or document that describes and explains a state of affairs or an incident that has taken place.

repressed inflation Alternative term for ***suppressed inflation***.

repudiation Act of informing the other party in a ***contract*** that one does not intend to honour the contract. Repudiation may also refer to the repayment of a debt, or to the termination of any form of agreement.

reputed owner Person who acts as the owner of a property, even if he or she is not. If the reputed owner becomes bankrupt, the property is divided among the creditors. *See also* ***bailment; estoppel; order and disposition***.

repurchase Situation that occurs when an issuer buys its own securities. It is most frequent in ***unit trust*** holdings.

repurchase agreement (repo) Transaction between a ***bond*** dealer and a bank. The dealer sells government ***securities*** while at the same time agreeing to buy them back at a specified time at a price high enough to allow the bank a profit margin. In this way, the repo may be looked upon as a form of loan.

resale price maintenance Practice whereby a supplier refuses to sell goods to a retailer unless the retailer agrees to sell them at a certain price, or above a minimum price. Resale price maintenance may be applied to prevent retailers from using the product as a ***loss leader***.

Resale price maintenance is allowable under the Resale Prices Act (1976) if the supplier can prove that it is in the interests of the consumer, as in the case of books and some pharmaceuticals.

research and development (R & D) Activity that aims to discover or invent new products or services. It covers pure scientific and technical research, applied research, product improvement and technological innovation.

Reserve, The Money held by the Bank of England as cash (coins and banknotes).

reserve asset cost *See* ***mandatory liquid assets.***

reserve currency Foreign currency held by a central bank in order to fund foreign trade.

reserve price Minimum price for shares sold by tender. *See* ***offer for sale by tender.***

reserves That part of a company's profits that are put aside for a particular purpose.

reserve for bad debts Money put aside against the possibility of unpaid debts.

reserve for obsolescence Money put aside to cushion a company against the possibility of its ***fixed assets*** becoming obsolescent or uneconomic.

resolution When a motion put before a meeting has been agreed upon, it becomes a resolution.

resting order Alternative term for an order ***good-till-cancelled.***

restitution Either the giving back of something to someone or a compensatory payment.

The court ordered the restitution of the property to its owner.

The court ordered the vandal to make restitution for the damage he caused to the building.

restraint order Court order preventing a person or organization from doing something. If issued to a bank, it cancels all customer ***mandates.***

restrictive Describing something that sets limits on something else.

restrictive covenant Agreement between two parties that restricts the activities of one. *E.g.* it may take the form of a ***clause*** in a ***contract*** to supply goods, that stops the supplier selling goods to a competitor of the second party. A restrictive covenant may not be upheld legally if it is seen to be against the general good (*e.g.* against the interests of free competition).

restrictive endorsement Endorsement that restricts the negotiability of a document.

restrictive (trade) practice Agreement made between two companies that aims to make restrictions regarding the supply of their goods, on such things as price, quantities, processes, geographical area, etc. On the whole, restrictive practices are assumed by the law to be against the public interest.

retail Sale of goods or services to the general public.

retail banking Banking activities where the main emphasis is on service for individuals rather than businesses and institutions. It is also known as consumer banking.

retail funds Funds that a bank, building society or other financial institution obtains from depositors and investors by post, telephone or over the counter at its branches.

retail price Price at which a good or service is actually sold through a retailer.

retail price index (RPI) Analysis of trends in retail prices, expressed as an index number and used to evaluate changes in ***retail prices*** with reference to ***inflation***.

retail repo ***Repurchase agreement*** (repo) in which money is lent to a bank, rather than to an individual or company.

retained earnings That part of a company's post-tax earnings not distributed to shareholders, and thus retained by the firm to finance the day-to-day running of the company and any future expansion. Retained earnings are added to reserves and hence appear on the firm's ***balance sheet***.

retained profit Profit remaining to a firm after the distribution of dividends and profit-sharing bonuses. Retained profit is generally used for the long-term expansion of the business, and is sometimes referred to as undistributed profit.

retention Holding back money to be used for a particular purpose.

retention money A buyer may hold back some of the payment due on completion of a contract, for a certain period of time, to allow him or her to check for possible defects in the work. The sum of money is known as retention money.

retentions Shortened form of either ***retained earnings*** or ***retained profits***.

retire a bill To withdraw a ***bill*** from circulation by having the acceptor pay it, either on or before the due date.

retirement Term with two meanings:

1. Payment of a debt.
2. Cancellation of a security because it has been redeemed or re-acquired.

return The comeback: profits and income from transactions or investments. It may also be a document (usually describing a financial situation) sent to an authority. *See* ***return on capital***; ***tax return***.

returned cheque Cheque returned to the bank it is drawn on because of lack of funds, death of the drawer, countermand, stale, etc. See also ***refer to drawer***; ***stale cheque***.

return on capital Measure of how well a company's capital is used, equal to 100 times the trading profit (before tax and interest) divided by the average capital used.

revaluation Practice whereby a company puts a new value on its ***fixed assets***, because ***nominal values*** and ***real values*** of such assets as property and machines have changed. Revaluation is also a change in the exchange rate of a currency so that its value against other currencies increases. *See* ***devaluation***.

revaluation reserve Reserve fund raised by a company by revaluing assets (at market price or replacement cost). Funds can also be raised by issuing shares at a premium above their par value.

revenue Money received from any transaction or sale, or money received by the government in the form of taxation.

revenue account Accounts of a business that state the amount of money received from sales, commission, etc.

revenue bonds Bonds issued by municipalities in the US with principal and interest payable from revenues or income from municipally- or state-owned plants, toll roads or bridges, or public works, such as water works, electric light and power plant, port authority, railroad, etc.

reversal Change in a company's fortunes (from being profitable to being unprofitable, or vice versa.

reverse arbitrage Paying off a bank overdraft by borrowing from the money market. *See* ***arbitrage***.

reverse repo Similar transaction to a ***repurchase agreement*** (repo) in which the dealer buys the bonds instead of selling them, so that in essence they are acting as ***security*** on the bank loan.

reverse takeover Purchase of control of a public company by a smaller, private company. This is often done in order that the private company may obtain a listing on the Stock Exchange.

reverse yield gap Situation in which low-risk assets provide greater returns that high-risk assets.

reversion Term with two meanings:

1. It is the return of property, goods or rights to their original owner.
2. It is the difference between the amount owing on a mortgage and the market value of the property (*i.e.*, it is the ***equity*** in the property).

revocable credit Credit facility extended by a banker who is willing to take ***bills of exchange***, but revocable (*i.e.* repayable) at any time.

revolver US term for ***revolving credit***.

revolving bank facility Another name for ***revolving credit***.

revolving credit Lending made by a bank that is automatically renewed at the start of each period (or as soon as the sum is repaid). *E.g.* a bank may arrange to lend a customer a certain amount each month. It will stop borrowing above that limit once it is reached, but allow borrowing to go on at the start of the next month. The US term for this arrangement is revolver.

reward packaging Method of presenting goods and other products to a potential purchaser so that the most desirable elements are evident immediately, from the best fruit at the top of the box in retailing to the best-selling (and most profitable) product in a financial proposal. *See also* ***switch selling***.

rider Addition to a document that follows logically from what has gone before.

RIE Abbreviation of ***recognized investment exchange***.

riesco Way of allocating income from one calendar year to two or more account years.

rigging the market Action that influences a market, by overriding market forces. *E.g.* it may be done by one dealer buying a substantial number of shares or a significant quantity of a commodity, thus pushing the market up.

right of establishment Under an EU ***directive***, the right of a bank or other financial institution to open offices in other EU countries.

right of resale A seller may, in certain circumstances, reclaim goods from a buyer and resell them, *e.g.* if a stoppage in transaction or a ***lien*** occurs and the goods are likely to perish as a consequence. In this case, the seller may sell to another buyer and give a lawful title to the goods.

rights issue Practice of offering existing shareholders the opportunity to buy more shares (*i.e.* subscribe more ***capital***), in order to raise additional capital. Rights issues act as a protection for the shareholder, in that the total number of shares issued increases without decreasing the percentage holding of each shareholder.

rim country One of the newly-industrializing countries in the eastern Pacific, *e.g.* Singapore and Malaysia, at present concentrating on assembly-based industries.

ring In general, a group of people who get together in order to illegally rig the market, *e.g.* by acting in concert to push prices up or down. *See also* ***bidding ring; concert party; rigging the market.***

A ring is also a method of trading on the London ***futures*** market or metals exchange.

ringgit Standard currency unit of Malaysia, divided into 100 sen. It is also known as the Malaysian dollar.

ring trading Method of trading adopted on the London Metals Exchange, whereby dealers sit in a ring and trade by open outcry. *See also* ***outcry market; ring.***

risk Amount one potentially stands to lose by a transaction.

risk arbitrage Practice of buying in to a takeover bid in the expectation that share prices will rise.

risk capital Capital invested in a company, or security, that presents a risk (*i.e.* the possibility of loss or, indeed, gain). The term is also used as an alternative term for ***venture capital.***

R

risk management Measures adopted to minimize financial risk (e.g., through insurance, ***hedging*** or spreading the risk).

risk premium Difference between the ***forward exchange rate*** of a currency and the expected future ***spot rate***.

rollover Movement of an investment from one institution to the owner of another institution.

roll-over relief Reduction in ***capital gains tax*** on the sale of a company's fixed assets if it is buying other assets in order to replace the first ones. *See also* ***deferred taxation***.

roll-up fund Offshore investment that reinvests interest so that it becomes part of the capital, thus providing tax advantages.

rotation of directors Process whereby at each ***annual general meeting*** (AGM) of a public company, a certain proportion of the directors retire (normally one third), although they may then be re-elected to the board. This enables shareholders to change a director without having to dismiss him or her.

rouble (US **ruble**) Standard unit of currency of Georgia, Kazakhstan, Russia and Uzbekistan (divided into 100 kopeks) and of Tajikstan (divided into 100 tanga).

roundabout production Alternative term for ***indirect production***.

round lot Number of (possibly mixed) shares or bonds traded at the same time, as a lot. The ***commission*** charged on a round lot is usually slightly less than on an ***odd lot***.

round trip On the futures market, the practice of buying and then selling the same investment or vice versa.

round turn An entire ***futures*** transaction from start to finish.

roup Term used in Scotland for an ***auction***.

Royal Mint UK government department with the sole responsibility for the minting of coins, under the direction of the Chancellor of the Exchequer. The US equivalent is the Bureau of the Mint. *See also* ***legal tender***.

royalty Sum paid to an inventor, originator or author, or owner of something from which a product may be made (such as an oilfield), and calculated as a proportion of the income received from the sale of the product.

She is still receiving royalties on a song she wrote ten years ago.

RPI Abbreviation of ***retail price index***.

rubber cheque Cheque that is drawn on an account that has insufficient funds to make the payment. In this event the cheque is "bounced'"back to the drawer.

rubel Standard currency unit of Belarus, divided into 100 kopecks.

rubilis Standard currency unit of Latvia, divided into 100 kopecks.

rufiya Standard currency unit of the Maldives, divided into 100 laari.

Rule 535 Stock Exchange rule concerned with permitted dealings. Clause (i) lists the items that can be dealt. Clause (ii) permits dealing in shares not listed, but with certain restrictions. Clauses (iii) and (iv) apply to overseas companies and exploration companies, respectively.

rummage Preventive search of a ship for contraband by Customs officers, often undertaken without warning.

running ahead Personal trading in a share by a broker immediately before following a client's instructions to do the same. It is illegal in the USA. *See also* ***tailgating***.

running broker Someone who acts as an intermediary between those who issue ***bills*** and the ***discount houses***.

running costs Alternative term for ***operating costs***.

running days A number of consecutive lay days including weekends and public holidays. *See* ***lay day; non-business days; weather working day***.

running expenses Also known as direct expenses or variable costs, expenses incurred in the running of a business and which vary with output. Running expenses and costs include those incurred in purchasing the factors of production and in the marketing, advertising and distribution of goods.

running margin Difference in rates of interest on money borrowed and on the same money invested.

running yield Alternative term for ***flat yield***.

run on a bank Situation that occurs when bank depositors lose confidence in a bank and in a short period of time (perhaps just one day) try to withdraw their deposits. Support from a ***central bank*** or other financial institution may be required if the bank is not to go out of business.

rupee Standard currency unit of India, Pakistan and Nepal (divided into 100 paisa) and of Mauritius, the Seychelles and Sri Lanka (divided into 100 cents).

rupiah Standard currency unit of Indonesia, divided into 100 sen.

rustbelt Also known as the rustbowl, the area in the US midwest and northeast regions where there is a high proportion of declining industries, such as iron- and steel-making.

rustbowl Alternative term for ***rustbelt***.

S

SA Abbreviation of ***société anonyme***.

safe custody Service sometimes provided by banks, by which customers deposit valuables in safe deposit boxes in the bank's care.

safe deposit Well-protected ***depository;*** one that is guarded and/or armoured to prevent theft, *e.g.* a safe deposit box.

safe haven currency National currency that is secure politically.

safe investment Investment certain to yield the expected ***return***.

salary Money paid to an employee, normally expressed as so much per year, but usually paid by cheque or directly into the employee's bank account on a monthly basis. *See also* ***wage***.

sale Formally, the act of transferring goods (or services) from one person to another, accompanied by the exchange of money.

sale and leaseback Sale of a property where the buyer agrees to lease the property back to its original owner. In this way, the seller is able to turn the property into liquid capital while at the same time remaining *in situ*.

sale or return Agreement whereby a distributor or retailer takes goods from a manufacturer or wholesaler on the understanding that he or she may return them if they are not sold within a specified period of time.

sales Colloquial name for a department within a company that deals with the sale of its goods and services.

An alternative meaning makes sales an abbreviation of sales revenue, synonymous with ***turnover***, as represented on a company's ***profit and loss account*** (especially in the USA).

sales account Document presented to a consignor when goods are sent to a foreign country for sale through an ***agent***. The agent submits to the consignor an account of the sales made, along with details of the agent's ***commission***, expenses and the final net ***profit*** on the sale.

sales audit Method of calculating the state of the ***retail*** trade, by comparing the throughput of money against stock.

sales drive Effort to improve ***sales*** and create ***demand***. Techniques include reducing prices, increasing the sales force or its commission, providing free samples and distributing point-of-sale advertising material.

sales journal In book-keeping, an account book in which the record of a sale is first made.

sample Product, or part of a product, that is sent to a prospective buyer so that he or she may decide whether or not to buy.

sandbag Defensive tactics for a ***takeover bid***, by which the ***target company*** agrees to negotiate a takeover, but lengthens talks in the hope that a ***white knight*** may ride by in the meantime.

sans recours *See* ***without recourse***.

satellite banking Division of a group of banks into large and small. The large banks provide a full range of services whereas the small ones (satellites) have a narrower function and need "large-bank" approval for certain activities (such as the granting of large loans).

satellite branch *See* ***sub-branch***.

saturation Situation in which something is completely full. *See* ***capital saturation***; ***market saturation***.

save as you earn (SAYE) UK government savings system whereby a proportion of a person's income is deducted at source and transferred to a ***National Savings Bank*** account.

savings Money put aside by individuals, often in a way that pays ***interest***.

savings account Account with a bank or building society in which people invest personal ***savings*** and earn interest. Often notice of withdrawal must be given. *See also* ***National Savings Bank***.

savings and loan US equivalent of a UK ***building society***. It is also known as a ***building and loan association***.

savings bank Bank in which personal savings may be deposited and interest received. *See* ***savings account; National Savings Bank***.

savings bond *See* ***income bond; National Savings First Option Bond; National Savings Income Bond***.

savings certificates *See* ***National Savings Certificate***.

SAYE Abbreviation of ***save as you earn***.

scarce currency Alternative term for ***hard currency***.

scheduled territory Official name for those countries that have tied their currencies to ***sterling*** by keeping it as their ***reserve currency***. It is also known as the sterling area.

Schilling National currency unit of Austria, divided into 100 Groschen.

science park Area, usually located near a university, that is set aside for industries with a technological or research base.

scorched earth Defensive tactics for a hostile ***takeover bid*** in which the ***target*** company sells its most attractive assets, or initiates adverse publicity about itself in an effort to make it seem a less than desirable acquisition.

SCOUT Abbreviation of ***shared currency option under tender***.

screw you money Informal US phrase for investments made by an entrepreneur as a cushion against his or her main business failing. The term is also used for money that enables an employee to leave his or her job without serious financial problems.

scrip issue Practice of issuing extra shares to existing shareholders free of charge. This is done by transferring reserves into the company's share account. In this way, the company increases its capitalization while at the same time reducing its share price and increasing the number of shares on the market. It is also known as a bonus issue, capitalization issue or free issue.

SDR Abbreviation of ***Special Drawing Rights***.

SDR-linked deposit Deposit of ***Special Drawing Rights*** (SDR) in a private bank account.

SEAF Abbreviation of ***Sock Exchange Automatic Exchange Facility***.

seasonal unemployment Unemployment caused by seasonal fall-off in demand for workers because of the nature of the occupation. *E.g.* the agriculture industry needs crop pickers only at harvest time. Even skilled workers are affected if their work cannot take place at certain times, but in this case wages must be high enough to carry skilled workers through times of unemployment, otherwise the industry would have difficulty attracting such workers. It has been argued that the term does not apply in this instance.

seasonal variations Statistical variations that occur during a particular season. These variations are often taken into account when calculating *e.g.* unemployment figures and trends. In these cases the figures are said to be seasonally adjusted.

SEAQ Abbreviation of ***Stock Exchange Automated Quotations.***

SEATS Abbreviation of ***Stock Exchange Alternative Trading Service.***

SEC Abbreviation of ***Securities and Exchange Commission.***

secondary bank Organization that offers such banking services as loans and mortgages, but not cheque accounts and so on.

secondary market Market in securities that have been listed for some time, rather than new issues. Secondary market trading occurs on the stock exchange. *See* ***primary market; tertiary market.***

secondary production Production of goods that have been manufactured as opposed to raw materials or foodstuffs. *See also* ***primary production.***

second mortgage Additonal ***mortgage*** on a property that is already mortgaged, granted only if the property has sufficient value to act as security for both loans.

second via Second (duplicate) document in a ***bill of exchange*** in a set, that is sent by a different route to avoid loss. *See* ***bills in a set.***

secretary In broad terms, somebody who prepares correspondence, keeps files and records and arranges appointments. *See also* ***company secretary.***

secret ballot Vote conducted by having voters mark their ballot papers in secret, as opposed to a public show of hands or other form of ballot.

secret reserves Alternative term for ***hidden reserves.***

sector Economic term for a part of the national economy or business activity.

secured creditor Bank or other creditor that has a legal charge on one of the debtor's assets. *See also* ***preferential creditor.***

secured loan Loan that is advanced against some asset (the security) of the borrower. In the event that the loan is not repaid, the creditor has rights to the security.

securities *See* ***security***

Securities and Exchange Commission (SEC) Organization founded in 1934 that regulates the securities market (brokers and stock exchanges) in the USA.

Securities and Futures Authority (SFA) Self-regulating oganization (SRO) established in 1991 to regulate the conduct of people who deal in debentures, futures, options and shares. It was formed by combining the functions of the Securities Association (TSA) and the Association of Futures Brokers and Dealers (AFBD).

Securities and Investment Board (SIB) UK financial watchdog, set up in 1986 by the Department of Trade and Industry to oversee the UK's deregulated financial markets. The US equivalent is the ***Securities and Exchange Commission*** (SEC). *See also* ***deregulation***.

Securities Exchange Act of 1934 An act (48 Stat. 881;15 U.S.C. 78a to 78jj) approved June 6, 1934, as amended, that seeks to outlaw misrepresentation, manipulation, and other abusive practices in securities markets and to establish and maintain "just and equitable principles of trade which would be conducive to open, fair and orderly markets."

Securities Management Trust (SMT Money) Bank of England subsidiary in which the bank places funds for its customers.

securities swill Informal US term for securities that are worth virtually nothing.

security Term with two meanings:

1. It is anything (usually property) pledged as ***collateral*** against a loan, or the document that sets out the terms of such collateral.
2. It is any financial ***instrument*** that is traded on a stock exchange and that yields an income. Securities represent a loan that will be repaid at some time in the future. In this sense the word is most often used in the plural, and securities include ***bills of exchange***, ***bonds***, ***debentures***, ***gilt-edged securities***, ***options***, ***shares*** and ***stocks***.

SEDOL Abbreviation of ***Stock Exchange Daily Official List***.

seed capital Capital used to determine whether a proposed project is viable.

seed money Money lent as ***venture capital*** to a company that is very young.

self assessment Scheme introduced in 1996 by the Inland Revenue that makes a tax payer responsible for calculating his or her own liability for income tax. The calculation can, however, be delegated to the Revenue.

self-employment Being in business on one's own account. The self-employed include those who run their own businesses, either alone or in partnership, and professional people such as doctors.

self-liquidating Describing something that has a predetermined life and liquidates itself at the end of that period. In the investment trust sector, for example, a closed-end fund with a stock exchange listing is self-liquidating.

self-regulating organization (SRO) In the UK, a non-governmental organization that governs a particular area of business activity, laying down codes of practice and protecting consumers and investors.

sell at best Instruction to a broker to sell shares or commodities at the best price possible. *I.e.* if the broker is selling, he or she must find the highest selling price. If the broker is buying, he or she must find the lowest price.

seller's market Market that is more favourable to sellers than to buyers. Such a market often arises when demand is greater than supply.

seller's option On the New York Stock Exchange, an option that enables the seller to deliver the relevant security at any time within a period of 6-60 days.

selling cost Extra expenditure required to increase ***sales***.

selling out If a person who has agreed to buy shares cannot close the deal, the seller is entitled to sell the shares for the best price possible and then charge the person who made the original tender the difference between the selling price and the original tender price, and any costs.

selling short Practice of making a bargain to sell securities or commodities the seller does not own. The seller does this in the hope that that before settlement is due, the price of the item will go down and he or she will be able to buy enough to cover the bargain at a lower price, thereby making a profit. The practice is also known as shorting or short selling. *See also* ***short bear***.

sell-side Those people who are on the market to sell, rather than to buy.

seller Person who exchanges goods or services for money.

sellers over Market in which there are more sellers than buyers.

sell price Alternative term for ***cash price***.

semi-variable costs Costs that include both ***fixed costs*** and ***variable costs*** in the reckoning. They are also known as stepped costs.

senior debt Oldest existing debt owed by a person or company, hence, the one that will be paid first, ***ceteris paribus***.

SEPON Abbreviation of ***stock exchange pool nominees.***

sequestration Act of seizure of property or other assets by the courts until a dispute has been settled.

service Something provided, usually for a fee, that may not be classed as manufacturing or production in any form (such as legal advice, brokerage, agency services, etc).

service a debt To pay interest on a ***debt***.

service economy The total output of the service, or tertiary, sector of an economy. It is also an economy that is based on services rather than manufacturing industries.

service industry Businesses engaged in the service, or tertiary sector, such as a shop or hairdressing business.

servicetill Another name for an ***automated telling machine*** (ATM).

servicing a loan Paying the interest due on a loan.

set of bills Alternative term for ***bills in a set***.

set-off In accounting, two parties that have an indebtedness of the standing to each other may set off both debts against each other by assuming that one debt has paid off the other and *vice versa*. This is known as a set-off.

settlement Act of paying in full for goods or services received, or of repaying a debt.

See ***settlement date***; ***settlement discount***.

settlement date (day) ***Account day***; the date on which stock exchange dealings must be settled. It falls ten days, or six business days, after the end of an ***account***.

settlement discount Discount offered for the early ***settlement*** of an account.

seven-day money Funds that have been invested in the money market for seven days.

sever To terminate a contract, especially a contract of employment. *See* ***severance pay***.

severance pay Sum of money given to an employee when he or she is made redundant.

SFA Abbreviation of ***Securities and Futures Authority***.

shakeout When a market cannot support the number of suppliers it has attracted, many of the less profitable suppliers leave the market, with only the more healthy operators remaining. This process of "natural selection"is known in the USA as a shakeout.

A shakeout may also be the reorganization of a company, e.g. after a ***takeover***, when the employee numbers are reduced and operations streamlined.

share *See* ***shares***.

share account ***Deposit account*** with a building society, usually requiring notice for withdrawals greater than a certain sum.

share broker Broker who charges commission on each share, rather than on a total transaction. *See also* ***value broker***.

share capital Capital raised by a company through an issue of shares. *See also* ***authorized capital; issed capital; uncalled capital.***

share certificate Document that proves a person's ownership of a company's shares.

shared currency option under tender (SCOUT) In situations where a foreign currency contract is under tender from several companies, SCOUT allows them to share a single ***hedge*** in the form of a currency ***option***.

share economy Aggregate value of companies quoted on the stock exchange. It is also known as "Quoted UK plc". It is also an economy in which many people are shareholders.

share exchange Alternative term for ***stock exchange***.

share exchange scheme Arrangement by which investors can use an existing ***portfolio*** of shares (instead of cash) as an investement in an ***investment trust*** or ***unit trust***.

shareholder Person who holds ***shares*** in a company.

shareholder democracy Either the notion that each shareholder is entitled to a vote, or the principle that as many people as possible hold shares in public companies and thus have a say in their management.

shareholder derivative suit Legal action taken in the USA, by a shareholder or a group of shareholders. against the directors of a company for mismanagement or breaches of responsibility.

shareholder relations Department within a US company, rather like customer relations, that concentrates on keeping shareholders up-to-date with company performance, etc.

shareholder's equity Equity held by shareholders rather than by the company itself.

share index Index that shows the average change in value of a number of individual shares. Share indexes therefore give an overall guide to movements in the financial markets. Examples include the Financial Times Stock Exchange 100 Index (FOOTSIE), the Nikkei-Dow Average and the Dow Jones Industrial Average.

share issue A limited company wishing to raise ***capital*** may issue a number of shares, each worth a fraction of the company's total value. The shares are placed on the market by a ***stockbroker*** acting on behalf of the firm in question and may, in most cases, be purchased by financial institutions, other companies and private individuals.

See also ***issued capital; issuing bank; issuing house.***

share option UK scheme that gives the employees the option to buy shares in their company at attractive prices (normally well below market price) at a specific future date. *See also* ***popular capitalism.***

share premium On a new issue of shares, a premium charged on the ***nominal value*** of the shares if it seems that the ***real value*** is likely to be much higher.

share pushing Hard selling of shares that may be worthless to investors.

share register Register of shareholders that is held by a company, giving names, addresses, details of shareholding, etc.

shares Form of security that represents the shareholder's stake in a business. Income on shares is in the form of a dividend rather than interest and is declared depending on the company's performance over the year. In the USA shares are known as common stock.

share shop Government-appointed bank, building society or stockbroker which deals with shares in a newly privatized industry. For the duration of the public share offer, share shops sell shares directly to the public without a commission charge (which the government pays to the shop).

share split If the market price of a share is thought to be too high, a company may decide to issue extra shares to its holders (known as a ***bonus issue***), increasing the number of shares on the market, and thus decreasing the price of each share. This process is known as a share split.

share warrant Certificate of ownership of shares, presented after shares are fully-paid.

shark Informal term for a person or company that may be preparing for a ***takeover bid.***

shark repellants Informal term for ***defensive tactics*** in the event of a ***takeover bid.***

shark watcher Consultant who studies the buyers of a company's shares in an effort to identify possible ***sharks.***

shell company Company that does not produce anything in the usual sense, but exists only in name. Shell companies may be set up and sold to people who are unfamiliar with the procedure for doing this, or may be the remnants of a defunct company that has been sold on to someone else. They may also be set up for use at some future time, or to operate as the holder of shares. *See also* ***paper company.***

shelter Investment instrument that gives little in the way of return but allows the investor to reduce income tax liabilities.

shequel Standard currency unit of Israel, divided into 100 agorot.

Sherman Antitrust Act One of the fundamental US Antitrust Laws, the pioneer federal statute in this field (passed July 2, 1890), and a cornerstone in the legal expression of public policy against restraint of trade and monopoly or attempts to monopolize.

shilling Former UK coin worth a twentieth of a pound (now 5p).

short bond Bond with less than five years to maturity. *See also* ***long bond; medium bond.***

short credit Loan that must be repaid over a short timescale. *See also* ***extended credit; long credit.***

short covering When a person is ***selling short***, the purchase of the security concerned in order to cover the bargain.

short-dated gilt ***Gilt-edged security*** with a redemption term of less than five years.

short-dated securities Fixed-interest securities that have a redemption date of less than five years. *See also* ***fixed-interest securities.***

short end That part of the market that deals with securities with relatively little time to go before payment is due. The amount of time varies from a few days to up to five years, depending on which security is being traded.

shortenings Loss by a bank of a small sum (usually a single banknote) from a large amount of cash (bundle of notes).

short hedge Hedge against a rise in interest rates on the ***futures*** market. *See also* ***long hedge.***

shorting Alternative term for ***short selling.***

short interest Interest rate charged on loans over a period of three months or less.

shorts Alternative term for ***short-dated securities.***

short sale A sale of a security that the seller does not own or any sale that is consummated by the delivery of a security borrowed by or for the account of the seller.

short selling Alternative term for ***selling short.***

short-term Loosely, something (in the financial world, a security) with only a short time left before maturity. In the USA, short-term generally means something with less than a year to run. A US alternative is near-term.

short-term capital Loan capital lent in the short-term, *i.e.* for less than five years. *See also* ***medium-term capital.***

short-term investment Investment for a short period. In the City, it refers to an investment for a period of days; elsewhere, the period may be up to three months. Short-term investments are usually made in return for interest rates slightly lower than those available on long-term investments. *See* ***long-term investment.***

short-termism Policy of a ***fund manager*** who invests in shares of a company whose performance is expected to improve in the short term to adjust a ***portfolio*** for maximum gain, rather than taking a long-term view of how share prices are likely to change.

show stopper Informal term for a court injunction initiated by the target company and served against the raider in a ***takeover***, stopping the hostile party from taking action any further.

shrinkage Mainly in retailing, a euphemism for theft (of goods or stock) by employees.

SIB Abbreviation of ***Securities and Investment Board.***

SIC Abbreviation of ***standard industrial classification.***

SICAV Abbreviation of ***société d'investissement à capital variable.***

side-by-side trading Prohibited practice in the USA of trading a share option at the same time as trading the underlying security on the same exchange.

sight deposit Term with three meanings:

1. It is a ***current account*** at a bank or an ***instant access account*** at a building society. *See also* ***time deposit***.
2. It is money ***at call***.
3. It is money on deposit overnight.

sight draft ***Bill of exchange*** payable on presentation (*i.e.* on sight).

silver wheelchair Terms sometimes written into the employment contract of a company's top management or directors, whereby the employee receives a large sum in compensation if he or she loses his or her position as a result of a ***takeover***. If the terms are generous enough, the silver wheelchair may act as a disincentive to raiders. *See also* ***golden parachute***.

simple debenture Alternative term for ***unsecured debenture***.

simple interest Rate of interest calculated by keeping interest that has already been paid separate from the capital sum. Thus, when calculating the next interest payment, the capital sum, but not the interest already paid, enters the calculation. *See also* ***compound interest***.

single capacity System that operated on the UK Stock Market before the ***Big Bang***, whereby the functions of ***jobber*** and ***stockbroker*** were kept separate. A jobber was not allowed to deal with the general public and a stockbroker could not trade in shares except through a jobber. Since Big Bang, the two functions may be amalgamated (***dual capacity***) and the people who perform these combined functions are known as ***market makers***. *See also* ***Chinese Wall***.

single-currency peg ***Exchange rate*** regime in which a country pegs its currency to the US dollar or some other stable currency and makes very few adjustments to the ***parity***.

sinking fund Sum of money set aside for a specific purpose and invested so that it produces the required amount at the right time.

six-month money Funds invested on the money market for six months.

sixpence Former UK coin worth 6/240 of a pound (2½p).

skinny bid Alternative term for ***thin bid***.

skittish Popular term describing a market that is extremely volatile.

skunk costs US term for costs already ascribed to a project, that will not be clawed back if the company decides to abort the project.

slate bull Non-profit making stock that is kept for a long time.

sleeping economy Informal term for an economy that contains substantial resources that are not fully exploited and having substantial unrealised trade potential. The People's Republic of China was usually quoted as an example of a sleeping economy.

sleeping partner Partner who invested capital in a firm but takes no active part in its management. He or she does, however, remain liable for the partnership's debts.

slice (of the action) Entitlement to a share in the profits of a company by being a shareholder, or of a transaction by taking a commission.

sliding scale Scale of charges that is based on the value of the thing upon which the charges are to be made. *See* ***ad valorem***.

slippage Under-performance of a ***start-up*** company. Slippage may lead to the need for additional capital.

Alternatively, it is the fluctuation in the price of a contract on a ***futures*** exchange.

slump Period of time during which the economy is poor, with high levels of unemployment and reduced economic activity.

small companies market Republic of Ireland's equivalent of the ***alternative investment market***.

small company fund Fund that puts ***unit trusts*** or other collective investments in the shares of various small companies.

smart card Plastic card that is provided with an computer memory chip (integrated circuit), which enables it to record financial transactions (debits and credits) without the aid of a central computer.

smoke-stack industry One of the "traditional" manufacturing industries, such as ironworks, mills, or engineering works. It is so-called because smoke stacks (chimneys) were typical features of the early industrial skyline.

SMT Money *See Securities Management Trust.*

snake Popular term for the European system that links the following currencies: the Belgian and French francs, the Danish krone, the Irish punt, the Dutch guilder, the German deutschmark and the Italian lira.

socialist commodity economy Technologically advanced socialist economy in which all the factors of production are controlled by the state.

social ownership Ownership of some or all of a country's industries by the government (on behalf of society in general). *See also* ***nationalization; privatization.***

société anonyme (SA) French equivalent of the UK ***public limited company*** (plc).

société d'investissement à capital variable (SICAV) French equivalent of a ***unit trust.***

société responsibilité limité (SRL) French equivalent of the UK ***private company.***

Society for Worldwide Interbank Financial Telecommunications (SWIFT) Non-profit making communications system, established in Brussels in 1977, that enables member banks to send funds and statements to each other.

socks and stocks Because of Federal Reserve regulations that do not permit branch banking, some US banks (popularly known as socks and stocks) have been set up to deal with either current account facilities or commercial lending, but not both.

soft arbitrage Movement of funds between the money market and bank deposits to benefit from the difference in interest rates. *See also* ***arbitrage.***

soft currency Currency of which there is a surplus on the market and which is thus relatively cheap.

soft dollars Dollars traded on the foreign exchange markets for which demand is persistently low because of a US ***trade deficit.*** The value of soft dollars tends to fall.

soft loan Loan that carries an unusually low rate of ***interest,*** often advanced as a form of ***foreign aid.***

softs Popular name given to traded ***commodities*** other than metals; *e.g.*

foodstuffs such as wheat and coffee.

sol Standard currency unit of Peru, divided into 100 centimos. It is also called the new sol.

sola *Bill of exchange* that does not have a duplicate as in ***bills in a set.***

sold contract note Alternative term for ***sold note.***

sold note Document sent by a broker to his or her client, confirming that a sale has been made. It is also known as a sold contract note.

sole agency Agreement by which only one party (***agent***) represents a principal either in a certain capacity or in a particular geographical area.

sole trader Person who trades on his or her own behalf and has not registered as a business.

In the financial and stock exchange worlds, however, the term has three precise meanings:

1. It is a trader involved in buying and selling securities ***short-term***, for his or her own account.
2. It is somebody who specializes in buying and selling securities on behalf of a broker or dealer, usually working as an employee.
3. It is a person who buys and sells contracts in financial ***futures*** without a ***hedge*** in the appropriate cash market.

solicitor In the UK, a professional person who gives legal advice and initiates legal proceedings on a client's behalf.

solvency State of a person or company that is cash positive, and able to pay all bills as they fall due; *i.e.* its assets are more than its liabilities. Its converse is insolvency.

solvency ratio For a bank, building society or other financial institution, its ***own funds*** divided by its liabilities.

som Standard currency unit of Kyrgyzstan, divided into 100 tyiyn.

sorting code Numerical code that identifies a bank or other financial institution. It consists of six numbers in three pairs (*e.g.*, 30-93-15); the first pair indicates the name of a bank, and the second two pairs a particular branch. The sorting code is printed in ***Magnetic Ink Character Recognition*** (MICRA) characters on cheques and other documents and speeds their progress through the clearing house.

South Sea Bubble *See* ***bubble.***

sovereign UK gold coin worth £1. It is ***legal tender*** but tends to be accumulated by collectors and traded for the worth of its gold content.

special agent *Agent* with authority to perform one particular action on behalf of another.

special crossing Crossing on a cheque that nominates a specific bank (as the only bank into which the cheque can be paid). *See also* ***crossed cheque***.

Special Drawing Rights (SDR) Form of ***credit*** extended by the ***International Monetary Fund*** (IMF) to its member countries as an addition to the credit they already hold. SDRs do not represent actual money, they are simply a form of credit, but they do not have to be repaid to the IMF and thus form a permanent addition to the reserves of each member country. Originally, they were allocated to member countries in proportion to their subscription to the IMF, but since then additional allocations have been made. At first SDRs were valued in relation to the value of gold, but have since been valued in relation to the member country's own currency. SDRs may be exchanged between member countries or between those countries and the IMF.

special manager Person with the requisite experience appointed by the court to run a business in liquidation.

special resolution ***Resolution*** (to the shareholders of a company) that is defined by the majority it needs and the notice that must be given. For example, a special resolution to change the ***articles of association*** of a company must usually be passed with a three-quarters majority.

special situation fund Fund that places ***unit trusts*** or other collective investments in a range of shares that are expected to rise sharply in value (perhaps because of a merger or takeover) or are believed to have bottomed out and are expected to recover.

specie Coins, rather than banknotes or gold bullion.

specific performance order Order made by a court to one party to a contract to fulfil the obligations to which that party is contracted. It may be made, for example, in place of the awarding of ***damages***.

speculation Discussion about a possible future event. Broadly, in finance, it is the practice of making investments or going into a business that involves risk. The term is sometimes used with pejorative undertones to apply to investment for short-term gain. In certain markets, such as ***commodities*** and financial ***futures***, speculation is clearly distinguished from transactions undertaken in the normal course of trading (physical buying or selling) or ***hedging*** (where the specific purpose is to minimize overall gains and losses arising from price movements).

spin-off A term with three meanings:

1. It is a company that has been formed from part of or separated from the ownership of a larger company.
2. It is merchandise that is produced to take advantage of one high-profile product. *E.g.* a television programme may have many spin-offs: a book; a recording of the theme tune; T-shirts; badges; etc.
3. It is a technology or product that arose as a by-product of another.

split Marketing exercise in which a company issues more shares to existing holders in order to reduce the price per share. *See also* ***bonus issue***.

spot Something that is carried out at once, on the spot. The term is most often used on ***futures*** markets, where its opposite is ***forward*** or highest (as in highest prices).

spot goods As opposed to ***futures***, spot goods are commodities available for immediate delivery, rather than forward delivery.

spot market Market in which the goods sold are available for immediate delivery. It is also known as the non-contract market. *See also* ***futures***.

spot price Price quoted for goods available for immediate delivery, usually higher than the forward price because it takes into account all costs except delivery.

spread Broadly, the difference between two (or sometimes more) prices or values.

springing warrant Alternative US term for ***exploding warrant***.

squeeze *See* ***bear squeeze***.

SRA Abbreviation of ***self-regulatory agency***.

SRL Abbreviation of ***société responsibilité limité***.

SRO Abbreviation of ***self-regulating organization***.

stabilizer Something that acts to keep *e.g.* the economy or prices stable. *See* ***automatic stabilizer***. Also known as a built-in stabilizer, it is also the part of a system that stabilizes it to keep fluctuations to a minimum without direct intervention.

staff management Management of support services that enable a company to fulfil its major function. Staff management is involved in the management of such activities as accounting, cleaning, maintenance, etc.

stag Person who buys new issues of shares in the hope that he or she will be able to make a fast profit by selling them soon after trading on the stock exchange opens. With the UK privatization programme of the later 1980s, the number of stags increased. It is not to be confused with STAGS (short for sterling accruing government securities). *See also* ***dolphin.***

stagflation US term for a combination of high inflation and economic stagnation.

STAGS Abbreviation of ***sterling accruing government securities.***

stale bull Dealer who has bought in the expectation that prices will rise but cannot then sell at a profit, either because prices have remained static or fallen, or because nobody wants to buy.

stale cheque Cheque that was drawn over six months before it was presented. Stale cheques are often refused by banks. *See also* ***out-of-date cheque.***

stamp duty Duty levied on the completion of certain transfer documents. *E.g.* stamp duty is paid (on property over a certain value) when a person signs property transfer documents.

standard Broadly, a norm against which other things are measured.

standard industrial classification (SIC) Method of classifying business, manufacturing and all commercial activity for statistical purposes.

standby LC Abbreviation of standby ***letter of credit.***

standby letter of credit A contractual arrangement guaranteeing financial or economic performance involving three parties - the "issuer" (bank), the "account party" (the bank customer) and the "beneficiary". The bank guarantees that the account party will perform on a contract between the account party and the beneficiary. *See also* ***letter of credit.***

standing order Also known as a banker's order, an order to a bank to make (usually) a series of payments on the customer's behalf. It is used to pay bills that are due at regular intervals. *See also* ***direct debit.***

stand on velvet Make a profit from speculation in stocks.

standstill agreement When bidding for shares in a ***target*** company, agreement that no more bids will be made for the time being.

staple commodity Alternative term for ***primary commodity***.

start-up Normally used to describe a company that is beginning from scratch. A start-up often needs ***venture capital*** financing to help it on its way.

stated account Account that shows how much one party owes another. It is agreed upon by both parties and is legally binding unless it can be shown to be false.

state enterprise Undertaking initiated and controlled by the government, generally for the benefit – direct or indirect – of all its citizens; *e.g.* a ***nationalized industry***.

statement Written report often taken as an official or legal document. *See also* ***bank statement***.

statement of account Not to be confused with ***stated account***, a document sent from a creditor to a debtor, detailing recent transactions and amounts owing, sometimes with terms for payment.

statement in lieu of prospectus If a company proposes to make a new issue of ***shares*** or ***debentures*** and does not issue a ***prospectus***, it must pass a statement in lieu of prospectus to the registrar of companies at least three days before the issue is to take place.

status inquiry Inquiry to a bank (often by a credit card agency) to determine the creditworthiness of one of its customers.

statute-barred debt Debt that may no longer be called in because it has been outstanding too long (more than six years) as defined by the Statute of Limitations Act 1939.

statutory company Company set up by Act of Parliament to produce essential services such as the provision of power and water.

stepped costs Alternative term for ***semi-variable costs***.

sterling UK standard currency. *See* ***pound sterling***.

sterling accruing government securities (STAGS) Form of ***zero-coupon bond***, denominated in sterling and backed by Treasury stock.

sterling area *See* ***scheduled territory***.

stipend Alternative term for ***salary***.

stock Term with four meanings:

1. It is a fixed-term security that is denominated in units of £100. *See* ***fixed-interest security***.

2. In the USA it is an alternative term for ***ordinary shares***.
3. It is sometimes also used in the UK to mean some types of ***ordinary share***.
4. It is a collection of raw materials or goods held by a manufacturer, wholesaler, retailer or end-user. It is also known as stock-in-trade or inventory.

stockbroker Someone who gives advice and buys and sells ***stocks*** and ***shares*** on the stock exchange on behalf of clients.

stock exchange Essentially a place where ***securities***, ***stocks*** and ***shares*** are bought and sold.

Stock Exchange Alternative Trading Service (SEATS) Service that displays quotations and orders for illiquid stock in which only one (or no) market maker is willing to trade.

Stock Exchange Automated Quotations (SEAQ) Electronic system on the London Stock exchange that displays in the offices of brokers and others up-to-date prices and information for all quoted securities. Only market-makers are permitted to quote prices on SEAQ, accepting certain obligations in return for the increased business that SEAQ offers.

Stock Exchange Automatic Exchange Facility (SEAF) Computerized system on the London stock Exchange that allows buying and selling of securities to be done at terminals in the broker's office. *See also* ***CREST; Stock Exchange Automated Quotations*** (SEAQ)***; Stock Exchange Pool Nominees*** (SEPON)***; TALISMAN***.

Stock Exchange Daily Official List (SEDOL) *See* ***Official List***.

Stock Exchange Pool Nominees (SEPON) Company that acts as a central pool for shares while they were being transferred from buyer to seller. Sold stock was deposited into SEPON and buy orders were fulfilled from it, through the ***TALISMAN*** system. In 1997 it was replaced by the Bank of England ***CREST*** system.

stock-in-trade Alternative term for ***stock*** (fourth meaning).

stockjobber Alternative term for ***jobber***.

stop-loss order Alternative term for ***stop order***.

stop-loss selling Sale of shares or futures contracts in a declining market, usually at a predetermined price, in order to prevent further loss.

stop order Instruction given by a client to a ***stockbroker***, to sell securities should they fall below a certain price.

stopped cheque Cheque that a bank will not pay because of an instruction from the drawer, possibly because it has been lost in the post or stolen.

story Security that is being actively traded on the US market at the present time, but which may lack underlying value.

straddle Practice of simultaneously buying forward and selling forward a ***futures*** contract or ***option*** in the same security in order to make a profit if the price of the security moves in either direction.

straight bond Also known as straight fixed-interest stock, a bond issued by a company.

straight-line depreciation Method of calculating the ***depreciation rate***. A fixed proportion of the total original value of the ***asset*** is written off in each accounting period, making allowance for its current resale value, either as a useful asset or scrap. *See also* ***write off***.

straight-line method In ***accounting***, method of calculating ***depreciation*** by writing off the value of the ***asset*** in equal amounts in each year of the asset's lifetime.

strangle Practice of buying out-of-the-money call and put ***options*** that are close to expiry at a relatively low ***premium***. If the price of the underlying ***future*** rises or falls suddenly, the buyer makes a profit.

Street, The Popular term for the New York Stock Exchange, referring to Wall Street.

striking price Also known as the exercise price, the price at which an ***option*** for the purchase or sale of a security is exercised.

strip Practice of taking US Treasury bonds, stripping the interest-bearing ***coupon*** and selling that and the principal separately. Such securities are said to have been stripped.

strong bear hug During a ***takeover***, a situation in which there is a high level of publicity surrounding the bid, putting pressure on the ***target*** company.

structural adjustment loan ***World Bank*** loan to a bankrupt or extremely poor country.

structural unemployment Usually high level of unemployment caused by the change from a labour-intensive to a capital-intensive economy.

student account Bank account made available to students, often with incentives such as lower fees and preferential interest rates.

sub-branch Small bank, often open for only a few hours or days per week, that is staffed and managed by personnel from a larger branch. The available services are also limited. It is sometimes known as a satellite branch.

subject bid (or **offer**) Bid (or offer) that is subject to stated conditions. *See also* ***firm bid***.

subordinated loan Loan that does not have repayment priority (compared to other loans).

subrogation The substitution of another person in the place of the creditor. The person so substituted succeeds to all the rights of the original creditor, all debts owing to the creditor becoming payable to the substituted person.

subscribed capital Alternative term for ***issued capital***.

subscriber On the formation of a company, a person who signs the articles of association and ***memorandum of association***. *See also* ***subscribed capital***.

subscription Sum paid to a company for shares in a new issue.

subsidiary company Company that is wholly or partly owned by another, called the ***parent company***.

subsidy Sum paid to companies in certain industries to enable them to sell their goods or services at a price close to the prevailing market price. A subsidy is also used to provide financial support to a commercial or quasi-commercial activity that would otherwise not be viable in narrow profit-and-loss terms, usually in order to sustain broader economic or social benefits.

substantial damages Damages designed by the court to place the plaintiff in the financial position that he or she would have enjoyed had the loss or injury not occurred. If the monetary value of the loss or injury can be precisely calculated, the substantial damages awarded are said to be specific; if precise calculation is impossible, approximate (general) damages are awarded.

sub-underwriter Bank, insurance company, market maker or jobber who accepts part or all of the commitment made by an ***underwriter***.

subvention In the UK, a payment made from one company to another (related) company in order to give a better picture of the group's performance.

In the USA, a grant made by the government, a company or other institution, to a non-profit making organization.

sucre Standard currency unit of Ecuador, divided into 100 centavos.

suicide pill Defensive tactics in the event of a ***takeover bid***. If the raider manages to acquire a certain percentage of the ***target*** company's shares, the remaining shareholders are automatically entitled to exchange their shares for ***debt*** securities, thus exchanging the company's ***equity*** to debt and making it seem less attractive to the raider.

sunlighting Practice of having two full-time jobs at once. *See also* ***moonlighting***.

sunrise industry Industry, such as those surrounding computer technology and biotechnology, that is rapidly becoming more important. *See also* ***senset industry***.

sunset industry Industry that, because of the march of technological progress, is becoming less important. *See also* ***sunrise industry***.

supermajority Between 70% and 80% of the voters. It is usual to demand a supermajority decision when deciding on such points as ***mergers*** or ***takeovers***.

superstock Share issue in the USA that gives the existing holders a large number of votes per share. Normally used as a defensive tactic during a hostile ***takeover bid***, superstock must be held for a certain period of time before the extra votes are credited to the holder.

supplementary benefit Payment made in the UK to someone who is either out of work but does not qualify for ***unemployment benefit***, or is on a low wage.

supplementary costs Alternative term for ***overheads***.

supply Provision of goods and services.

supply and demand Two market forces that in microeconomic theory determine the price of goods, services or investment instruments. If supply is low and demand high, the price increases. Conversely, if demand is low and supply high, the price falls (unless price controls are in operation).

Supply-Side Economics The school of economics that developed in the US in the late 1970s and early 1980s, emphasizing supply instead of demand in economic analysis, and particularly the disincentive effects of high taxes upon productivity, investment, and growth.

support Practice of actively buying securities or foreign exchange by an "official" in order to stop their market value from falling. This most often happens when the ***central bank*** buys its own securities to stop the price falling and thus forestall a rise in interest rates.

suppressed inflation Inflationary trend that has been slowed down or completely halted, usually by extensive government intervention in the economy. It is also known as repressed inflation.

surety Alternative term for ***guarantee***.

surveyor Person whose job is to examine buildings etc. and report on their condition, perhaps for a mortgage provider.

suspension notice Notice published by a company that wants, for a defined period, to suspend the facility of converting ***loan stock*** to ***share capital***.

swap Alternative term for ***bed-and-breakfast deal***.

sweat equity US practice of providing labour in exchange for shares when personal ***capital*** is unavailable.

sweep facility Bank service whereby it routinely transfers funds from a deposit account into a current account when its balance falls below a particular amount. Similarly, funds over a certain amount in the current account may be automatically transferred to the deposit account.

SWIFT Abbreviation of ***Society for Worldwide Interbank Financial Telecommunications***.

Switch Computerized ***debit card*** system that permits a customer to pay a shopkeeper or other supplier who has an ***electronic point of sale*** (EPOS) or ***electronic funds transfer at point of sale*** (EFTPOS) terminal. Founded in 1988 by the Midland Bank, NatWest and the Royal Bank of Scotland, the facility is now offered by many banks and building societies.

switching Practice of transferring investment from one security to another (in a comparable class) in order to take advantage of price fluctuations or to improve a tax position.

switch selling Salesperson's technique whereby, if a potential buyer resist a particular product, another (equally attractive) one is suddenly made available.

syndicate Group of people that come together to work for a common aim, *e.g.* in underwriting large risks for Lloyd's of London. *See also* ***consortium.***

syndicated loan Large bank loan made by a group of banks to a single borrower.

syndication Practice of dividing investment risk between several people in order to minimize individual risk.

Syndication is also the practice of distributing information (especially news information and newspaper and magazine articles) to several outlets.

synergy Additional benefits to be gained by the combination of hitherto separate activities. It is sometimes colloquially expressed as "2 + 2 = 5", and cited to justify the takeover or merger of companies with complementary or mutually reinforcing activities or resources.

T

tailgating Act of a broker who recommends purchase of a stock to one customer on the basis of another customer having just expressed faith in the stock by making a purchase. The term also includes the personal trading in a share by a broker immediately after taking an instruction from a client to do the same. *See also* ***running ahead***.

tailspin Sudden plunge in market prices.

This week's crash sent equity prices on several European markets into a tailspin.

taka Standard currency unit of Bangladesh, divided into 100 paisa.

take back When a US company is sold, the take back is a situation in which the owner must accept payment in something other than cash.

take in Accept stocks as loan security in order to postpone a sale until the next ***settlement date***.

takeover Buying of a proportion of another company's shares so that the purchaser gains control of the company or its assets. *See also* ***merger***.

takeover bid Offer by one company to buy the shares of another, thereby gaining control of the target company. It is often shortened to "bid".

takeover panel Stock Exchange body responsible for seeing that the City Code on Takeovers and Mergers is observed by parties wishing to make a ***takeover bid***.

takeover stock Shares that are bought by a raider during a takeover battle.

taker-in Person who is willing to take up a commitment made by a ***bull*** dealer, in the event of the dealer being unable or unwilling to pay for it at that time.

TALISMAN Abbreviation of Transfer Accounting, Lodgement for Investors, Stock Management for Jobbers. It was a central computerized system for settling equities, and also facilitated the transfer of stock from the central Stock Exchange pool and the issue of new certificates. In 1997 it was replaced by the Bank of England ***CREST*** system.

tally Originally a notch made on a piece of wood as a record of a debt or payment, now most often referring to a distinguishing mark on an item of merchandise.

tallyman Term with three possible meanings:

1. It may be an accountant (*e.g.* one working for a bookie on a racecourse).
2. It is a person who gives credit to be repaid in instalments (traditionally by going round housing estates door-to-door).
3. It is a person responsible for checking merchandise as it is loaded and unloaded from a vessel.

talon Slip that accompanies a sheet of coupons of ***bearer bonds***, which may be sent to the issuing company when more coupons are required.

tangible assets Literally, assets that may be touched, such as buildings or stock. They may be contrasted with intangible (or invisible) assets, which are those that are not visible, such as a company's goodwill or the expertise of its staff.

tangibles Another term for ***tangible assets***.

tap When the government makes a new issue on the gilt market, it is very rarely fully subscribed. The remaining gilts in the issue are gradually released by the ***government broker*** and this action is known as a tap. *See* ***gilt-edged security***.

tap buying In certain circumstances, the government will buy back gilts before they have matured. This known as tap buying. *See* ***gilt-edged security***.

tap issue Issue of government securities direct to government departments rather than onto the open market.

tap stock Gilt-edged stock released onto the market in a ***tap***.

tape dancing Unethical method of manipulating share prices in the USA in which a dealer reports a deal inclusive of his commission. This seems to make the share price rise.

tare When the weight of goods is being established, the tare is the weight allowed for the packaging. Tare is also the weight of a (goods) vehicle without fuel; its unladen weight.

target Objective towards which somebody or an organization is working. In corporate finance, it is a company that is the object of a ***takeover bid***.

All the sales representatives met their sales targets for the year.

Having been made aware of the imminence of a hostile takeover bid, the board of the target company met to discuss defensive tactics.

target price Average price for commodities fixed by the Common Agricultural Policy of the EU and achieved by purchasing goods at the ***intervention price***.

tariff List of charges made in return for goods or services. There are also two more particular meanings:

1. It is the list of dutiable goods and duty payable, issued by Her Majesty's Customs.
2. It is a system of charges in which a certain rate is payable up to a certain point (*e.g.* a certain quantity of goods) and then the rate changes beyond that point.

tariff barrier Alternative term for ***customs barrier***.

TAURUS Abbreviation of transfer and automated registration of uncertified stock, a computer system that was intended to enable stocks and shares to be transferred by computer, making contract notes and certificates unnecessary. After a series of failures, it was abandoned in 1993 and replaced three years later by ***CREST***.

tax Money paid to central or local government to cover its expenditure. Various kinds of taxes are collected by the Inland Revenue (the Internal Revenue Service in the USA), HM Customs and Excise (in which case the tax is known as a duty) and local government authorities. *See also* ***duty; rates; value-added tax***.

tax abatement Reduction in the rate of tax. It should not be confused with a tax ***rebate***.

taxable income Income on which taxes are levied. It is calculated by deducting ***personal allowances*** from ***gross*** income.

tax and price index (TPI) Index launched in 1979 to compare levels of ***taxation*** with ***retail prices*** and relate them to average wage levels. The TPI is used to calculate the real spending power of the nation.

taxation Imposition and subsequent collection of a ***tax***.

taxation schedule One of six categories into which income is divided for the purposes of calculating taxes.

tax avoidance Use of loopholes in tax legislation to minimize tax liability. Unlike ***tax evasion***, tax avoidance is legal.

T

tax base The form of income upon which tax is calculated. *E.g.* the tax base for income tax is a person's taxable income.

tax bracket The percentage of one's income that one pays in tax depends on the level of income. Incomes are divided into brackets for the purpose of calculating tax. The term is also applied to people in that bracket.

She is in a higher tax bracket than he is.

tax credit That part of a ***dividend*** payment on which a company has already paid ***tax***, thus relieving the ***shareholder*** of the necessity of doing so.

tax concession Allowance made by the Inland Revenue to taxpayers in certain categories, which means that these people or companies pay less tax than they would otherwise be liable for. *E.g.* tax concessions are often used by the government to induce companies to relocate in areas high in unemployment.

tax deduction card In ***pay as you earn*** (PAYE) income tax, a record of all deductions made by the employer at source, submitted for each employee to the Inland Revenue annually.

tax deductions Money removed from a person's salary or wages to cover income tax. In the USA, however, tax deductions are expenses that are deductible against tax.

tax-exempt special savings account (TESSA) Type of tax-free investment, introduced in 1990 to encourage people to save. Up to £9000 can be invested, and interest is tax free as long as no withdrawal is made for a period of five years. After five years, up to £9000 of the money can be reinvested in another TESSA. In 1997 the government announced that TESSAs would lose their tax-free status in 1999, apparently to persuade investors to transfer to the planned new ***Individual Savings Accounts*** (ISAs).

tax evasion Evasion of tax liabilities by providing false information to the ***Inland Revenue***. Tax evasion is a criminal offence in the UK. *See also **tax avoidance***.

tax exemption Not having to pay tax. In the USA, however, it is the proportion of income upon which tax is not payable.

tax exile Person who lives abroad in order to minimize liability for tax.

tax gap Difference between the amount somebody owes the Inland Revenue (the Inland Revenue Service (IRS), in the USA), and the amount they actually pay.

tax haven Country with liberal tax and banking regulations. In some instances it benefits companies to set up their registered offices in such a country, to avoid paying taxes in their own country.

tax holiday Period during which a start-up company need not pay taxes.

tax loss Loss sustained by a person or business which may, once incurred, be offset against a demand for ***income tax***, ***capital gains tax*** or ***corporation tax***. Tax losses are frequently incurred deliberately in an attempt to reduce the real cost of tax-paying.

taxpayer identification number (TIN) A taxpayer's identification number in the US represented by a nine-digit number with no alphabetic characters. A TIN is usually an individual's Social Security number or an employee identification number.

tax point Point at which ***value-added tax*** (VAT) is payable.

tax relief Concessions made to taxpayers in respect of certain liabilities.

He expected to get tax relief on his mortgage.

tax return Document submitted to the ***Inland Revenue*** annually, stating an individual's earnings and expenses for the year and used to calculate that person's tax liabilities.

tax shelter Investment instrument that does not attract tax.

tax year Period of twelve months, specified to start at any calendar month, for tax and accounting purposes. It is also known as the ***financial year***. *See also* ***fiscal year***.

T-bill Abbreviation of US ***treasury bill***.

TCV Abbreviation of ***total contract value***.

teaser Initial low rate of interest offered on an adjustable rate mortgage (ARM), which may seem very attractive at the time of arrangement, but which inevitably rises.

technical analysis Analysis of the changes in price of a company's ***stock***, based on past movements in the value of its shares; also called chartism.

technical market analyst Someone who studies the stock market and predicts changes on the basis of market trends and the state of the market as a whole.

technical office protocol (TOP) Scheme aimed at standardizing computer systems that link design and engineering functions within manufacturing industries.

technopole Derived from technopolis, meaning a society dependent on high technology, a technopole is a place where business dealing with high technology products have congregated.

teddy bear hug Situation in which the target company approves of a ***takeover bid*** in principle but requires a higher price.

Ted spread Difference between the price of a US ***treasury bill*** and the price of the ***Eurodollar***.

telebanking Method by which bank customers may make financial transactions from their homes or offices, using a computer linked by a ***modem*** to the bank's computer.

telecommuting Increasingly common practice whereby people work at home, "commuting" by computer link-up rather than by car or public transport. *See also* ***electronic cottage***.

telegraphic transfer Method of transferring money to a transferee abroad. The transferor instructs his or her bank, who will then contact their agent in that country to pay the transferee.

telemarketing Advertising, selling and conducting market research over the telephone, person to person.

telemarketing system Computer system that canvasses people in their homes over the telephone. Dialling is done electronically and a voice-activated audio-tape carries on the "conversation".

telesales Selling a product over the phone. It is a branch of ***telemarketing***.

telephone banking Method of using a bank, often at any time of the day or night, without visiting its premises. Enquiries and requests are made by telephone, using a ***personal identification number*** (PIN) if necessary.

teleshopping Service whereby a store's customers may order goods for delivery, either over the telephone or, increasingly, using a home or personal computer.

teletext output price information computer (TOPIC) Computerized system that provides stock dealers with up-to-the-minute information on market prices. *See also* ***quote machine***.

teller Bank employee whose function is to take and pass out money over the counter. *See also* ***automated teller machine*** (ATM).

temporary employment Full- or part-time employment in the short term, sometimes with a specified time-limit, and often without a formal contract.

temporary exports Short-term "export" of cash or goods to an ***offshore*** location, often for the purpose of ***tax avoidance***.

tenancy Either an agreement whereby a person is entitled to occupy a property, usually in return for ***rent***, or the length of time agreed for such occupancy.

tenancy in common In principle, a situation in which two people are entitled to tenancy of the same property and may do as each wishes with their part of it. If one tenant dies, his or her share of the property is passed on to the heir, rather than to the other tenant(s). Now, however, tenancy in common applies only to groups of four or more people. *See also* ***joint tenancy***.

tenant's fixture Fixture provided by a tenant, which may be removed before his or her tenancy ends.

tender Generally, an offer to supply goods or services at a certain price and under certain conditions. A tender is usually submitted in response to an invitation to do so and is normally made in competition with other potential suppliers.

tender bills ***Treasury bills***, issued by the government each week to cover short-term finance. Tenders for these bills are made by discount houses and financial institutions. *See also* ***tap***.

tender offer Offer for sale by ***tender***. In the USA, it is an offer made to the shareholders of a public company to buy their holding at a certain price, normally above the current market price. This may be done by a company in order to effect a ***takeover***.

tender pool One of a series of groups into which an acquisitive company may divide its target company's shareholders, in order more successfully to persuade them to take up a ***tender offer***. It is a form of divide and conquer.

tenor Period of time before a ***bill of exchange*** has to be paid. In effect it is the "life" of the bill.

term Period of time during which something is valid.

terminal The end of something. In computing, it is where data can be inputted to or outputted from a system. *e.g.* a keyboard or VDU screen.

terminal date Date of expiry of a ***futures*** contract.

terminal market Financial market in ***futures***.

terminate To finish something, often used in regard to a contract or agreement.

They terminated his contract of employment after he was caught trying to defraud the company.

term loan Fixed loan made for a specified number of years.

terms Conditions attached to an agreement or contract.

term shares Funds deposited with a building society for a stated number of years, to earn higher than usual interest.

terms of trade Indication of a country's trading position, based on a comparison of its imports and exports.

territory Geographical area covered by a sales representative or by a company's operations.

tertiary market Market in listed securities traded by non-exchange brokers on the over-the-counter market. *See also* ***primary market***.

TESSA Abbreviation of ***tax-exempt special savings account***.

The Opening ***Call-over*** at the start of each trading session on some exchanges. Otherwise, the term is used as shorthand for ***opening price***.

thin bid ***Takeover bid*** backed by an aggressor who holds only a small number of shares. It is also known as a skinny bid.

third class paper Corporate debt issued by companies with a low ***credit rating***. Third class paper is a hazardous investment.

third market Stock Exchange market introduced in January 1987, with less stringent entry requirements than the ***unlisted securities market*** (USM). It is also known as the third tier.

three-six-three Late-lamented lifestyle of the US banker: "Pay interest at 3%; lend at 6%, be on the golf course by 3 pm".

threshold Limit or point at which something changes.

threshold agreement Agreement between an employer and employees (or the representative union) that wages will increase only if the rate of ***inflation*** reaches or exceeds a certain level, the threshold.

threshold company Company that has moved out of the ***start-up*** stage and is moving towards becoming secure and more profitable.

threshold price Price fixed under the Common Agricultural Policy (CAP) by the European Commission, below which the price of agricultural imports from non-member states is not allowed to fall.

thrift Shorthand in the USA for ***thrift and loans***.

thrift and loans Financial institutions in the USA that are backed by an insurance fund and oriented towards the customer. They are also known as industrial banks. *See also* ***savings and loan***.

tick Minimum price movement on a financial futures contract. *See also* ***uptick***.

tied loan Loan made by one country to another on condition that the money concerned is spent on the lending nation. Tied loans are a common form of ***foreign aid***, because they create employment and have no effect on the lending nation's ***balance of payments***.

tied outlet Retail outlet that is financially backed by a manufacturer on the condition that the outlet sells the manufacturer's goods. *E.g.* most public houses are tied outlets.

tie-up Arrangement whereby a large company helps to finance a smaller company, thus gaining rights in some or all of its developments. Tie-ups most often occur where the receiving company is developing in high-technology areas. *See also* ***accord***.

tigers *See* ***Treasury Investment Growth Receipts*** (TIGRs).

tight money Money available only at a high rate of ***interest***. Tight money is created when the authorities reduce the ***money supply*** in an attempt to curtail the level of activity in the economy; funds therefore become scarce and thus attract high interest rates.

TIGRs Abbreviation of ***Treasury Investment Growth Receipts***.

till money Coins and banknotes held by a bank, called vault money in the USA.

time and motion Study of the way in which a particular job is carried out, in an effort to streamline the physical actions involved and so save time.

time bargain Deal struck on the understanding that settlement will be postponed until the next ***settlement date***.

time deposit Deposit or investment that cannot be withdrawn without giving notice. It is also an alternative US term for ***fixed deposit***. *See also* ***sight deposit***.

time preference Theory of interest that suggests that interest is the price paid by a borrower for immediate consumption, and a compensation to the lender, who loses the opportunity to use the articles or money lent for his or her own purposes. Therefore, time preference is a person's preference for current rather than future consumption, or *vice versa*.

time rate Payment for work done based on the amount of time the job takes. *See also* ***piece rate***.

time server Worker who has lost sight of any promotional ambitions and has no motivation to work with any interest or initiative. The time server freewheels until he or she retires.

time sharing Term with slightly different meanings in the fields of computing, property and employment:

1. In computing, it is the use of data and facilities of a mainframe computer by several different users at the same time.
2. In property, it is an arrangement whereby people buy time during which they are entitled to use a property. *E.g.* it is becoming increasingly common to buy a two-week time-share in a holiday villa abroad.
3. In employment, a time-share job is a full-time job shared by two or more people, each performing the same function, but working at different times. It is also known as a job-share.

time value of money Theory by which one's money is more valuable now than at any time in the future, whether it be in an hour's time, next week or next year.

tip Cash given to someone who has rendered a service, over and above the payment agreed. Tipping customs vary from country to country, but those who are normally tipped include taxi-drivers, waiting staff, beauticians and hairdressers. It is also known as a gratuity.

A tip may also be a piece of information passed to someone to whom it may be of advantage.

tithe Literally meaning "one-tenth", a tithe was originally a payment of that portion of one's income to the Church. Now, it has come to mean payment of a fixed sum at regular intervals.

title A person's right to something.

title deed Legal document giving the holder ***title*** to a land or (more loosely) to property. Title deeds are often accepted as ***collateral*** for a ***loan***. It is also known as deed of title.

toehold purchase First acquisition of up to 5% of a target company's shares in an attempted ***takeover bid***.

token coin Coin whose exchange value is more than the value of the metal from which it is made. Some gambling and vending machines take token coins.

tolerance In manufacturing, the degree to which a product differs from the ideal specification, without giving grounds for it to be rejected.

tolar Standard currency unit of Slovenia, divided into 100 stotin.

toll Payment made for the use of a facility such as a bridge or tunnel. In some countries there are also tolls payable for the use of motorways. The toll is normally charged to cover the cost of maintaining the service.

toll call Long-distance telephone call in the USA, charged to the caller.

toman Standard currency unit of Iran, worth 10 rials.

tombstone Informal term for an advertisement, placed in the press, giving details of those involved in a securities issue. A tombstone is not normally an offer to buy.

TOP Abbreviation of ***technical office protocol***.

top copy First (and most legible) sheet of a document of which several carbon copies have been made.

TOPIC Abbreviation of ***teletext output price information computer***.

top up To improve the benefits gained from an existing arrangement, *e.g.* by increasing contributions to a pension or assurance scheme.

top-up mortgage Alternative term for a ***margin loan***.

total contract value (TCV) Figure applied to ***futures*** markets and calculated by multiplying the size of the contract (*e.g.* 10 tons of cocoa) by market price (*e.g.* £1,000/ton) to give the value of the contract (£10,000).

total quality management (TQM) Management concept in which employees at every level are involved in quality and product control.

touch For any security, the difference between the best ***bid price*** of one market maker and the best ***offer price*** of another. *See also* ***spread***.

touch signature Check on the identity of a person cashing traveller's cheques in the USA using fingerprints (because the bearer has no passport as proof of identity).

town clearing (bank) Clearing of cheques in London. Town clearing takes place in two stages. The first, in the morning, deals with cheques of less than £500, received the previous day. The second, deals with cheques of over £500.

toxic waste Informal US term rating a security as a very bad investment. *See also* ***junk bond***.

TPI Abbreviation of ***tax and price index***.

TQM Abbreviation of ***total quality management***.

tracker bond Lump-sum account invested in equities that guarantees the capital and often guarantees also a minimum return.

trade Business of buying and selling in general. In the USA, a trade may also be another term for a ***bargain*** or deal.

trade advertising Advertising that is restricted to one section of the public *i.e.* those people (such as retailers) who operate within the advertiser's own industry.

trade agreement Agreement between two or more countries or two groups of countries regarding general terms of trade.

trade balance Alternative term for ***balance of trade***.

trade barrier Something that restricts or discourages trade, such as high levels of import ***duty*** or low import ***quotas***.

The leaders of the car industry in the UK called for trade barriers to be set up to restrict foreign competition.

trade bill ***Bill of exchange*** between traders. The value and acceptability of a trade bill depends upon the standing of the accepting trader.

trade credit Credit one company or business gives to another, usually in the form of time to pay for goods or services supplied.

trade creditor Company or person to whom money is owed as a result of normal trading. *See* ***accounts payable***.

trade debt Debt incurred by a company during the normal course of business as the result of the non-payment of bills.

trade debtor Company or person who owes money for goods or servics received. *See* ***accounts receivable.***

trade deficit Excess of a country's ***imports*** over ***exports***, resulting in a negative ***balance of payments.***

trade delegation Group of delegates sent to promote trade and negotiate agreements with a foreign trading partner.

trade discount Discount offered to trade customers, *i.e.* to customers likely to place large and regular orders. A trade discount therefore recognizes the value of the customer concerned.

trade gap In an adverse ***balance of trade***, the difference between the values of imports and exports.

trade investment Investment in ***capital goods*** related to existing business, or in a new business in an established sector.

traded option Unlike ***traditional options***, traded options are transferable and the terms of the option are fixed. Thus, it has been possible to form a market for trading the options themselves, as well as the underlying security, commodity or future.

trade mark Logo or name (trade name) used to distinguish one manufacturer's product from another's. Registered trade marks may not be used by another manufacturer in the country of registration.

tradeoff Exchanging one thing for another. Goods may be traded off against each other, but so may many other things such as the terms of an agreement.

After five hours at the negotiating table they decided on a tradeoff of terms to break the stalemate.

trade references List of trading partners to whom a company may refer if they wish to confirm the creditworthiness of a potential customer.

trade terms Special conditions (usually discount prices) available to people working in the same industry or trade.

trader Person who concerns himself or herself in trade.

trading Activity of a ***trader*** in all its meanings.

trading account First section of a ***profit-and-loss account***, in which income and expenditure concerned in a company's trading activities are detailed. The final figure on this account is the company's ***gross profit.***

trading bank Australian term for a ***commercial bank***.

trading day Day on which trading takes place on a stock exchange. On the UK stock exchange, every day is a trading day with the exception of weekends and public holidays. *See also* ***non-business days***.

trading certificate Certificate handed to a new company by the Registrar of Companies to enable it to begin trading.

trading cheque Voucher paid for by instalments which can (when paid for) be used to buy goods from specified shops.

trading crowd Group of dealers interested in trading in a particular security.

trading estate Area of land, usually situated just outside a town or city, set aside for warehouses and light industrial units. It is also known as an industrial estate or industrial park.

trading floor The area within an exchange building where trading takes place.

There was panic on the trading floor of the Exchange today as prices began to fall sharply.

trading halt Temporary stoppage in trading on a securities or options market.

trading loss Loss incurred while taking a principal (trading) position in a ***market***. The loss must be recorded on a ***profit and loss account*** of a company. A trading loss is thus often disguised, where possible, by such tactics as "redefining" it as a ***fixed asset*** investment or including it as an extraordinary or ***below-the-line*** item in the accounts.

trading post On the ***trading floor*** of the New York Stock Exchange, an area where dealers congregate to trade.

trading stamps Discount given by a retailer to its customers in the form of stamps. The stamps have a redemption value (in cash or goods) and the discount is represented by this value.

traditional option Non-transferable option that has been available on a market for over a century, written on a variety of shares listed on the exchange. Each time a dealer wishes to buy a traditional option, the terms are re-written.

tranche Slice or portion. In general, one of a series of payments which when put together add up to the total agreed.

The author received his advance as five tranches of £1000 each.

More specifically, a tranche is a block of a stock issued before or after (and sometimes at a different price to) another block of identical stock.

tranche funding Method of providing finance by which successive sums of money are forwarded, each dependent upon the financee attaining prearranged targets.

tranchette Small block of ***gilt-edged securities*** issued to the market, as an addition to stock already on the market. *See also* ***tranche***.

transaction Act of carrying out a business deal.

Considering the lengthy negotiations involved, they concluded the transaction surprisingly swiftly.

transaction charge Charge payable to the London International Financial Futures Exchange on each transaction made.

transaction costs Costs incurred in buying and selling securities, such as the brokers' commissions, taxes, etc.

transfer Legal movement of something (*e.g.* property, shares, etc.) from one owner to another.

transfer deed Document proving the sale of a property or registered stock. To make the transfer official, the seller must sign the deed. In the case of a registered stock the document is also known as a stock transfer deed or a transfer form.

transfer payment Payment made by the UK government that is not in return for goods or services: *e.g.* state pensions and unemployment benefit.

transfer stamp duty Duty levied on the transfer of securities on the stock exchange. It is therefore a form of capital transfer tax. Transfer stamp duty is not imposed upon government stocks, nor on securities bought and sold within one ***account***.

travel allowance Amount added to a person's ***salary*** to cover the cost of travelling to work, or journeys undertaken in the course of work.

traveller's cheques Cheques used by people going abroad. They are issued by banks, building societies and travel agents in round-number denominations in major international currencies. They are guaranteed against loss or theft. The purchaser signs the cheques when they are bought, and overseas countersigns a cheque in the presence of the person to whom it is being paid; usually a proof of identity (such as a passport) is also required. They may be exchanged for foreign currency or used to pay for goods and services. A commission is charged when they are issued and when they are cashed.

treasury Government department that deals with national finance and government funding, and is responsible for the execution of the government's economic policy. Some large companies also have treasury departments.

Treasury bill In the UK, a government ***bill of exchange*** issued in £5,000 denominations to discount houses at a discount on its face value and repayable on a certain date (usually 91 days hence). In the USA, often abbreviated to T-bill, it is a short-term ***bill of exchange*** issued by the US Treasury in $10,000 denominations.

treasury bond Alternative term for a ***government bond***.

treasury investment growth receipts (TIGRs, propounced tigers) Form of US ***zero-coupon bond*** in dollar denominations.

trend Direction of a price movement, which may be measured over periods of time.

trial balance In accounting, test that the books of account are accurate, by extracting a balance and checking that the debits equal the credits. This may take place monthly, but must be carried out at least annually, during an ***audit***.

Trial of the Pyx Annual test made at the Royal Mint in the UK, to check that coins contain the correct quantities of the relevant metals.

triangular trade Trading system in which a nation uses the profits from exports to another country to pay for imports from a third country.

tribunal Special court set up to make a judgement on specific problems.

trickle-down theory Theory whereby the money put into the pockets of those who are already rich through government policy is thought to seep down into the hands of those who are less well off. Trickle-down is thought to be a more efficient method of re-distributing wealth than ***transfer payments***.

triple-A In the rating of US stocks and bonds, a triple-A rating is the highest rating a stock may achieve.

Turnover was light in most bonds, but triple-A rated issues continued to be in demand.

triple-witching hour Last hour before quarterly futures and options expire, during which turnover increases considerably, causing drastic changes in market prices.

troy weights System of weights most commonly used to weigh precious metals and gemstones. *See also* ***avoirdupois***.

true and fair Describes the ratification of an ***account*** in auditing. *See* ***audit***.

trust Term with three meanings:

1. It is a group of companies that join forces to create a ***cartel***, or in some cases a ***monopoly***. In the latter sense it is more often used in the USA, *e.g.* in the term ***anti-trust law***.
2. It is a sum of money or property placed into the care of a group of trustees, to be managed (although not necessarily invested) for the benefit of an individual or organization such as a charity.
3. In the securities industry, a trust is an investment operation that is managed by a group of trustees on behalf of other people, such as a unit trust.

trustbusting US government action taken to prevent trusts (in the US sense) forming, and to break them up if they are already in operation in an apparent effort to stimulate competition.

trust deed Legal document that transfers property into the hands of trustees and sets out the terms of the trust.

trustee Person managing a ***trust***.

trust letter Document that a bank requires when somebody uses goods as security for a loan.

TSA Abbreviation of The Securities Association, a former self-regulating organization (SRO) now replaced by the ***Securities and Futures Authority*** (SFA).

tugrik Standard currency unit of Mongolia, divided into 100 mongos.

turn Difference between the price at which a security is bought and the price at which it is sold. It is thus the gross profit on the transaction.

turnkey Situation, especially in the computer and construction industries, in which a supplier provides a complete customized package to a customer.

turnover Gross value of all sales made by a company during the accounting period. On the Stock Exchange, the turnover is the total number of shares changing hands during a certain period of time.

turnover rate Rate at which something moves, *e.g.* goods in a retail outlet. More specifically it is the number of shares to change hands on the Stock Exchange in a year, compared to the number of shares in issue.

two-part tariff System of charges comprising two elements. In some cases, a fixed sum is supplemented with a variable sum (*e.g.* a taxi driver makes a fixed charge and then adds a certain amount depending upon the time of day and the time the journey has taken, or upon the distance travelled).

tycoon Someone who has amassed a large fortune and a great deal of personal and professional power through business or inheritance.

U

UCITS Abbreviation of ***undertakings for collective investments in transferable securities***.

ullage Potentially a confusing term which may be used in two different senses:

1. It is the difference between the capacity of a cask and the volume of its present contents.
2. It is now used by Customs officials to refer to the actual contents of a cask. In this case the term ***vacuity*** is used to describe the difference between capacity and actual volume.

ultimo Commercial Latin for "of the previous month", sometimes abbreviated to 'ult'.

ultra vires Meaning "beyond the power of", a phrase that denotes an act that goes beyond or against the acting company's objectives as defined in its ***memorandum of association***.

umpirage In cases of ***arbitration***, there may be more than one arbitrator. A group of arbitrators are governed by an umpire and in the event that the arbitrators are unable to reach a unanimous decision the umpire's decision is always final. The act of referring to the umpire in this way is known as umpirage.

umpire *See* ***umpirage***.

unabsorbed cost In accounting, the cost of production may be allocated to each unit over a specified level of output and represented as a percentage of that unit's overall cost to the producer. If the specified level of output is not reached, then some of this cost is not paid for, and is known as unabsorbed cost.

unbundling Separation of a broker's prices from his services. It is also a term in the computer industry that denotes sales of parts (often software) separately from the main machine.

uncalled capital Money owing to a company on ***partly-paid shares***. Uncalled capital exists as a reserve to be called upon at any time by the directors of a company.

uncertificated units In ***unit trusts***, the dividends from the trust may be reinvested, to form new units. In most cases the dividends are too small to justify the issuing of a new certificate and so uncertificated units are held on behalf of the investor until the units are surrendered.

unconnected depositor Person who makes use of a bank merely to deposit interest-earning funds (and makes no use of any other available services).

unconscionable bargain Bargain that turns out to be unfair because one party has not had the time to consult an expert. Unconscionable bargains may be made void in law.

uncrossed cheque Cheque that is not crossed, indicating that it may be exchanged for cash. It is also known as an open cheque. *See also* ***crossed cheque***.

undated stocks Fixed interest security with no redemption date attached.

undercapitalization Situation of a company that does not have enough capital to take it through the initial burn-out period immediately after ***start-up***. *See also* ***burn rate; capitalization***.

under contract To be bound by the terms of a contract.

underground economy That part of an economy controlled by organized crime. The underground economy is better-controlled and more concentrated than the ***black economy***.

underlying security Security that is the subject of an ***options contract***.

underpin To strengthen something, *e.g.* the current trend in market prices, a current way of thinking, etc.

This month's government deficit data is expected to help underpin the gilt market.

undertaking Agreement or promise to do something.

They have given us a written undertaking to supply the goods within ten days.

They have undertaken the new brief for the job.

undertakings for collective investments in transferable securities (UCITS) ***Unit trusts*** that may be traded in any of the EU countries.

underwater Describing shares that drop in value after the initial public offering. *See also* ***discounted value***.

underwater option Stock ***option*** offered to US employees. The shares are normally offered at a discount on the market rate, but when the market price falls below the ***grant price***, the option goes underwater.

underwriter Person or institution that agrees to take up a proportion of the risk of something. *E.g.* an underwriter may take up the shares of an issue that are not taken up by the public, in return for a commission (known as an ***underwriting commission***). For the issuer, the underwriter represents the guarantee that the whole issue will be subscribed.

A Lloyd's of London underwriter agrees to take liability for a certain proportion of the insurance required.

undischarged bankruptcy Occurs when the debts of the bankrupt have not been paid. In this case the individual has no property that may be called his or her own and is barred from public office, and from holding management positions or directorships.

undisclosed Describes an action performed for various reasons without others knowing about it or without knowing the reasons behind it.

undisclosed principal Person represented in a business transaction by an agent or broker, and whose identity is therefore unknown to the person with whom the intermediary is conducting business.

undistributed profit Alternative term for ***retained profit***.

undue influence If a party to a ***contract*** can be shown to have been influenced by a third party, such as a relative or close friend, so that the third party has some benefit from the contract, then undue influence may be declared and the contract made void.

unearned income Income received from investments (and not from the provision of goods or services), including ***dividends*** and ***interest*** payments.

unemployment benefit Commonly known as the dole, unemployment benefit is a payment made in the UK by the State to someone who is out of work and has previously paid a certain number of national insurance contributions.

unfair dismissal The removal of a person from his or her job for reasons that are unfair. To discover whether these reasons are indeed unfair, the case may be brought before an industrial tribunal.

unfunded debt That portion of the ***National Debt*** that is in the form of fixed-term securities. It consists of the ***floating debt***, listed securities and small-scale savings.

unit Term with three meanings:

1. It is one single item produced for sale. *See also* ***unit cost***.
2. It is the name given to a single area of factory or retail space, especially on industrial estates.
3. In finance, it is a share (in the everyday sense) in an investment or series of investments. *See* ***unit trust***.

unit bank Bank with only one office (and no branches), usually run by the owner.

unit banking Banking system that operates in the USA, whereby banks are not permitted to open branches. *See also* ***branch banking***.

unit cost Cost of producing one item. Unit cost is calculated by taking the total cost of production and dividing it into the number of units produced. Unit cost helps a company to determine ***price***.

unitization Conversion of an ***investment trust*** into a ***unit trust***.

unit trust Trust into which investors may buy by acquiring units. The capital thus collected is invested in various securities in a wide range of markets. Contributors to unit trusts benefit from the diverse nature of the ***portfolio*** built up, and from the expertise of a ***fund manager***.

universal agent ***Agent*** with unlimited authority to close contracts on behalf of the principal.

See also ***power of attorney; warranty of authority***.

universal bank Type of bank, not yet realized, that would provide a complete range of services, including (in addition to ordinary retail banking) bond issues, investment advice and management, loans, share dealing and stockbroking.

universal banking Type of banking that, in addition to providing the usual services, involves company investments. It is uncommon in the UK and illegal in the USA.

unlawful The formal difference between an act that is unlawful and an act that is illegal is that an illegal act is forbidden by law, whereas an unlawful act is not protected by law. E.g. most forms of wagering are unlawful.

unlimited company Company that consists of members who are all liable for the total of the company's debts.

unliquidated damages Amount of damages determined by a court, rather than specified by a contract.

unlisted securities Those securities not listed on the stock exchange. *See* ***Unlisted Securities Market***.

Unlisted Securities Market (USM) Former market for shares in companies that do not fulfil the requirements for a full quotation on the Stock Exchange, or that do not wish to be quoted, but which do fulfil certain less stringent requirements. It closed in 1996 to be replaced by the ***Alternative Investment Market*** (AIM).

unloading Practice of putting on the market large quantities of a certain product (or certain shares) at a low price. *See also* ***dumping***.

unlocking agreement Agreement, often attached to a contract, by which one party may, under certain conditions, requires the other to buy him or her out, thereby ending or unlocking the agreement between them.

unpaid cheque Cheque returned to the payee after having been through the clearing process, usually because of lack of sufficient funds to cover the cheque (*see* ***refer to drawer***).

unpaid services In calculating the national product, unpaid services are not taken into account. Such services are those provided by people who do work for themselves, such as gardening and DIY, wives who look after children and manage households, and carers who provide nursing services for relatives who are ill.

unpresented cheque Valid cheque not yet presented for payment (and therefore not reflected in a ***bank statement***). *See also* ***stale cheque***.

unquoted Normally describing shares or debentures not quoted on the Stock Market.

unquoted company Company that does not have its shares quoted on a stock exchange.

unquoted investments Alternative term for ***unlisted securities***.

unquoted securities Alternative term for ***unlisted securities***.

unrequited transfer Gift of finance made by one country to another.

unsecured No formal security held. If a loan is unsecured there is no guarantee it will be repaid.

unsecured creditor Person who has made a loan but received no ***security***.

unsecured debenture ***Debenture*** that gives the holder no guarantee that repayment will be received by a specified date. In such a case, the holder of an unsecured debenture must wait until the company has been wound up before claiming payment. For this reason, most debentures are secured against company property or financial assets. It is also known as a simple or naked debenture.

up or out (position) High pressure job or position. In such a job an executive is either promoted very quickly or replaced equally speedily.

The job of brand manager is an up or out position.

upside The bright side – the possibility of things getting better.

Trade figures will have to be very bad indeed to affect the dollar. Upside potential in this case is far greater than downside potential.

upstairs deal Deal arranged behind closed doors – usually in the boardroom. Many ***takeovers*** are settled by upstairs deals.

upstream Movement, e.g. of funds, from a ***subsidiary company*** to its ***parent company***. *See also* ***downstream.***

upstream activity Activity within an industry or company that extends beyond basic manufacturing and marketing. Upstream activities are generally more expensive than these ***downstream*** activities, but are important in that they help to expand activities in general. Two examples of upstream activities are research and development in any industry, and exploration in the oil industry.

Higher crude oil prices bolstered earnings for upstream activities, such as oil exploration and production, while downstream activities showed steep declines.

uptick Describing a transaction (such as a sale of shares) that is made at a higher price than the one obtained immediately before. It is also known as a plus tick. Uptick is also used to denote a (short-lived) rise in a price or value.

There was a small drop in sterling late in the day, which seemed to be caused by a slight uptick in the dollar.

See also ***down tick; tick***.

uptrend Improvement of some general kind, e.g. in market prices.

The company's executives expected a small setback in profits in the short term, but were optimistic that the uptrend would continue.

usance Term with three meanings:

1. It is the rate of interest charged on a loan.
2. It is ***unearned income*** derived from the ownership of wealth or capital.
3. It is the amount of time customarily allowed for payment of short-term ***bills of exchange*** between two foreign countries. The usual period is 60 days.

user-friendly Originally, describing computer software that is easily used, even by a novice. The term is now often used for anything that is easy to use.

USM Abbreviation of ***unlisted securities market***.

usufruct The right to the use of property belonging to someone else, but not the right to diminish its value in such use.

usury Moneylending at an excessive rate of interest, not in itself illegal. *See* ***moneylender***.

utility stock Share in a company providing utilities such as water, electricity and gas.

V

valium picnic Popular term for a quiet day on the New York Stock Exchange.

valuation Estimate of what something is worth. More particularly, it is a summary of the value of a ***portfolio*** of investments at a given time.

value Term that is not as precise as it might seem. The value of something is the price a buyer is prepared to pay for it, but this can fluctuate according to all sorts of variables, *e.g.* whether it is a ***buyer's market*** or a ***seller's market***, to what use the buyer will be putting the goods, etc. Usually the term is qualified, to minimize possible confusion.

value added Difference between the price a company or industry pays for its materials and the price at which it sells its product. *E.g.* a used-car dealer may acquire a car, recondition the engine and repaint the body. When he sells it, the added value is the value of these operations as reflected in the new (higher) selling price of the car. *See also* ***value-added tax***.

value-added tax (VAT) Form of indirect taxation by which the producer, seller and consumer pay a percentage of the value added of the product or service. *E.g.* if a manufacturer buys raw materials at £10 per unit and sells each unit for £20, the value added is £10. The manufacturer is required to pay a percentage of the £20 in VAT, and can claim back the VAT paid on the £10-worth of materials. VAT for most things is 17.5% in the UK, although some goods and services are exempt and some ***zero-rated***. *See also* ***ad valorem***.

value broker Broker who charges a commission on a total transaction, rather than per share. *See also* ***share broker***.

value in exchange Value of something as a form of exchange, rather than as an object of use. *E.g.* precious stones are worth virtually nothing in terms of real value in use but because they are rare and desirable, they command a high price. *See also* ***value in use; value paradox***.

value in use Value of something to the person using it, which may be different to the sale value of the object. *E.g.* a machine may be valuable to its owner because it produces goods for sale, whereas it may be valueless in itself, perhaps because it cannot be moved. *See also* ***value in exchange; value paradox***.

value paradox An object or commodity may be valuable in terms of exchange, but totally worthless in terms of use. Equally, a thing may be extremely valuable in use but is inexpensive to acquire. *E.g.* salt or water are very useful commodities, but are fairly cheap. Most precious stones may be said to be totally useless, but are expensive to buy because they are rare. The value paradox is this apparently illogical assignment of value. *See also* ***value in exchange; value in use.***

variable costs Expenses, incurred in production, that vary depending on output.

variable-rate mortgage *Mortgage* with a rate of interest that may be varied by the mortgagee to suit conditions on the money market.

variation margin When dealing in contracts on a ***futures*** market, the gain or loss at the end of a trading day that is recorded on a person's account. If the variation margin falls below the ***initial margin*** required, the trader is required to deposit more funds.

VAT Abbreviation of ***value-added tax.***

vatu Standard currency unit of Vanuatu, divided into 100 centimes.

vault money *See* ***till money***.

vehicle currency Currency used to make payments and quotations in international investment and trade, most often the US dollar.

vendor Person who sells goods or services.

venture capital Also known as risk capital, capital invested in a venture (usually a young company, often in high-technology areas) that presents a risk.

VER Abbreviation of ***voluntary export restraint.***

verba chartarum fortuis accipiuntur contra proferentem Maxim used in legal circles, meaning that where the wording of a contract is imprecise and open to misinterpretation, it will be taken in the sense that goes against the party that drew up the contract. It is also known as the contra proferentem rule.

verification Checking that a statement is accurate. More particularly, the term refers to the checking of statements made by a company in its ***prospectus***. Verification is undertaken by the company's solicitors in order to protect the company's directors. When a prospectus is sent for verification, it is often accompanied by ***verification notes***, clarifying each statement.

vertical diversification Diversification into industries or businesses at different stages of production to the diversifying company. *See also* ***horizontal diversification***.

vertical integration Amalgamation of companies involved in different stages of production in the same industry, *e.g.*, to produce one company capable of extracting raw materials, using them to produce goods and then distributing and selling the manufactured product.

vested interest Reason (*e.g.* an investment) or possible benefit that a person may have for maintaining a certain state of affairs.

viability Ability of a person, a company or even a country to support itself, or of a product to survive in a market and generate a profit.

vicarious performance Situation that occurs when a party who has contracted to supply something passes the work onto someone else to be done. In this case, the legal responsibility under the contract still lies with the supplying party. *See* ***assignment of contract; delegatus non potest delegare***.

vigilantibus non dormientibus jura subveniunt Maxim meaning that if people think they have a claim to make, they should go ahead and make the claim, as soon as possible. *See also* ***laches***.

VISA Worldwide ***credit card*** organization whose facilities are included with the cards issued by several major banks, including ***Barclaycard***.

visible Describing something that can be seen, identified or counted, such as visible exports and imports.

visible balance Alternative term for ***balance of trade***.

visible exports Also known as visibles, goods sold to foreign buyers and shipped abroad. The difference between the value of visible exports and ***visible imports*** is the ***balance of trade***.

visible imports Tangible products imported; imports of goods rather than services. *See also* ***invisible imports*** .

visibles *See* ***visible exports***.

visible trade Trading in ***visible*** goods between countries.

voidable contract Contract that may be voided by one or other of the parties to it. *E.g.* if one party fails to make known all information relevant to the contract, it may be deemed voidable. *See also* ***void contract***.

void contract A contract that is deemed in law never to have existed. *See also* ***voidable contract.***

volatility Measure of the stability of a particular instrument. If, say, a share price or a market index moves often and vacillates wildly, then it is said to be volatile.

volume Term often confused with ***turnover***, although in some instances they may be used to mean the same thing. Strictly, volume is the number of units traded, whereas turnover refers to the value of the units traded.

The stock exchange saw today the third largest drop in terms of points, but volume was moderate at about 650 million shares.

On the commodities market, however, volume refers to the quantity of ***soft commodities*** traded, and turnover refers to the tonnage of metals traded over a particular period of time (normally over a day of trading).

voluntary export restraint (VER) The limiting of certain types of exports from one country to another (or group of countries) in order to forestall the imposition of import quotas or other restrictions by importing countries. It is often preceded by a voluntary restraint agreement, stating that this is what the exporting country intends to do.

voluntary liquidation Liquidation of a company that has decided to cease trading, rather than one that has gone ***bankrupt***.

vostro account Bank account held with a UK bank by a foreign bank. *See also* ***nostro account***.

voting rights Right of a shareholder to vote at a company's ***annual general meeting*** (AGM). This right depends on which type of shares are held; generally, ***ordinary shares*** carry voting rights whereas ***debentures*** do not. The articles of association and the company's ***prospectus*** detail which shares carry voting rights and which do not.

voucher Generally, a paper given in place of money, such as a gift voucher or a ***luncheon voucher***.

In ***accounting***, a voucher is more precisely a document (such as a ***receipt***) that supports or proves entries in ***books of prime entry***.

VRA Abbreviation of ***voluntary restraint agreement***.

vulture capitalism Pejorative view of ***venture capitalism***, whereby investors lure talented people away from established companies, encourage them to set up on their own, work hard and be ingenious and then face a demand for a high return on the investment.

W

wage Payment made to a worker, normally fixed as a rate per hour, day or week (and usually paid weekly).

wage differential Difference between levels of wages, caused by many variables, *e.g.* occupation, industry, sex and age of the employee, geographical location, experience and qualifications of the employee, etc.

wage economy Informal term for the total ***earned income*** in an economy. It is also an economy in which the majority of people's income is from wages.

wage freeze Situation in which wages are fixed for a certain period of time, either by government authority on a national level or by agreement within a single company or industry.

wage-price spiral Form of ***inflation***. If a producer is forced to increase wages, he or she must increase the price of the product to cover the increased wages costs, which in turn leads to new wage demands.

wager Bet. Essentially, a wager is a contract between two parties, that one will give the other something of value depending upon the outcome of some future event.

waiter Person on the London Stock Exchange or at Lloyd's who runs errands, takes messages and looks after the day-to-day running of the exchange. Historically, the first waiters were those in the coffee houses at which dealings first took place.

waiting time Time an employee spends not working, *i.e.* waiting for a machine to warm up or be repaired, or waiting for another employee to finish the previous stage of a job.

waive To give up a right or remove or overrule conditions of an agreement.

walks department Clearing bank section that deals with cheques delivered by messengers (who arrive on foot) and drawn on non-clearing banks.

wallflower Stock that is no longer favoured by stock market investors.

Wall Street Another name for the New York Stock Exchange (Wall

Street is the street in Manhattan on which the exchange is located). Sometimes the name is further abbreviated to The Street.

wall, the Popular name for the problem encountered by some US bankers when trying to persuade customers to make use of the ***automated telling machines*** (ATM).

warehousing Term with three meanings:

1. With reference to shipping, warehousing is the business of storing, examining and sorting goods which takes place in a warehouse before they are released into the country in question.
2. In more general terms, it is the storage of goods on behalf of a manufacturer, distributor or retailer.
3. On the stock market, using funds invested in insurance or unit trusts to buy shares that are falling in price, often as a precursor to a ***takeover bid***. *See* ***concert party***.

warrant Term with three meanings:

1. It is a receipt that describes goods held in a warehouse, transferable by endorsement. In this sense a ***wharfinger*** warrant (also known as a wharfinger receipt) is a similar receipt describing goods on a wharf. *See also* ***wharfage***.
2. It is a long-date ***option***.
3. It is a security of a specific market value that may be exchanged for a certain share at a predetermined price. The warrant's value lies in the difference between the predetermined conversion price and the ***market price*** of the share.

warranty Term with two meanings:

1. It is a statement or guarantee that goods are in working order or that workmanship is not faulty.
2. In a ***contract***, it is an implicit or explicit guarantee that the premises upon which the contract is based are factual or true. If the warranty turns out to be false, the contract is not voidable, but the injured party may seek damages.

warranty of authority Power given to an ***agent*** to act under the instructions of a principal.

wash sale Tax-avoiding fake "sale" of shares between two brokers (which also inflates the price). It is illegal.

wasting assets Assets that inevitably diminish in quantity, such as coal in a working mine.

watered stock Stock that has become a smaller percentage of a company's total share capital because of subsequent share issues.

waybill Document, normally drawn up by the carrier of goods, describing the goods, naming the sender and addressee, and the conditions of carriage.

ways-and-means advance Advance paid by the Bank of England to the *consolidated fund*.

wealth Total of a person's or country's ***assets***, both tangible and intangible.

wear and tear Popular and legal term for ***depreciation***. Wear and tear is the decrease in value of an item due to deterioration through normal use rather than through accident or negligence.

weather working day Day on which work is able to go ahead because the weather conditions are favourable, *e.g.* in construction work or in loading or unloading a ship in port.

weekend effect Theory that prices of stocks and shares do better on a Friday than on a Monday, because of such influences as the way in which dealers time their settlement of purchases, etc.

weighted ballot Ballot (for shares) that is in some way biased towards a certain type of investor.

The issuing house was instructed to weight the ballot for shares in favour of small investors.

wharfage Payment made for placing goods on a wharf during loading or unloading a vessel.

wharfinger Someone who is responsible for the running of a wharf, similar to a warehouseman.

whipsaw Violent movement (or series of movements) in prices on any market.

Today's whipsaw action reflects nervousness in the foreign-exchange market.

Whipsawed by the dollar, blue-chip stocks managed to end another volatile session yesterday little changed, but many other stocks fell.

white collar Employee who does office work rather than factory work. *See also* **blue collar**.

white knight When a company finds itself the target of a ***takeover bid***, it may seek an alternative company or person to whom it offers to sell itself in preference to being taken over by the original bidder. This friendly company is known as a white knight and the tactic is known as a white knight defence. *See also* ***grey knight; white squire defence.***

white squire defence In a ***takeover*** situation, a ***target*** company may place a significant number of its shares with a friendly party in order to prevent the ***raider*** from acquiring them. *See also* ***white knight.***

wholesale banking Large-scale banking activities (mainly borrowing and lending) undertaken for government departments, international organizations and other banks and financial institutions. *See also* ***retail banking.***

wholesale deposit Large amount of money deposited in a bank or other financial institution.

wholesale market Interbank ***money market***, especially for short-term loans.

wholesaler Person who buys goods in bulk from a producer and then sells them in smaller quantities to retailers or other wholesalers, earning a profit either by charging a commission to the retailer or by adding to the manufacturer's price.

wife's earnings election In personal ***taxation*** in the UK, it may be advantageous for a wife to have her earned ***income*** taxed separately from that of her husband. The husband, however, continues to pay tax on her unearned income although they are essentially paying tax as single people. There have been moves recently to have all married couples taxed separately and to abolish the wife's earnings election.

will Legal document drawn up by a person (usually under the advice of a solicitor) giving instructions as to how the person's estate is to be distributed after his or her death. The signature on a will has to be witnessed by two people, neither of whom is a beneficiary but can be an executor. *See also* ***intestacy.***

windbill Alternative term for ***accommodation bill.***

windfall profit A profit caused by fortuitous circumstances outside the control of the recipient, such as that caused by a rise in stock prices or an inheritance.

winding-up Cessation of business activity on the part of a company and the start of that company's liquidation.

windmill Alternative term for ***accommodation bill.***

window cheque *See* ***counter cheque.***

window-dressing In ***accounting***, a (legal) method of making a set of accounts seem better than they are by presenting them in such a way as to make the usual comparisons between figures difficult.

wiping Passing a ***credit card*** or other type of ***plastic*** through a card reader to access the information on it in order to carry out a transaction, often a purchase at a shop or store (*see* ***electronic funds transfer at point of*** **sale** (EFTPOS)).

wire house Informal US term for a large stockbroking firm.

withholding tax Tax on the interest on a deposit or investment deducted at source (the depositor or investor receives net interest).

without recourse Note on a ***bill of exchange*** indicating that in the event of non-payment of the bill, the current holder may not blame the person from whom he or she bought it. It is also sometimes written in French as sans recours.

won Standard currency unit of North and South Korea, divided into 100 chon.

working assets All the assets of a company except its ***capital assets.*** Working assets include outstanding debts, stocks of raw materials, stocks of finished product and cash in hand. It is also known as current assets.

working capital Capital available for the day-to-day running of a company, used to pay such expenses as salaries, purchases, etc.

working director Director who takes an active part in the management of a company.

work in progress In accounting, the value of goods currently under manufacture or services being supplied, but not completed at the end of the accounting period.

work study Study carried out to minimize effort put into a particular task; similar to a time-and-motion study.

World Bank ***Central bank*** of the United Nations.

worst moment concept In preparing financial projections and budgets, the worst moment concept takes into account the worst times in ***cash-***

flow, *e.g.* periods when large bills must be paid, as well as the easier times.

writ Notice served by a High Court, normally signalling the beginning of a court action, informing a person that he or she is either to appear in court at a certain date or that he or she must perform (or refrain from performing) a certain action. Failure to comply with a writ is punishable by the court.

write down In accounting, to take the cost of an ***asset*** and deduct the amount by which the asset has depreciated in capital terms. This is the write-down or ***book value*** of the asset.

write off (US **charge off)** To delete an ***asset*** from the accounts because it has depreciated (or been written-down) so far that it no longer has any book value. *See also* ***write down***.

writer to the signet In the Scottish legal system, a person who performs the same function as a ***solicitor*** in England and Wales.

writing down allowance Another term for ***capital allowance***.

wrongful dismissal Redundancy that a court of law decides was illegal. A company responsible for wrongfully dismissing an employee is normally expected to re-employ the person concerned, and may also be liable to pay some form of ***compensation***.

WT Abbreviation of ***warrant***.

X

XA Abbreviation of ex all, denoting shares that have been bought minus rights to any benefits being offered, *e.g.* participation in a ***rights issue***, rights to ***dividends***, etc.

XC Abbreviation of ex capitalization, denoting a share that has been bought minus the right to participate in a forthcoming ***scrip*** issue.

XD Abbreviation of ex dividend, denoting a share that has been sold without the right to receive the next ***dividend***.

XR Abbreviation of ex rights, denoting a ***share*** that has been sold, but does not entitle the new holder to participation in a forthcoming ***rights issue***.

Y

yankee Slang term on the London Stock Exchange for US ***securities***.

yankee bond Bond that is issued in dollar denominations to attract US investors.

yard Slang term for a ***billion***.

year-earlier Previous year.

A & G Electronics posted a pre-tax profit up 20% on year-earlier pre-tax profits of £20 million.

year-later Next year.

yearling bond UK fixed-interest security that has a life of under five years; issued through banks and stockbrokers on a weekly basis.

year's purchase Method of calculating the value of a purchase (of, say, a company) by relating it to the anticipated year's ***income*** from the purchase; *i.e.*, the price of a business in relation to its average annual profits or the price of a property in relation to the average annual rent.

Yellow book Popular term for a publication entitled *Admission and Securities Listing*, issued by the London Stock Exchange Council, setting out regulations of admission to the Official list and the obligations of securities admitted.

yen Standard currency unit of Japan, divided into 100 sen.

yield Return on an investment, taking into account the annual income and the capital value of the investment, usually expressed as a percentage.

yield gap Difference in average yield between investments in ordinary ***shares*** and in ***gilt-edged securities***.

York-Antwerp rules Voluntary code, drawn up in 1877, for those involved in shipping cargo by sea.

yo-yo stock Stock whose price fluctuates widley in an unpredictable way.

Z

zaire Standard currency unit of Congo (formerly Zaire), divided into 100 makuta.

zai-tech Japanese and US stock market practice of borrowing money in order to invest in stocks and bonds.

zebra Form of ***zero-coupon bond.***

zero Shorthand for ***zero-coupon bond.***

zero-balance account Cheque account operated by a company by which cheques are drawn against the account balance, which at the start of the day is always zero. At the end of the day the value of all cheques drawn is totalled and the amount is transferred into the account, so that the account balance reverts from a ***debt*** to zero.

zero-base budgeting Method of ***budget*** management whereby each manager assigns a priority rating to each budget request. Zero-base budgeting forces each manager to justify every request.

zero-coupon bond US ***bearer bond*** that pays no ***dividend***, but is issued at a substantial discount. A capital gain is made by the bearer when the bond matures, and so tax on the proceeds is paid at a lower rate than if the proceeds were in the form of dividends. Zero-coupon bonds are not issued in the UK. *See also* ***bond washing***.

zero-dividend preference share Type of share sold by an ***investment trust*** that pays no dividend to the investor, who receives payment only when the trust is wound up.

zero-rated In the UK, describing an item that attracts no ***value-added tax*** (VAT).

For the time being, books continue to be zero-rated.

zip-code Post code usued in the USA comprised of state abbreviation and five figures, used in much the same way as a post code in the UK.

The company's zip-code is NY 10016.

zloty Standard currency unit of Poland, divided into 100 groszy.